THE SCIENCE OF EVALUATION

A REALIST MANIFESTO

RAY PAWSON

D0002411

Los Angeles | London | New Delhi
Singapore | Washington DC

Los Angeles | London | New Delhi
Singapore | Washington DC

SAGE Publications Ltd
1 Oliver's Yard
55 City Road
London EC1Y 1SP

SAGE Publications Inc.
2455 Teller Road
Thousand Oaks, California 91320

SAGE Publications India Pvt Ltd
B 1/I 1 Mohan Cooperative Industrial Area
Mathura Road
New Delhi 110 044

SAGE Publications Asia-Pacific Pte Ltd
3 Church Street
#10-04 Samsung Hub
Singapore 049483

Editor: Katie Metzler
Assistant editor: Anna Horvai
Production editor: Ian Antcliff
Copyeditor: Jennifer Hinchliffe
Proofreader: Jill Birch
Marketing manager: Ben Griffin-Sherwood
Cover design: Wendy Scott
Typeset by: C&M Digitals (P) Ltd, Chennai, India
Printed by: MPG Printgroup, UK

© Ray Pawson 2013

First published 2013

Apart from any fair dealing for the purposes of research or
private study, or criticism or review, as permitted under the
Copyright, Designs and Patents Act, 1988, this publication
may be reproduced, stored or transmitted in any form, or
by any means, only with the prior permission in writing of
the publishers, or in the case of reprographic reproduction,
in accordance with the terms of licences issued by
the Copyright Licensing Agency. Enquiries concerning
reproduction outside those terms should be sent to the
publishers.

Library of Congress Control Number: 2012942929

British Library Cataloguing in Publication data

A catalogue record for this book is available from the British
Library

ISBN 978-1-4462-5242-0
ISBN 978-1-4462-5243-7 (pbk)

Library
University of Texas
at San Antonio

To Wendy

Contents

About the Author

---**Ego**---

Ray Pawson is Professor of Social Research Methodology in the School of Sociology and Social Policy, University of Leeds. His main interest, perforce, is in research methodology and he has written widely on the principles and practice of research, covering methods – qualitative and quantitative, pure and applied, contemporaneous and historical. Publications include *A Measure for Measures* (1989), *Realistic Evaluation* (1997) and *Evidence-Based Policy: A Realist Perspective* (2006). He was elected president of the Committee on Methodology of the International Sociological Association (1994–98). He has served much time in prison (for research purposes), being a former UK director of the International Forum for Education in Penal Systems (1995–97). He has held the post of visiting professor at the University of Rome, University of Victoria, Canada and the Royal Melbourne Institute of Technology, as well as visiting fellow at the UK Economic and Social Research Council's Centre for Evidence-Based Policy and Practice. He is best known for his writing on evaluation methodology, research synthesis and evidence-based policy, work which has been supported over the years by four ESRC senior fellowships. Research income exceeds £3.5 million. He has acted as researcher and consultant on programme evaluation for the various UK and European government departments and agencies.

---**Alter Ego**---

'God save you, dear reader, from an *idée fixe*, better a speck, a mote in the eye.'
Joaquim Maria Machado de Asiss – *The Posthumous Memoirs of Bras Cubas*

Ray Pawson's idée fixe, which goes by the name of *realist inquiry*, has travelled through thirty years and three previous books – one on measurement, one on evaluation research and one on research synthesis. And now here he is in 2013, with *The Science of Evaluation*, doggedly, stubbornly, unendingly writing manifestos in the name of realist social science. A number of institutions have supported this work and along the way he has been fortunate enough to receive several fellowships and visiting positions. He is world famous in Italy, Tasmania and Vancouver Island. Happily, the idée fixe remains controversial. Other bodies (unnamed for the purposes of this sketch) have not been so enamoured and social inquiry has fragmented into a thousand rival fragments. Undaunted, he is already working on a new book – *How to Think like a Social Scientist*.

I am some kind of realist, some kind of critical, hypothetical, corrigible, scientific realist. But I am against direct realism, naive realism and epistemological complacency.

Donald T. Campbell, *Methodology and Epistemology for the Social Sciences*, 1988

Preface: The Armchair Methodologist and the Jobbing Researcher

What enables and yet constrains research? What is both medium and outcome of research? What do researchers reproduce without even knowing it? What is supposed to unite researchers but may divide them? What empowers researchers to speak but is never fully articulated? What is played out in the routine of research but can never be routinised? What is the responsibility of all researchers but for which none has a mandate?

The answer to all of these riddles is METHODOLOGY. Methodology provides what has been variously described as the procedures, the rules, the codes and the laws of scientific research. But methodological procedures are unlike the exacting drills followed, say, by airline pilots in readying a plane for take-off. Methodological rules are unlike, for instance, those in official rulebooks enforced by referees and followed by sports teams for fear of the penalty. Methodological codes are unlike, for example, the highway code with its compendium of regulations and advice designed as behavioural conventions for all road users. Methodological laws are quite unlike the legislative decrees sanctioned by governments, written in statute and sustained by enforcement regimes.

Scientific methodology shares with these other regimes the ambition to clarify and organise. But the crucial difference is the extent to which the procedures, rules, codes and laws are formalised. In all of our other cases, there is a manual to follow or a handbook to be thumbed or a rulebook to be consulted or an authoritative tome to be pondered. To be sure this guiding documentation is often in a state of steady evolution, with even the two hundred and fifty-year-old Marylebone Cricket Club, the driest and dustiest of regulatory bodies, responding with continued clarifications and amendments to the rules of that game. The crucial point in these other cases is that vested authority is marshalled via a codified set of decrees and propositions.

Consider, by contrast, the rules of the scientific game. Each time the researcher dreams up a project, responds to a tender, enters the field, draws conclusions, makes observations and pens a paper, that individual too will work under a set of expectations. Indeed many researchers consider that they operate under the sternest of requirements – that of producing scientific truths about the fragment of the world selected for study. But whether they are peering down a microscope or into the human psyche, whether they are smashing atoms or counting heads, they do not begin the day by consulting the manual. They have no rulebooks to which to refer, no regulators to affirm standards and no sanctions to keep them honest.

There are methodological rules, of course, but they are soft centred and mutually applied. They exist within the institutional norms and tacit knowledge of the research community. There is no executive body. There is no hard and fast division between legislator and legislatee. Self-scrutiny, peer review and organised distrust provide the levers of control. If science was merely a matter of routine and compunction, of compliance and rule following, it would be pre-programmed – done already or awaiting completion in the pipeline. In reality, scientific research undergoes constant change as fresh discoveries are made and new fields open up. Accordingly, methodological rules cannot be carved in stone. They must allow for creativity and indeed they must innovate as the natural and social worlds change about us and so fashion novel investigative challenges. Methodological rules are therefore adaptive – principle informs practice but innovative practice may yield fruit and gradually embed back into the principles. Each time the researcher dreams up a project, responds to a tender, enters the field, draws conclusions, makes observations and pens a paper, that individual will seed minute modifications to the methodological rules.

I begin this book with this brief soliloquy on methodology as a solemn memorandum to myself of the challenges to come – for I am about to pontificate on the procedures, rules, codes and laws of a little corner of scientific inquiry known as evaluation research. I am about to write a book on methodology – and not for the first time. How does this work? Or, to put it more combatively – if the rules of science are adaptive and collegial who vested you, dear author, with the authority to codify and formalise them?

I think it works like this. The wellspring of methodology is the repetition of certain procedures from investigation to investigation. Let us take as an example the most commonplace of social science methods, the interview. An author might take part in many interviews across many studies and thus reflect on instances that had been more successful and less successful. Further consultations follow with colleagues who have plied and pondered the same trade. The result may well be a textbook, which gathers together the rules of thumb and tricks of trade, so presenting what a group of investigators perceive as best practice. Recall that textbooks, for Kuhn (1962: 2), are crucial to the consolidation of scientific paradigms. Not only do they establish the philosophical footing and provide exemplars, they proselytise for a particular perspective.

Kuhn held a rather dim view of such monographs in the physical sciences, noting their tendency to convey a somewhat conservative, wrinkle-free, wrangle-free view of laboratory life. The same cannot be said of the social science 'methods' textbook. Some texts may be celebrated and regarded as authoritative. But the words of the armchair methodologist only remain definitive as long as the jobbing researcher continues to operate on the same foundations. The principles are sustained in practice. Given the untold complexity of society and the potentially limitless ways of studying it, there are always reasons why that practice may not be sustained. To return to our illustration, an interview may try to tap anything from mundane, face-sheet variables to the subject's innermost thoughts, so leading to the enormous, present-day portfolio of available methods (Gubrium et al., 2012). Jobbing interviewers may thus pick and choose. The result is that social science methodology is rather febrile. In Kuhnian terms, it is 'pre-paradigmatic' – unable to settle on a definitive set of first principles. Given the huge terrain of social inquiry, it is hardly surprising that there is a multitude of theories and methods. It is hardly surprising that some of these come and go. As anecdotal evidence of the fickle fate of methodological strictures in the field of interviewing, I note a marooned attempt of one scholar to persuade the world of the merits of the 'realist interview' (Pawson, 1996 – Google Scholar citation count 34). Before its time, no doubt!

It would appear, then, that there is something of a 'methodology market' in the social sciences and this brings us back to the issue of what it is that licenses methodological authority. What is it that generates the staying power of a particular approach? Occasionally, this is attempted by institutional closure. The methodological armchair becomes a throne. A group declares itself to be the executive and attempts to lay down the law on a particular sphere of operations. For an example here we come closer to home and consider the modus operandi of groups such as the Cochrane and Campbell Collaborations (www.cochrane.org/; www.campbell-collaboration.org/). Having devised what they consider a 'gold standard' approach to a particular form of research, namely systematic review, they then lay down the procedural rules. Hierarchies of evidence must be observed, protocols must be followed and study designs must be approved. If all of this is in place, then an inquiry is authorised and authenticated. Follow this formula and you will find yourself with an accredited, trade-marked publication.

Thankfully, in the febrile, pre-paradigmatic world of social science inquiry, researchers are mostly independent and not so regimented; they still pick and choose their methodology. The guiding and appropriate impulse is to tailor the method according to the perceived requirements topic under study. In other words, methodologies are sustained under the choices and preferences of those jobbing researchers designing the next inquiry and the next and the next. What is more, each inquiry will require a gentle adaptation of the strategy to meet the peculiarities of each situation studied. Methods gain their spurs by thoughtful adaptation rather than mindless replication. Methods come and go but some are more adaptable and thus sustainable. The underlying dynamic of the methodological market, it would seem, is one of the 'survival of the fruitful'.

And this is where I find myself. This book is about the stamina and staying power of the realist approach to evaluation research. Nick Tilley and I published *Realistic Evaluation* in 1997, following a good five years of forethought and deliberation. That book was about methodological choice, for at that time we considered the programme evaluation market rather limited: outcome driven, quasi-experimental approaches imported from clinical trials, processual studies uncovering the formative minutiae of local programmes, mixed in with a bit of constructivist tomfoolery. We proselytised for an alternative, focused on explanation and based on research designs which extracted, tested and refined programme theory. Other key authors shared and championed that mission (Henry et al., 1998; Mark et al., 2000). Other researchers began to share the labour and the terminology, analysing findings by 'context', 'mechanism' and 'outcome'. And even the policy community began to pay heed to the realist slogans, commissioning research to discover 'what works for whom in what contexts?'.

The strategy was further expanded in 2006, with the publication *of Evidence-based Policy: A Realist Perspective*. This book was prompted by the observation that evaluative studies have become industrial in proportion and by the thought, still very much with me, that even more power can be brought to the realist elbow and to the policy table, by extracting, testing and refining programme theories via existing evidence culled from the evaluation factory. And with this step 'realist synthesis' was born. The explanatory principles remain the same but with a different technical application – realist reinterpretations of all the operational stages of a systematic review were provided: establishing the review question, searching for primary studies, assessing their quality, extracting the data, synthesising the evidence, disseminating the findings, and so on.

The present text is intended to be a sequel to these two volumes. One can gain a crude measure of the staying power of ideas through citation counts and it is true to say that it would have knocked the socks off Pawson and Tilley in 1997 and Pawson in 2006 had they an inkling of the weight of present-day bibliographic references to *Realistic Evaluation* and *Evidence-Based Policy* (Google Scholar citations at the time of writing being 2668 and 488 respectively). But all of that is history and the aim of *The Science of Evaluation* is to progress, refine and extend key realist themes throughout applied social inquiry. To do so I have had to ponder on exactly what it is that leads to the survival of the methodologically fruitful. In this spirit, I have in mind four simple motifs to guide the development of the method and with which to infuse this book: i) practice what you preach; ii) share ownership; iii) stimulate debate; iv) address the most difficult challenges.

The first developmental strategy is easy to describe and, given sufficient time, the easiest to put into use. Since empirical practice is both medium and outcome of methodological principle, it is always important to combine the two in explaining the realist perspective. It is important for the armchair philosopher to become the jobbing researcher. Methodological wisdom, perforce, has been aided and abetted on each occasion that I have dreamt up a project, responded to a tender, entered the field, made observations, drawn conclusions and penned a paper. In the final chapter of the book I present a version of the latest, the most extended, and (I like to think) the best crafted of my attempts at realist synthesis (Pawson et al., 2011a). Previous publications on this research have concentrated on the specific policy implications, namely – is there evidence to support the effectiveness of a potential ban on smoking in cars carrying children? Here, the research is reported in two different ways: i) as an exemplification of all the practical steps and decisions that have to be made in conducting a realist synthesis, and ii) as a study of the limits to knowledge that emerge and always emerge from research synthesis.

This second developmental strategy, opening the method to collective ownership, happens, if it happens, under its own steam. At the time of writing there are over a hundred published studies utilising realist evaluation and more than a score of realist syntheses. It is these empirical investigations, rather than any methodological commentary, which embody the sustainability of the strategy. These evaluations and syntheses are located right across the policy waterfront – development studies, social care, urban regeneration, public health, crime reduction, agricultural extension, information science, wildfire prevention and so on. Accordingly, inquiries cover a bewildering array of 'whats' that may work, 'whoms' who may benefit and 'circumstances' that might respond to intervention. As each inquiry progresses, there will be a fresh challenge, one that the researcher deems untouched by previous investigations and unremarked in the existing texts and guidelines. Other researchers will confront similar challenges and collectively they, too, expect a piece of the methodological action.

One example of this, current at the time of writing (Greenhalgh et al., 2011), is the project: *Realist and meta-narrative evidence synthesis – evolving standards* (RAMESES). The aim is to spread ownership of these newer methods of systematic review by having a Delphi Panel, currently numbering 28 individuals with experience in realist synthesis, brainstorming, submitting personal views, exchanging theoretical and empirical papers, and using a simple voting system in order to try to establish some publication standards for these approaches. Whilst I cannot trace all of these developments between the covers of this book, Rameses can expect to leave his fingerprints. In short, there is a club out there of which this is an invitation to join.

The third development strategy, encouraging debate, sounds unremarkable but is truly a cornerstone of the scientific method. As each new realist inquiry progresses there is some resonance and some dissonance with the principles set down in the foundational texts, for as we have seen, real researchers do not simply rehearse scripts or follow recipes. Inevitably, it is the dissonance that is of interest and all the more so when the departure from the method constitutes a challenge to the method. Not all users of a method become wedded to a method. It is under such challenges, or under the scrutiny of what Campbell (1988: 513) calls 'the disputatious community of truth seekers', that methodological progress emerges.

Accordingly, in the second chapter of the book I examine some of the dispute that has gathered in the minds of would-be users of realist evaluation. As a preview, let me mention my favourite migraine-inducing issue – 'I can perceive endless b***** mechanisms and contexts in my programme but I cannot tell one from the other'. In short, some researchers have found it impossible to practise what I preach. My aim in this respect is to engage in conceptual clarification, to refine the exposition of some key realist concepts in order to make them more user-friendly. However, I should make it clear that the medium of clarification here is hard-headed debate. I respond to what I perceive as errors in the application of the method. Readers may be experiencing a whiff of contradiction here and would be correct in thinking that this hardly sounds like 'sharing control' of the method. Because the methodological debate will take place within the covers of this book, won't I load the debate? But sharing control of a method is not the same as ceding control. Methodological debates are there to be won and lost and they should be battled out in the open. To this end Chapter 2 is subtitled 'A Realist Diagnostic Workshop'. It is intended as a platform for further debate that, thanks to the brave new world of online communication, can be continued elsewhere. Here then is another invitation providing a right to reply, an opportunity to add further challenges, and a chance to enlarge the debate. This is all organised under a Sage website called *Methodspace*, which can be accessed at www.methodspace.com.

The fourth strategy for methodological development is to expose a strategy to its most difficult challenges. And where might realism stick out its chin? One methodological challenge dominates this book. It is the feature that generates headaches, triggers migraines and beckons frontal lobotomies for all hard-pressed evaluators and not just realists. I refer, of course, to the problem of complexity. It is the task of Chapter 3 to unravel the different layers of complexity confronting the evaluator but let us foreshadow the mission by noting that programmes are complex by dint of their multiple ambitions and multiple stakeholders, and on account of their long, adaptive and disputed implementation chains, and because the problems they seek to resolve are often interconnected, long-standing and deep-seated, and by reason of the diverse rules, customs, histories in the institutions and contexts in which they operate. And so on!

Now, how has realism fared in the face of complexity? Realist evaluation has many virtues but a mixed blessing is that it adds to the complexity of evaluation research. *Realistic Evaluation* encouraged researchers to dive into the black box and search out what it is about programmes that makes them work. So, to return to a favourite example, readers were urged to understand that CCTV cameras were only dumb, unthinking bits of glass, metal and electronics stuck on the side of buildings, which actually worked to reduce crime through the reasoning of the criminals, operators, ground staff, police and passers-by who encountered them. In this simplest of interventions a flurry of real explanatory mechanisms was thus identified – immediate arrest of those caught in the act, improved detection of those caught on camera, better deployment of police and security staff, increasing perceived risk for would-be offenders, promoting natural surveillance by creating safer environments, reducing the time for crime and so on (Pawson and Tilley, 1997b: 78). Complexity blossoms.

Another realist invective – apply contextual thinking – also increases the complexity of evaluative inquiry, and abundantly so. Realism urges evaluators to consider that all of the characteristics of all participants plus all of its institutional, cultural and historical surroundings were part of the programme. All might be decisive in its success. Previously, programme evaluation had a tendency to treat these factors as either confounding variables to be controlled out of outcome calculations or as immutable, pre-existing features that were not part of the implementation process under scrutiny. The contextual penny has now dropped. All evaluators now understand that what works in Wigan on a wet Wednesday will not necessarily work in Thurso on a thunderous Thursday. The problem, of course, is that contextual conditions are infinite and hardly limited to the British towns, climatic conditions, and weekly rhythms in this little jingle. Complexity snowballs.

The second book, *Evidence-Based Policy*, represents a move from single to multiple inquiries. The conduct of an evidence review, by its very nature, forces researchers into a headlong confrontation with complexity. Synthesis spreads inquiry, inevitably and inexorably, along the implementation chain and across the contextual landscape. One discovers that although a family of programmes carries the same name and harbours the same ambitions, it will never be implemented in the same way twice. For instance, in reviewing the effectiveness of Megan's Law in the USA (under the law the identity of a released sex offender is made known to the community in which he settles), the book examined the manifold decisions required in enacting the legislation (Pawson, 2006a, chapter 5). Which released sex offenders constitute a risk? When, where and how should the local community be notified of their presence? How can community response be channelled and controlled? How and to what extent should probation and police practices change? It soon becomes clear that there is little common ground in the way such decisions are made from state to state, and from county to county, and indeed from official to official. Complexity skyrockets.

In short, it can be said that the realist perspective, having called for an opening up of the 'black box' of interventions, now needs a way of replacing the lid. The entire second part of the book is devoted to that task. The way ahead is marked by an admixture of ambition and caution. Evaluation science needs to be more venturesome in widening the focus of inquiries from that of 'the programme' and should begin to consider 'policy ideas and their history' as its subject matter. It needs to avoid the perpetual, regressive habit of 'starting from scratch' and should expect each new investigation to respond to and develop from 'what is already known'. At the same time it is necessary to make absolutely clear that the terminus of evaluation research is, always and perforce, partial knowledge. Accordingly, the central task in all that follows is to defend and indeed to celebrate the never-ending pursuit of unobtainable truth.

Under the challenge of such a fine motto, I now offer a speedy rehearsal of the thesis to come. It is produced in three parts, which I like to think of as prequel, midquel and sequel. I am pretty sure, *Star Wars* apart, that there is no such word as 'midquel' but the idea is to suggest sequence in the argument and growth in the storyline. Part One looks back to the foundations of realist evaluation. Part Two wrestles with the present day challenges and with that tenacious opponent going by the name of complexity. Part Three contemplates the future and a wider, cinemascopic role for evaluation science. Each chapter has been designed to be read independently and so takes the bother to explain itself at the outset.

Part One. We begin in prehistory, before evaluation research had been weaned, with a brief chapter on the emergence and the present-day relevance of key realist ideas in philosophy and social science. Next is a chapter dealing with the methodological headaches left behind by the previous ministrations of Drs Pawson and Tilley. Hearty debate is joined as I seek to refine the basic conceptual apparatus of realism via a critique of the misadventures of other researchers who have found their own ways of conducting 'realist' evaluations.

Part Two. Complexity takes its bow in Chapter 3, with a concerted attempt to articulate its every nook and cranny as seen from a realist perspective. Given that the issue of complexity tops the agenda in all schools of evaluation and social science, Chapter 4 compares notes and seeks out the strengths and weaknesses of the rival 'solutions'. This is followed by the pivotal chapter of the book, an attempt to rewrite the principles of evaluation science under the challenge of complexity. I venture to suggest that evaluation research should significantly enlarge its explanatory ambitions, whilst acknowledging that its findings and policy recommendations will always remain partial.

Part Three. Chapter 6 is the first of three seeking to pursue some grander challenges of the now widened realist manifesto. It produces a programme theory for the much coveted ambition of 'behavioural change'. Revealed is the wave after wave of 'invisible mechanisms' that must be fired in shifting wavering, havering programme subjects and a sharp contrast is drawn with the naive pronouncements of the 'nudge' theorists. Clinical interventions, at large and as a whole, are the target of Chapter 6 under the argument that they are every bit as complex as social interventions. It follows that evidence-based medicine would benefit from a healthy dose of realism. Finally we come to the denouement of the tale, the circumambulatory Chapter 8, which attempts to practise in the space of a single investigation, all of the earlier preaching on the science of evaluation.

A brief conclusion contemplates dialogue with the chattering classes. It asks – how will the complex and partial truths of realist inquiry fare amidst the political clamour? A mixed picture emerges personified by two characters – the Steady Eddy of Realism and the villainous One-armed Scientist.

With the content described, I am now ready to commence my self-appointed task of refining the principle and practice of evaluation science. As I've tried to explain, methodological progress is a process that no one superintends. Methodologists do their thinking rather noisily – out loud, in texts, on the rostrum and the soap box. For jobbing researchers methodological decisions are muted and ceaseless and made in confronting the *next* fieldwork problem. Both ways are true ways and I have tried to infuse and balance the book with work on both the principles and practice of realist inquiry. For a methodology to advance, its philosophers and practitioners, its arm-chair dwellers and field-workers, and its farmers and cowmen should be friends.

Speaking of which, it is a pleasure to introduce and thank the many colleagues who have roamed the realist prairies with me and who, according to the cunning alibi I have concocted above, share co-responsibility for all the blunders and pratfalls that I am about to make. Geoff Wong, Lesley Owen, Sanjeev Sridharan, Trish Greenhalgh, Gill Westhorp, Joanne Greenhalgh and Ana Manzano have joined me in several recent projects and publications and their ideas, their labours, and some of their words are imprinted onto the following pages. Mark Monaghan, Jenny Hewison, Nick Emmel, Frans Leeuw, Nicoletta Stame, Elliot Stern, Mike Kelly, Kieran Walshe, Rob Anderson, Mark Pearson, Alex Clarke, Patricia Rogers, Greg Ogrinc, Paul Batalden, Don Berwick, Dave Byrne, Malcolm Williams, and Martyn Hammersley have all proved valuable allies in a variety of intriguing sub-plots. Last and hardly least, thanks to Nick Tilley for joining me in that initial, insightful stroll in Meanwood Park. One must never omit the vital institutional support and I hereby acknowledge awards from two UK bodies, the ESRC (Economic and Social Research Council) and NIHR HS&DR (The National Institute of Health Research: Health Service and Delivery Research programme). Thanks also to Katie Metzler and Anna Horvai, the new team at Sage. Much better than the old bloke. My unedited texts can be a pain and I am grateful for the painstaking work of Ian Antcliff, Jennifer Hinchliffe and Jill Birch, the production team at SAGE for bashing it into shape. For further proof that one can judge a book by its cover, grazie ancora a David dalla Venezia. With apologies from my forgetful brain to anyone omitted from a now lengthy list of sympathisers, there is one final lexicographical task before we enter the labyrinth.

'Realism' – What's in a Name?

Once again, I've produced a book marching proudly under the banner of 'realism'. It has become increasingly problematic to do so because as realist inquiry has flourished it has also divided. It is useful, therefore, to attempt to clear up a little terminological confusion at the outset. Donald Campbell (1988: 444) found himself in a similar difficulty some three decades ago in an utterance I have used as the epigraph for this book: 'I am some kind of realist, some kind of critical, hypothetical, corrigible, scientific realist. But I am against direct realism, naive realism and epistemological complacency.' It would take a chapter or two to sort through this little lot of realisms, so I will settle for noting that Campbell's (1988) critical realism is not the same as Bhaskar's (1979) critical realism: the former being about promoting criticism and counter criticism in the community of scientists; the latter being about the possession of a privileged, normative standpoint with which to criticise other interpretations of the world. Campbell's other realisms are based on a view that science is a perpetual process of theory testing, thus always beginning in the 'hypothetical' and still ending in the 'corrigible'.

My own usage of realist terminology has also wobbled in wordage if not in meaning. The strategy developed here was first termed 'scientific realist' analysis (Pawson and Tilley, 1997a). We used the phrase because the mantle of science has been grabbed, wrongly in our opinion, by these favouring experimental trials. We also favoured it because the method was identified squarely with a generative view of causation which had come to the fore in the philosophy of science.

A couple of years later Tilley and I dropped the prefix 'scientific' and settled on the phase 'realistic evaluation', though this was intended as a title of a book rather than the name for the method. We still insisted on pursuing the high scientific objectives of objectivity and generative causal explanation but also wanted to emphasise that evaluation research had a different cause from other social sciences, namely to have realistic ambitions to inform real-world policy and practice.

Thereafter, the simpler phrase 'realist evaluation' became the norm, partly because it was also the preferred nomenclature of other authors (Henry et al., 1998; Mark et al., 2000). I continued in this usage when I enlarged the approach to cover systematic review methodology, which in realist guise, for obvious reasons, became 'realist synthesis'. In other outlets I have referred to 'middle-range realism' (Pawson, 2000) in order to stress membership of the theory-driven school of evaluation research and usage of an explanatory formula following closely upon Merton's middle-range theory.

In the present text, I had a sneaking ambition to return to my original term, 'scientific realism', based on continuing solidarity with and the further development of Mertonian and Campbellian methods. As this would only have seeded further confusion I have decided to stick, and proudly so, to the terms 'realist evaluation' and 'realist synthesis'. Though to mark some broadening ambitions I also introduce the term 'evaluation science' in an attempt to decouple evaluation research from its moorings in the analysis of single interventions. Evaluation science has ambitions to shape the widest domains of policy inquiry and is served by the methods of realist evaluation and realist synthesis.

In the spirit of Campbell I close this lexicon by noting that I, too, am 'some kind of realist'.

PART 1

Precursors and Principles

The aim of Part One is to establish the book's realist foundation and, to the best of my ability, create a level playing field for all readers. Realism, as a form of scientific explanation, has a long history. Realist evaluation and realist synthesis are new kids on the block. They should be understood as workaday research strategies that have done their utmost to embody the principle of realist explanation. They are attempts to remain faithful to key tenets from the philosophical page and to apply them in the practical struggle to make sense of the policy mêlée.

Chapter 1 establishes some key realist principles, the seven pillars of realist wisdom no less. I've chosen to do this with some economy by selecting seven key authors and highlighting their particular contributions. Drawing up the shortlist was something of a headache. Lavish excuses are made to those not making the cut. The point to note is that the realist endowment belongs to the philosophy of science, the sociology of science and to social science methodology more generally. Only two jobbing evaluators are encountered and, even here, discussion revolves around their Herculean ideas on evaluation's guiding principles. The Pillars of Hercules appear on the cover page of Sir Frances Bacon's *Novum Organum* (1620), with the inscription, 'Many will pass through and knowledge will be the greater.' I like to think the same applies to anyone encountering the foundations established here.

Chapter 2 pays close attention to the founding concepts of realist evaluation. As with any other method, realist inquiry develops its own terminology. Realist evaluation centres around exploring the 'mechanisms', 'contexts' and 'outcomes' associated with an intervention. For any would-be users of the method, questions immediately erupt – what are these things, how do I spot them, how many of them need to be dealt with, how should I understand their balance? Although, I have striven to make all of these matters clear, it is inevitable that in other hands these core ideas will be reshaped. The purpose of the chapter is to thus further refine the key apparatus of realist evaluation by engaging in debate with other realist evaluators and other realist inquiries. As explained in the preface, the whole point is to collectivise ownership of the strategy.

Chapter 1 represents work done in the realist armchair. Chapter 2 transfers realism to the field. The aim of Part One is to make them equally comfortable environments.

ONE

Precursors: Seven Pillars of Realist Wisdom

A couple of years ago Elliot Stern asked me to make a contribution to the journal *Evaluation* under the title 'From the library of Ray Pawson', with the aim of describing some of the intellectual precursors to my work. The intention was to provide a lighter-hearted coda to the other, more closely-textured papers evaluating water purification programmes in Swaziland, value-for-money local government schemes in Stoke-on-Trent, cheese production improvement in Switzerland, and so on. I took a little bit of persuading, fearing that it might read like a vanity publication, 'About Ray Pawson'. My feeling was that one's ideas should do the talking and that one's texts should speak for themselves. Better to watch Wayne Rooney play football than to have someone explain why he is good at it. Better to suffer prolonged, agonising torture than hear Wayne Rooney describe the influences on his game.

In the end humility faltered and the influences on *my* game were described (Pawson, 2011). Given that one of the aims of this book is to test the stamina of realist inquiry, it struck me that that little paper would make a fine starting point. I've adapted it by extending each pocket description as well as adding two further intellectual heroes. Rather than just describe their key ideas, I've also emphasised their value to evaluation research and evidence-based policy. With some partial exceptions, these are not the musings of evaluators. Most of these authors are writing to a philosophical remit and throughout the book I will call on the principles established in this chapter to provide the platform for a practical science of evaluation.

———— **1. Bhaskar, R. (1978) *A Realist Theory of Science.* London: Verso** ————

This, his first text, is on the philosophy of science and is unlike his remaining work which reaches into the social sciences and humanities. It gives pride of place in natural science explanation to the concept of the 'generative mechanism'. Physicists explain the relationships such as the gas laws through knowledge of the kinetics of molecular action. The attributes of compounds, such as gelignite's capacity to explode, is explained by their underlying chemical composition. Biologists explain evolutionary change through the mechanism of natural selection. In medicine, the 'mechanism of action' of a drug is what enables it to attack viruses, kill cancerous cells, heal bacterial infections, and so forth.

Bhaskar's moment of glory lies in showing that the laws of physics are not discovered through observational routines, nor through the mechanical application of measuring instruments. Rather, laboratory work attempts to reproduce a set of processes that we expect theoretically will give rise to an empirical regularity. Scientific experiments trigger a hypothesised mechanism in a known set of conditions in order to see if the expected uniformity comes to pass. Consider an early example, recounted by another realist (Harré, 1983) in a book on *The Great Scientific Experiments*. The experiment in question aimed to refine our understanding of the earth's geomagnetic field. It had been known (through observation) that magnetised compass needles always pointed in the same direction, originally considered to be towards 'Heaven' and then, more mundanely, to the 'North'. The prevailing theory explained this as a result of the north acting as a 'point attractive', which physically pulled magnetised objects in that direction. Norman's 1581 (Harré, 1983) experiment consisted of inserting a magnetised wire into a cork and suspending the floating compass in a beaker of water. As expected, the needle continued to point north. However, it also dipped in the direction of the North Pole but without descending to the bottom or moving to the north end of the beaker.

What this experiment does is to help confirm one theory at the expense of another. The conclusion drawn was that 'the direction is not produced by attraction but by a disposing and conversory power existing in the earth as a whole' (Harré, 1983: 53). The crucial experimental manipulation is the release of the compass needle from its fixed anchorage. Under this condition, we can then see clearly that it is not physically dragged off to the point attractant. Rather, its angle of rest means that the earth itself must have a magnetic field and that a free-floating compass simply aligns itself to the field. Our understanding of geomagnetism, it may be said, has advanced somewhat from the sixteenth century but this simple experiment has all the classic ingredients. Experiments are made by designing rather than observing a closed system, the design being informed by theory. The results of the manipulations are foreshadowed and interpreted by theories of underlying generative mechanisms which organise the observable properties.

There is a vast gulf between this account and the basic understanding of experimental manipulation at large in the world of randomised trials. Under the latter logic, laws are discovered through experimental manipulation and observation. The idea is to create (by randomisation or matching) two identical systems into one of which a new component is introduced. Observations are then made of outcome differences that occur between the experimental and control conditions and should a change occur, it is attributed to the one difference between them, namely the introduction of the experimental stimulus. The manipulation does not require any understanding of why the control situation behaves as it does and why the introduction of a new component might change it. The findings are expected to speak for themselves.

The message is clear. If evaluation is to follow the *Great Experiments* it would be wise for it to start with a theory of how the intervention affects the system into which it is introduced. As Bhaskar puts it, 'Theory without experiment is empty. Experiment without theory is blind' (1978, 191). From this pioneering study we glean a core concept, generative mechanism, and a pleasing motto to carry forward into the book. Note that following this groundbreaking work, Bhaskar's philosophical outpourings turned increasingly to the normative, the emancipatory, and, ironically, towards the point attractive heavens. Evaluation practitioners beware.

2. Archer, M. (1995) *Realist Social Theory.* ——— Cambridge: Cambridge University Press

This is the first of several volumes whose task is to comprehend the nature of causality in the social world. Here we move from physical systems to social systems and from sub-atomic generative mechanisms to ... what? Archer's message is clear – social science should commence with an understanding of how people come to make choices, for their collective decision making constitutes the underlying mechanism that generates all social outcomes.

But there is a twist – society is made by, but never under the control of, human intentions. As she put it in a memorable phrase: 'Society is that which nobody wants, in the form they encounter, for it is an unintended consequence'. Our choices are set in a fascinating relay race. At any given time, choices are conditioned by pre-existing structures, institutions and opportunities. Those choices, once applied, then go on to remould a novel social structure, which in turn conditions a fresh round of choices for a slightly different cohort of choice makers. And so on. Society is thus in a state of permanent self-transformation (termed 'morphogenesis' by Archer). It is patterned and re-patterned by wilful action but without confirming anyone's wishes, even those of the most powerful.

This is the permanent state of society. This is how life goes on. There are major implications for evaluation research. The things we study – policies, programmes, interventions – are inserted into systems which are already fluid and changing. Interventions are often heralded as 'instruments for change' – but what they actually try to do, all they can do, is to change the course of change. This dynamic plays havoc with one of the time-honoured themes of evaluation research – counterfactual logic. Evaluation has traditionally been asked to pronounce on whether a programme makes a difference 'beyond that which would have happened anyway'. We always need to keep in mind that what would have happened anyway is change – unavoidable, unplanned, self-generated, morphogenetic change.

Evaluation will always struggle with the idea of an incessantly renewing world and it is worth setting down some of the initial implications. The first is to consider the nature of programmes. They are part of society and thus they too obey the iron law of self-transformation. Interventions will always mutate (thanks to sage practition-ers, who always want to improve them) and can never be exactly reproduced (to the chagrin of dogmatic trialists who require them to be standardiseable). Then, there is the matter of what programmes do. Programmes seek to change the way that the subjects make choices. But, according to Archer's model, the collective choices of those so changed begin to make up a new social order. In short, programmes may well change the conditions that made them work in the first place and so can be expected to have a limited 'shelf life'.

Morphogenesis places a cap on the overall ambitions of evaluation. Programmes induce change but without conforming to the wishes of any particular stake-holder, even those of the most powerful. The changes generated can never be fully anticipated and are not entirely predictable. But this is no cause for hand-wringing; neither is social change haphazard and random. The social world stum-bles between stability and change and it is the relatively enduring features that imprint a pattern. This world of 'demi-regularities' is the subject matter of realist evaluation and synthesis.

——— 3. Elster, J. (2007) *Explaining Social Behaviour.* Cambridge: Cambridge University Press ———

Realist evaluation is a form of theory-driven evaluation. But its theories are not the highfalutin' theories of sociology, psychology and political science. Indeed, the term 'realistic' evaluation is sometimes substituted out of the desire to convey the idea that the fate of a programme lies in the everyday reasoning of its stakeholders. Good evaluations gain power for the simple reason that they capture the manner in which an awful lot of participants think. One might say that the basic currency is common-sense theory.

However, this should only be the starting point. The full explanatory sequence needs to be rooted in but not identical to everyday reasoning. In trying to describe the precise elbow room between social science and common sense one can do no better that to follow Elster's thinking. He has much else to say on the nuts and bolts of social explanation, but here we concentrate on that vital distinction, as mooted in the following:

> Much of science, including social science, tries to explain things we all know, but science can make a contribution by establishing that some of the things we all think we know simply are not so. In that case, social science may also explain why we think we know things that are not so, adding as it were a piece of knowledge to replace the one that has been taken away. (2007: 16)

Some of the things we all know, posits Elster, are encapsulated in the form of 'pro-verbial folk wisdom' and proverbs illustrate prettily how we must build on but also build beyond everyday understanding. So, if someone is stirred to observe that 'too many cooks spoil the broth' they are constructing a clever piece of everyday generative explanation about how over-staffed and chaotic work routines may lead people inadvertently to duplicate an action (the soup gets over-salted). Alas, posits Elster, proverbial reasoning has a tendency to mislead. The salty broth outcome is akin to but not consonant with another piece of metaphorical wisdom, namely that: 'too many shepherds make a poor guard'. Here, over-staffing is such that people choose not to act under the assumption that someone else has already done the job. An even more contradictory proverb has it that 'many hands make light work'. Forms of work organisation remain the explanatory mechanism. In this case, workers' choices are preordained and fixed but their separate and individual functioning brings efficiency to a collective task. Finally, moving to tasks requiring uniform behaviour for all members of a group, we discover a further metaphorical twist to the proverbial repertoire on teamwork, namely the advice: 'no member of a crew is praised for the individuality of his rowing'.

The point of comparing these everyday maxims is that they provide an evaluation challenge in miniature. They are all, so to speak, programme theories rooted in practitioner wisdom. They all point to outcomes, sometimes unintended, which are frequently discovered in collective work routines. They all feature mechanisms which tell us what it is about teamwork that generates a particular outcome. But no one proposition is universally correct; sometimes they are 'so' and sometimes they are 'not so'. All depends on context. It is the realist evaluator's task, and the added value of social science, to identify and explain the precise circumstances under which each theory holds.

4. Merton, R. (1967) *On Theoretical Sociology:* ——— *Five essays old and new.* New York: Free Press

Evidence-based policy has become associated with systematic review methods for the soundest of reasons. Most programmes have a history and it makes sense to comb the historical records to see if we can discern reasons for success and failure. It always provides something of a shock in conducting such exercises to come upon the atomised and fragmented nature of programme-building. One digests report after report in which the same old programme theory is presented as an innovative intervention, with a shiny new acronym, aimed at a hitherto neglected social group, located in some previously overlooked corner of Never Never Land. Most evaluation research complies with this little conspiracy, tackling the one-off intervention using designs that start from scratch. One is led to wonder, under such a regime, whether lessons are learned, whether policy reflection has been deepened and whether programme implementation becomes more skilled.

But there is solace. There is a research domain, which is even longer in the tooth, and in which this problem is even more pressing and which foreshadows a solution. I refer to sociology, noting in passing that all of the social sciences trouble over whether they can be said to have progressed. Enter any sociology library and peer across the groaning shelves, enter cyberspace and download from all the countless sociology journals and similar questions are prompted. There are countless, separate inquiries but can they be said to cumulate? Has each author and each generation added to the wisdom of its forebears? Inquiry is older, but is it wiser? Answers to these questions seem to range from an unquestioning 'yes' (just look at all that work!) to a hostile 'no!' (why look for conflux when the job is social criticism?). To be sure, the issue of 'accumulation' raises a moot question but at least, for sociology, a solution has been mooted.

The blueprint for a progressive, accumulative social science has been long established. In one of his five essays, Merton puts forward the notion of middle-range theory, suggesting that we should produce explanations that: 'are sufficiently abstract to deal with different spheres of social behaviour and social structure, so that they transcend sheer description' (1967: 68). The key step comes with the ability to 'confederate' seemingly diverse empirical phenomena:

> An army private bucking for promotion may only in a narrow and superficial sense be regarded as engaging in behavior different from that of an immigrant assimilating the values of a native group, or of a lower-middle-class individual conforming to his conception of upper-middle-class patterns of behavior, or of a boy in a slum orienting himself to the values of a settlement house worker rather than the values of the street corner, or of a Bennington student abandoning the conservative beliefs of her parents to adopt the more liberal ideas of her college associates, or of a lower class Catholic departing from the pattern of his in-group by casting a Republican vote, or an eighteenth century French aristocrat aligning himself with a revolutionary group of the time. (1968: 332)

He suggests here that all of these seemingly diverse behaviours have a common thread. That dynamic is explained under an idea known as 'reference group theory'. This is based on the simple, abstract idea that people base their own actions on the standards of 'significant others'. In order to discern where an individual's life-chances lie one has a common investigative challenge – to figure out which is his/her relevant 'in-group' and 'out-group', how much she/he aspires to the in-group, and how high are the barriers forbidding in-group membership?

Evaluators would do well to seek confederation across their findings. The penny might then drop that their gleaming intervention is not new at all and will have been tried before – and that the place to start evaluation is with the well-travelled programme theory that underpins it. Available policy levers are not that numerous and so programme theories are repeated ad nauseam. The starting point is to consider much more tenaciously the similarities between seemingly diverse programmes – what do they hold in common?

───── ## 5. Popper, K. (1992) *The Logic of Scientific Discovery.* London: Routledge ─────

Having a background in social science methodology has made me very wary about strong claims for evidence. Social research is supremely difficult and prone to all kinds of error, mishap and bias. One consequence of this in the field of evaluation is the increasingly strident call for hierarchies of evidence, protocolised procedures, professional standards, quality appraisal systems and so forth. What this quest for technical purity forgets is that all scientific data is hedged with uncertainty, a point which is at the root of Popperian philosophy of science.

Popper preferred the term 'critical rationalism' to describe the considerable reach of his philosophical perspective. Here we pick up the 'post-empiricist' thread of the work. Like Bhaskar, he argued that scientific laws are not established in experiment and observation. For Popper such a viewpoint committed the error of induction, for no run of favourable data, however long and unbroken, is logically sufficient to establish the truth of an unrestricted generalisation. Black swans lurk in prey of the 'law' based on the million observations that swans are white.

For Popper, as with Bhaskar, it is our theories which make sense of observable regularities. But empirical evidence still plays a vital role in scientific research for it is capable of falsifying or limiting the scope of those theories. Accordingly, he moves away from the 'one hypothesis, one test at a time' view of scientific inquiry and regards it as a continuous or 'evolutionary' process. Scientists face a puzzling set of observational patterns; they apply their creative imagination by putting forward a bold set of conjectures to explain the apparent uniformities; they then test the theories in observation and measurement, the tests revealing more complex empirical work than first envisaged; some explanations are then preferred according to their ability to explain the patterns as well as the exceptions to the patterns; certain theories survive which are then put to further testing and development as new puzzling observations come to light. For Popper (1992: 94), as with Merton, science grows with the cumulation of explanation, rather than on the bedrock of observational facts:

> The empirical basis of objective science has thus nothing 'absolute' about it. Science does not rest upon rock-bottom. It is like a building erected on piles. The piles are driven down from above into the swamp, but not down to any natural or 'given' base; and when we cease our attempts to drive our piles into a deeper layer, it is not because we have reached firm ground. We simply stop when we are satisfied that they are firm enough to carry the structure, at least for the time being.

What is good enough for natural science is good enough for evidence-based policy, which comes with a frightening array of unanticipated swans – white, black and all shades of grey. Here too, 'evidence' does not come in finite chunks offering certainty and security to policy decisions. Programmes and interventions spring into life as ideas about how to change the world for the better. These ideas are complex and consist of whole chains of main and subsidiary propositions. The task of evaluation research is to articulate and refine those theories. The task of systematic review is to refine those refinements. But the process is continuous – for in a 'self-transforming' world there is always an emerging angle, a downturn in programme fortunes, a fresh policy challenge. Evidence-based policy will only mature when it is understood that it is a continuous, accumulative process in which the data pursues, but never quite draws level with, unfolding policy problems. Enlightened policies, like bridges over swampy waters, only hold 'for the time being'.

———6. Campbell, D.T. (1988) *Methodology and Epistemology for Social Science: Collected Papers.* Chicago: University of Chicago Press (edited by S Overman) ———————

Campbell is rightly venerated for his classic texts on quasi-experimentation, known fondly in the trade as the 'old testament' (Campbell and Stanley, 1966) and the 'new testament' (Cook and Campbell, 1979). These books devised research designs and statistical techniques to reduce threats to the validity of field experiments and they form the basis of all modern work in that domain. However, Campbell was also an eminent philosopher of science and laboured for over thirty years in developing an approach that he variously describes as 'evolutionary epistemology' and 'post-positivist, critical realism'. And it is this contribution that is represented here by a volume of his collected writings.

His name lives on in the evaluation community, being celebrated by a group of scholars attempting to organise systematic review methodology under the auspices of 'The Campbell Collaboration' (www.campbellcollaboration.org/). Somewhat mischievously, I want to suggest that Campbell would have had his doubts about membership. In particular, there are two Collaboration shibboleths that do not accord with the writings of Campbell the philosopher. The first is the insistence on 'procedural uniformity': the idea that in order to achieve objectivity and reproducibility reviews must be carried out in the same fashion to the same protocol. The second is the 'hierarchy of evidence', the concentration on evidence gleaned from Randomised Controlled Trials (RCTs), the low credit rating afforded to qualitative research, and the virtual detestation of local, tacit knowledge.

To advance my sceptical case I turn to Campbell's own words. Here is what he has to say on: i) objectivity and ii) qualitative method:

> The objectivity of physical science does not come from turning over the running of experiments to people who could not care less about the outcome, nor from having a separate staff to read the meters. It comes from a social process that can be called competitive cross-validation and from the fact that there are many independent decision makers capable of rerunning an experiment, at least in a theoretically essential form. The resulting dependability of reports … comes from a social process rather than from the dependability of any single experimenter. Somehow in the social system of science a systematic norm of distrust, combined with ambitiousness, leads people to monitor each other for improved validity. Organized distrust produces trustworthy reports. (1988: 302)

> Qualitative knowledge is absolutely essential as a prerequisite foundation for quantification in any science. Without competence at the qualitative level, one's computer printout is misleading or meaningless. We failed in our thinking about programme evaluation methods to emphasise the need for a qualitative

context that could be depended upon. One example is the frequent separation of data collection, data analysis, and programme implementation that was once characteristic of Washington's funding of programs ... This easily lead to a gullible credulity about the numbers on the computer tape, with the analyst in total innocence about what was going on in the program implementation ... To rule out plausible hypotheses we need situation specific wisdom. The lack of this knowledge (whether it be called ethnography or program history or gossip) makes us incompetent estimators of programme impacts, turning out conclusions that are not only wrong, but often wrong in socially destructive ways. (1988: 366)

The implication for evaluation and systematic review could not be clearer. Here is a clarion call to scavenge for evidence of all forms, quantitative and qualitative, outcome and process, measurement and gossip! But then there is the glorious twist represented by the first quotation. However high this evidence is piled, it will not lead to objectivity. What counts are the hypotheses that drive us to the data and the inferences that are drawn from the data. In order to harden such inferences, Campbell argues that theories must be tested and tested again, sometimes to destruction and sometimes to live another day. Above all, we need to attend much more closely and collectively to the quality of the reasoning in research reports rather than look only to the quality of the data.

7. Rossi, P. (1987) 'The Iron Law of Evaluation ———— and Other Metallic Rules', *Research in Social Problems and Public Policy*, 4(1): 3–30

Rossi has made many fine contributions that would grace any evaluation library. More obvious candidates for an accolade might be the two pioneering papers with Chen, which make the earliest claims for the utility of a theory-driven approach (Chen and Rossi, 1980; 1983). Another classic is the punctilious, *Money, Work and Crime*, which eats up 348 pages in evaluating a single programme (Rossi et al., 1980). This intervention, the 'transitional aid research project' (TARP), was based on the idea of providing released prisoners with small, limited term financial incentives to facilitate their adjustment to life beyond the prison wires. Early trials of the programme were highly promising, the revolving door of reincarceration turning significantly more slowly for the intervention recipients than for the unsupported control groups. But, as with many demonstration projects, disappointment followed – with a later, larger trial based in different penitentiaries failing to show any net impact.

Rossi's team had collected sufficient data to peer, nay pour, into the black box of this programme. The intervention is a simple incentive, the 'money' of Rossi's title. Now, as with all programme theories, incentives work through their perceived utility to the subject. In the case of TARP, aid could be used to support job search, namely 'work', or conversely, it could negate the immediate need to find paid employment and so initiate a return to old habits, namely 'crime'. Indeed, within limits, the payments could be used to support any chosen vice or virtue. In realist terms, the intervention triggers opposing mechanisms and it is the balance of choices in the population under study that determines the net outcome of the programme. Such balances can be expected to differ from instance to instance, trail to trial. Different mechanisms may, as here, cancel each other out.

Rossi came upon *countervailing mechanisms* in much of his evaluation research career and was thus inspired to compose the 'Metallic Laws of Evaluation'. The most tyrannical insists on the following:

> The Iron Law of Evaluation: The expected value of any net impact assessment of any large scale social program is zero.

Rossi's tongue was firmly in cheek in the naming of his laws. His brain was firmly engaged, however, for he insists, with the iron law, that programmes work only when implemented in a particular way and only when targeted at well-defined outcomes, for the right subjects, in appropriate circumstances. Why Rossi thinks that this formula impels us towards zero aggregate impact is that 'large scale programs' generally overreach themselves. In other words, a programme theory finds favour, sometimes on the back of good news from a pilot investigation, and a huff and puff of activity breaks out in its wake, encouraging it into the hands of inexperienced practitioners, and expanding its market to ill-defined outcomes, tougher subjects and inauspicious contexts. Few interventions can survive that journey.

Emboldened by this maverick paper, I conclude with a further decree:

> *A Golden Rule for Evaluators and Policymakers*: Instead of imagining your job is to choose the most effective interventions, better to follow the iron law and to treat a chosen programme as a blank canvas in which your task is to choose the best means for its targeting and implementation.

All good advice manuals should end at the magic number seven and so I cut short my tour of the library at this point. It goes without saying that many other volumes and many other authors could equally have taken pride of place. I am thinking, for instance, of the master of generative explanation, Raymond Boudon, whose sociological work is a model for evaluative inquiry, being a perfect amalgam of principle and practice. Fortunately, I have had the opportunity to say this elsewhere (Pawson, 2009a). Another unforgivable omission is Carol Weiss, also a founder of the theory-driven approach in evaluation and the scholar who has best explained its utilisation potential – the 'enlightenment approach'. No excuses here – other than that this entire book may be said to be given over to her question – 'which links in which theories should we evaluate?' (Weiss, 2000).

As explained, the real purpose of this chapter is to examine the infrastructure of a methodology and thus the real motive for the above selection is to demonstrate that realist evaluation and realist synthesis stand on the shoulders of giants.

TWO

First Principles: A Realist Diagnostic Workshop

The realist approach can now be said to be part of the repertoire of evaluation methods. There has been a corresponding shift in methodological focus. Polemical thrust and counter-thrust about the realist contribution as compared to that of other evaluative approaches such as randomised trials and meta-analysis have given way to closer examination of its practice 'on the ground'. This chapter seeks to clarify some core principles through a constructive critique of recently published 'realist evaluations'. The approach followed here was prompted by a remark made by a candidate for a post on a project requiring, as it was put in the job description, 'experience in realist approaches to evaluation'. Sagely, he remarked that realist evaluation was in danger of becoming the 'new grounded theory'. He was referring, one supposes, to the overabundant and carefree use of a convenient methodological tag – one that bestows some contemporary vogue on the research, one that distances the writer from vile positivism and one, most significantly, that allows the researcher to pursue a blend of close empirical analysis combined with a modicum of careful theory development. The parallel is not exact of course. Grounded theory experienced a rather major hiccup when the two founding authors (Glaser and Strauss, 1967) fell out on finer points of method – thus leaving followers to choose between them (e.g. Walker and Myrick, 2006). I can report, by contrast, sweet harmony in the Pawson and Tilley camp.

The charge, however, remains. The years since the publication of *Realistic Evaluation* (Pawson and Tilley, 1997b) and *Evidence-Based Policy: A Realist Perspective* (Pawson, 2006a) have seen the publication of more than a hundred papers claiming to be realist evaluations and over a score of systematic reviews declaring themselves to be realist syntheses. A glaring question arises – are they really realist? It turns out that this is a tough question and arguably the wrong question to ask. It has always been stressed that realism is a general research strategy rather than a strict technical procedure (Pawson and Tilley, 1997b: chapter 9). It has always been stressed that innovation in realist research design will be required to tackle a widening array of policies and programmes (Pawson, 2006a: 93–99). It has always been stressed that this version of realism is Popperian and Campbellian in its philosophy of science and thus relishes the use of the brave conjecture and the application of judgement (Pawson et al., 2011a). From these vantage points, it can be seen that realist inquiry is a broad and welcoming church.

The question, however, will still not go away. For a strategy to be regarded as paradigmatic, there has, by definition, to be a family resemblance within the paradigm. Whilst the core strategy is always capable of development under new challenges, realist inquiry has and must have unique and distinguishing family features. The paper goes back to basics in documenting and explaining some of these meta-theoretical essentials. It does so, however, in a ruthlessly practical manner. Acknowledging that there is a core framework implies that out there in the field there are likely to be better and worse approximations. One of realist evaluation's tasks is to improve programmes by distinguishing between situations with effective and ineffective implementation. By the same logic, it follows that methodological refinement will be generated by examining applications of the method with exactly the same critical and differential focus.

This brings us more precisely to the task of the present chapter, which provides a close examination of some published examples of 'realist evaluation' in order to diagnose potential weaknesses and to consider how these interpretations of the approach might be strengthened. Readers will appreciate that the author is treading on collegial eggshells here and it should be stressed that studies selected below are chosen with a diagnostic purpose – to improve the generic programme of realist research. What follows is not a crackdown on counterfeit goods and the examples are not featured to name and shame particular authors. Rather, the purpose of the chapter is to clarify realist evaluation's core strategies and to elucidate its core terms by examining their commission and omission in a series of studies.

There is no such thing as the perfect inquiry, realist or otherwise. The case studies that follow are chosen to represent examples of common drawbacks, the difficulties that many authors have faced in trying to render realist principles into realist practice. Accordingly, the case studies are grouped to investigate three shortcomings: i) absence of an explanatory focus; ii) working in one data medium method rather than being multi-method; iii) failure to investigate contexts, mechanisms and outcomes in configuration. Note finally that I have investigated each case only against specific published outputs and the diagnosis, here apart, fails to mention one of the biggest drawbacks of all to realist ambitions, namely the journal requirements in many a field to publish in three or four thousand words. Little wonder that realist contributions fail to find room for all that occurs within the black box and in the contextual surrounds of an intervention.

Realist evaluation has its own slogan – 'what works for whom in what circumstances'. Since it was coined in the first text, this phrase has gradually been embellished to capture the multiple, contingent outcomes of all interventions. A more meticulous, if less snappy, version thus goes: 'what is it about a programme that works for whom, in what circumstances, in what respects, over which duration'. The most significant rendition, however, adds a vital realist signature – 'what works for whom in what circumstances … and why'. We know there will be a complex footprint of outcomes; the trick is to explain it. Why are the winners winners and why are the losers losers? Why does a programme work in Wigan on a wet Wednesday and why does it then fail in Frinton on a foggy Friday?

Realist evaluation is avowedly theory-driven; it searches for and refines explanations of programme effectiveness. One can find, however, several self-professed realist studies that lack this essential process. Kazi et al. (2011) provide a typical example. The evaluation traces the outcome patterns associated with a care coordination programme called 'Wraparound'. The intervention is described as a 'strength-based, family-driven process that works to empower families and decrease or eliminate the need for service providers while increasing and maximizing families' connection and use of natural support' (2011: 59). The programme theory, as described, is about assisting families to identify their strengths as well as their needs and thus to engage a bespoke team from local agencies and their immediate community who will work collectively to address those needs. The working hypothesis is a familiar one in the social care field, namely that the bridgehead to recovery should be assembled on the pre-existing stanchions of family potential. The actual implementation of Wraparound is not explained other than in passing descriptions noting that the requisite care develops over several months and in 'any place the family suggests' (2011: 59). In short, we sit squarely in realist territory here – long implementation chains, multiple and varied stakeholders, bottom-up ambitions and tailored and differential access to services.

Impact is assessed by the programme team using the Child and Adolescent Functionality Assessment Scale (CAFAS). This is described by the authors in the following terms:

> used to assess a youth's functional impairment, rated as severe, moderate, mild or minimal/no impairment … a tool to determine day-to-day functioning that might be impacted by emotional, behavioral, psychological, psychiatric or substance use problems … a compilation of subscales: role performance (subdivided into school/work roles, home roles and community roles), behavior to others, moods/self harm (subdivided into moods/emotion and self-harmful behavior), substance use and thinking. (2011: 59)

I start with the lustrous aspect of Kazi, et al.'s paper. As part of their work routine Wraparound 'professionals' completed the CAFAS assessment for each participating youth on a quarterly basis. These repeated measures provide the research team with a real time indicator of progress (or lack of it) through the period of the intervention. Rather than concentrating on the net performance of all participants, the research team apply realist logic, breaking down the analysis of outcomes using a variety of contextual and processual variables. And it is through this analysis that the realist motif, 'what is it about the intervention that works for which participants in what respects' comes into full force.

These contingencies are listed in great detail, of which three are reproduced to give a flavour of the main findings. Note the close texture of the findings. The first outcome relates to the CAFAS school subscale, the second and third monitor change on the behaviour subscale:

1   Those with greater impairment denoted by the total score on their baseline CAFAS measure improved at a greater rate than those with lower levels of impairment ($r = -.283$; $p < .05$; $n = 57$, power = .59);
2   85.7% ($n = 18$) of female youth improved in this outcome compared to 55.2% of males ($n = 16$) who improved ($r = .323$: $p < .05$, $n = 50$, power = .57);
3   The mean age of those who did not improve was 15 ($SD = 3.12$, $n = 16$) compared to a mean of 16.93 for those who did improve ($SD = 1.2234$; $n = 35$).

A plethora of similar sub-group, subservice, subscale differences are noted on the basis of which, the authors claim: 'having real time access to this information is vital for the continuing evaluation of services, especially where immediate attention to significant patterns may lead to production of greater improvement in outcomes' (Kazi et al., 2011: 65). Once again a realist ambition is strongly echoed – the notion of strengthening implementation and improving the targeting of interventions on the basis of careful attention to outcome patterns. But is this particular analysis a sound enough basis on which to do so?

There are reasons to disbelieve. The first is that variations in sub-group success are potentially infinite. Clients may be subdivided on any of the familiar facesheet variables but also by finer distinctions marking their family, neighbourhood, peer, criminal, cultural backgrounds and so on. Given that the scheme is adaptive, service delivery can also be measured in very many different ways – what particular ministrations are encountered? in which way are they delivered? by whom? where? over what duration? and so on. Finally, of course, there are outcomes and, as noted, although CAFAS is already a veritable jewellery box of indicators, there are many other ways of testing impact through self-report, psychological tests, institutional records, performance indicators and so on.

Given that the potential permutations are inexhaustible, how can we know the research has latched onto the really significant outcome patterns? One way is by 'data dredging'. Kasi et al. (2011) employ this method using the limited data matrix manufactured by the project. The outcomes noted above are indeed the ones which pass sophisticated and time-honoured tests of statistical significance. Yet some standard drawbacks apply here (Lieberson, 1985). A significance test can only respond to the particular indicator chosen to measure a particular input or output. Choosing an alternative indicator may mean that the relationships fall in or out of statistical significance. In the present instance, before pronouncing on 'progress' or 'improvement' care must thus be taken to acknowledge that the particular measurement modality, 'professional opinion on Y', may not necessarily square with other potential measures of Y listed above. What is more, in all multivariate analysis the significance of any particular covariate depends on which other variables have been included and controlled for in the model. As we have seen above, the list of candidate variables is endless (X_1 ... X_∞) and by including (X_{17} ... X_{23}) or excluding (X_{31} ... X_{37}) it is again possible that any particular covariate may fall in or out of significance (see also Kazi et al., 2011: 61). In short, for the realist, variations in programme performance are a crucial first step but outcome patterns considered alone are only surface 'markers' or 'traces' (Byrne, 2002: 32), namely the potential outward signals of inner workings of programme in a particular manifestation.

The practical significance is only revealed by explanation building. The lack of the anchor role of explanation building can be seen immediately in examining the report's key findings noted above (Kazi et al., 2011). One needs to superimpose the 'why' question:

1 Why, for instance, do those with greater CAFAS-scored impairment at baseline improve their School Assessment more than those with lower recorded deficiencies? Could it be that they receive more attention on the programme? Could it be that they are more appreciative of the scheme? Could it be because it is the very first time they have been so encouraged? Or, could it be a measurement artefact – regression towards the mean?

2 Why do females outstrip males in the practitioners' assessments of improvements in behaviour due to the programme? Might it be that girls find 'empowerment' less embarrassing than boys, are more practised at 'talking things through', and are more willing to interact outside their immediate group of peers? And might programme practitioners respond more fulsomely to these points of potential? Or, might it be an artefact of the research act, girls being more guileful under observation and the scorers falling back on stereotypes of placid female demeanours?

3 Why do older participants outpace the young in their behavioural improvement? Might it be because they have seen more of the consequences of continued delinquency? Might it be because of growing awareness that life's difficulties will multiply as they come to the end of their school career? Might it be that they are more mature in their responses to practitioners? Might they be better practised in manipulating care workers and extracting services? Or, might there be a measurement artefact – with older subjects being more practised at 'faking good'?

The point of these instant conjectures is to show that statistically significant relationships don't speak for themselves. They are capable of multiple explanations and sometimes contradictory explanations and sometimes perverse, artefactual explanations. Without knowing which explanation applies, it would be grossly premature to adapt or retarget the programme. Sadly, it is still necessary to point out that correlation does not equal causation and that this ancient maxim also applies to the 'forward conditional binary regression models' applied in this research. Correlations must not be mistaken for explanations because variables do not have causal powers. For instance, it is not the 'age' of these young people's bones, which acts to improve behaviour whilst on the programme. Age bestows the person with certain experiences and it is the store of preconceptions that they bring to a programme that lead them to interpret it and act on it in different ways. In all cases, the outcome patterns come to be as they are because of the collective, constrained choices of all stakeholders. In all cases, investigation needs to under-stand these underlying mechanisms in order to capitalise on the gains accrued in charting the differential effectiveness of the intervention. We need to know why the older, female and the most functionally impaired respond differently.

How might this be achieved? How can the study be nudged into being more firmly realist? Whilst there is no exact protocol for doing so, this particular design might have been buttressed as follows:

1 Realist research is theory driven and in this study could have usefully begun in prior quali-tative work eliciting, articulating and formalising some hypotheses about why outcomes are so varied. It is the task of programme practitioners to guide allcomers through every assumption and turn of an intervention. Typically, they have an abundance of expertise on who prospers in relation to which programme feature and, crucially, why this might be so. This is intensely practical theorising and it would, incidentally, knock the spots off my 'top of the head' conjectures accounting for the three outcome configurations listed above. This is not to say that these 'folk conjectures' are perfect but they can provide a legitimate focus for the investigation – an alternative to the happenstance of dredging through the infinite programme disparities.

2 A second strategy is to strive for what I have previously described as a 'footprint' of outcomes. Rather than a statistical trawl to discover which sub-group or sub-service or sub-scale difference is significant, pursuing a theory can drive the analysis to look for further 'cross item' corroboration. If we begin, for instance, with a theory that a certain level of maturity is needed for a youth to benefit from a 'wraparound' of service provision, we might speculate that this might show up in a pattern where age relates to behavioural improvement (as in finding 3). But we might also expect that age (as a proxy for maturity) would also relate to the youth's ability to deal with more services. Is there further quantitative evidence to suggest that age correlates with increased access with the agency office, school, residential treatment facilities, family court, church and community groups? Realist analysis accounts for 'outcome patterns' rather than provid-ing a tally of discrete effects (see also Trochim, 1985).

3 A third strategy, in the respondent validation tradition, would be to further deepen the working hypotheses by consulting those on the receiving end of the programme theories (Pope and Mays, 2006). The recommendation so far begins with practitioner folk theories and seeks to corroborate them in the rich evidence on outcome patterns. If the original hypothesis posits that sub-group X prospers (or fails) because of their preference set Y, then it is also useful to ask members of sub-group X whether they too concur with the conjecture – do they recognise the broad theory as a description of their motivations? This evidence may be gleaned in follow-up qualitative research with selected sub-groups where participants are able to reflect back on their experiences of the programme.

4   A fourth strategy for making sense of the outcome patterns is to compare notes with (or formally synthesise) existing research on the same family of programmes. Although Wraparound is unique in time and place, its ambitions and structures are very well known in community social work. Whilst such programmes never reproduce exactly, we already know quite a lot about for whom and in what circumstances and why its ingredients (mentoring, out-of-home placements, care coordination, etc.) work (Philip and Spratt, 2007).

In short, Kazi and colleagues are quite correct to pinpoint the discernment of rich, dynamic outcome traces as a cornerstone of realist evaluation but have failed to see that it is theory that sustains and develops the observational pattern – a point made many years ago by the distinguished philosopher Abraham Kaplan: 'The pattern can be indefinitely filled in and extended: as we obtain more and more knowledge it continues to fall into place in this pattern and the pattern itself has a place in a larger whole' (Kaplan, 1998: 335).

Winners and ... winners? ————

Long before realist evaluation entered the fray, there was always friction between exponents of outcome and process evaluation, which rested in turn on the old antagonism between quantitative and qualitative research. Those preferring quantitative evidence regarded qualitative data as dangerously subjective. Those preferring qualitative evidence regarded quantitative data as providing crude oversimplifications of the human response to interventions. Readers will remember those days and perhaps regard them as a thing of the past given that the current orthodoxy, realist evaluation included, recommends a multi-method approach. As a first approximation one can say that mining mechanisms requires qualitative evidence, observing outcomes is quantitative, and that canvassing contexts requires comparative and sometimes historical data. The requisite balance, however, is precarious and there are 'realist' studies that attempt to cover all angles in an essentially descriptive and thus qualitative manner. Artificial results often follow.

The ensuing difficulty has long been dubbed as the tendency to produce 'good news' stories. In old parlance, the problem involved authors of rich, qualitative accounts of the participants' positive interpretations of a programme going on to proclaim that it 'works' (and should be extended, funded further, etc.) without the benefit of any quantitative data on whether behavioural outcomes had actually changed.

Under the new species of 'qualitative realism' the embellishment is more subtle – the careful elaboration of how a programme may work carrying over into assertions that it has worked. An example is a study by Priest (2006) of a community capacity-building programme, 'Motor Magic', which seeks to address motor and sensory impairments in preschool children. The programme 'uses a setting approach within a kindergarten environment, aiming to provide easy access to occupational therapy for children and to maximise opportunities to engage with, and build the capacities of parents and kindergarten staff to support those children' (2006: 221). Again we find ourselves with a multi-objective, multi-component, multi-stakeholder programme, which Priest approaches in the realist manner, beginning by breaking Motor Magic down in its programme theories. A dozen subtle strategies are discerned within the black box – embedding occupational therapy classes within the standard curriculum, parents observing and participating in specific activities, formal training in therapy for kindergarten staff, etc., etc.

Next, as music to realist ears, each strategy is then unpacked in the form of context, mechanism, outcome (CMO) conjectures (Pawson and Tilley, 1997b: chapter 4), of which I paraphrase a couple of specific examples:

- The strategy of grouping children together with similar needs, is hypothesised to work best for 'children with language as well as fine motor difficulties' (Context) by allowing children 'to watch and copy others to develop their own fine motor skills' (Mechanism) with the result that there is increased willingness to attempt new activities at kindergarten and home, increased participation in fine motor activities at home, etc. (Outcomes) (Priest, 2006: 226).
- The strategy of 'parental inclusion in activities using their non-dominant hand' is said to work best for 'parents with limited understanding of their child's particular developmental needs' (Context) by generating 'more positive attitudes and increased pleasure and appreciation of their child' (Mechanism), with the result that there is an improved relationship with the child (Outcome) (Priest, 2006: 229).

Now we come to the matter of the empirical corroboration of the many such hypotheses. Two focus groups were conducted with kindergarten staff and parents, led by an external facilitator (not the evaluator) exploring the various programme theories. Interviews were audiotaped, transcribed and analysed using the CMO hypotheses as the thematic frames. The methodological problem, in short, is that this same body of qualitative evidence is made to speak to the Cs, the Ms and the Os.

In the case of mechanisms, unsurprisingly, some compelling data is unearthed. Mechanisms are embodied in the subjects' reasoning and they are best investigated therein. The classic analytic device chosen is to quote passage after passage in which parents and staff articulate how they have interpreted and acted upon the resources provided by Motor Magic. To pursue just one example, a parent recounts the following experience of participating in motor skills activities: 'We were made to cut with the opposite, our left hand or right hand regardless ... and write our names ... and that really was an eye-opener for me to show how difficult for me it was as an adult, but as a child having to do these things right from scratch and not knowing how. That was a real eye-opener' (Priest, 2006: 228). Programme mechanisms change minds. They open eyes. And such close qualitative research is an ideal way of revealing such processes.

In the case of charting outcomes and contexts, other forms of data have more authority and qualitative data is stretched to breaking point in being made to measure and compare. In respect of the outcomes, the study does great initial service in hypothesising the wide range of benefits that might follow (willingness to participate, improved relationships, readiness for school, behavioural change, etc.). But for each output or outcome, the evidence is compiled under exactly the same narrative strategy of reproducing statements from proud parent or positive practitioner: 'I think that his self-esteem, his confidence that all just grew and he was a completely different little boy' (Priest, 2006: 223). And no doubt he was. But even setting aside all problems to do with selectivity, social desirability effects, chatty bias, researcher partisanship, and so on, the problem is that hand-picked, personalised descriptions of outcomes cannot reveal collective outcomes patterns. Realist evaluation presupposes pattern. There will be winners … and losers.

Since the task here is to refine the realist approach we move to correctives, which in this case are straightforward. Realist evaluation works by explaining outcome patterns and these cannot be determined through anecdotal remarks (on the part of subjects) or wishful thinking (on the part of evaluators). Outcomes should be carefully conceptualised and indicators thought through; baselines should be established; before and after measures should be plotted; complete cohorts of subjects should be followed. None of these requirements necessitate a fundamental reorientation of research strategy. Many of them are also the prerequisites of good administrative data, which can often be harnessed in the close confines of case study research. The key point is to address theory and if, to repeat the examples above, the theory says that there will be an 'increased participation in fine motor activities' or 'an improved relationship with the child' then such increases or improvements should be monitored and apportioned.

I must make it clear that Priest's study bears all the hallmarks of a preliminary inquiry and doubtless the author would regard it as a modestly funded pilot, designed to raise insightful explanatory hypotheses. In its research strategy, however, it does typify one mistaken interpretation of realist evaluation – as just another form of qualitative inquiry, opposed to positivism and designed to penetrate the intervention black box. It is interesting to note that Priest's inquiry is almost the mirror image of the first case study (Kazi et al., 2011). There, outcome data proliferated but without theory or qualitative evidence. Both of the latter appear in study two – in the complete absence of outcome data. Put the two strategies together and realist evaluation begins to be realised.

Configurations not catalogues

The most unlovely term in realist terminology is the 'context, mechanism, outcome configuration' – the CMOc. It is an ugly circumlocution but it is there for a purpose. The phrase attempts to convey the idea that evaluation tests programme theories and to do so the theory must be cast as an *if–then* proposition. The idea is to render the programme theory into its constituent and interconnected elements. In plainer, if more elongated prose, a CMOc is a hypothesis that the programme works (O) because of the action of some underlying mechanisms (M), which only comes into operation in particular contexts (C). *If* the right processes operate in the right conditions *then* the programme will prevail. To emphasise the causal and conditional nature of this conjecture the idea was presented as the 'equation': $C + M = O$ (sometimes better rendered $C + M \rightarrow O$).

As such, a CMO is a proposition and testable one to boot. There are different ways to construct the test, though in essence a realist investigation will hypothesise, monitor and seek to explain how the same programme resource is interpreted and acted upon in different ways by different participants in different positions. As a simplified example, I depict this process of investigation in Figure 2.1. A programme based on, say, payments, loans, grants or giveaways may have started with the elemental proposition that the incentive (M_1) will encourage participants (C_1) to change their behaviour (O_1). Theory building continues, leading to a refinement, say, that the same incentive (M_1) may be squandered (O_{1A}) by the rich (C_{1A}) and seized upon (O_{1B}) by the needy (C_{1B}). A more sophisticated theory and a tougher test would, of course, be provided by contemplating further sub-groups who might use the incentive in further ways, leading to the discovery of many other configurations as in Figure 2.1. In short, and in the familiar jargon, CMO propositions specify what it is about the programme that works, for whom and in what circumstances. The specificity of these elements increases with inquiry but their form does not change.

This propositional and proposition-building function of the CMO has not always been fully understood. The problem is that programmes never offer up a single theory. In realist terminology, there will always be multiple Ms – a proliferation of ideas within a programme, creating different resources which trigger different reactions amongst participants. There will always be multiple Cs – a huge range of different individual circumstances and institutional conditions, which shape the action of the assorted mechanisms. There will always be multiple Os – an extensive footprint of hits and misses, an uneven pattern of success and failure associated with the underlying causal dynamics.

$C_1 M_1 O_1$

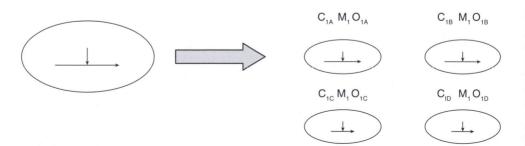

Figure 2.1 CMO before and after testing

In order to anticipate this inevitability, Pawson and Tilley (1997b) devised 'the CMOc table' as a way of incorporating multiple hypotheses within any investigation. Table 2.1 illustrates the general format. If–then propositions are displayed horizontally. For illustration's sake let us imagine a youth job creation programme. One of the ways in which it might work is by offering incentives to continue training, described in the table as M_1. It is supposed that this resource will only have an effect on certain subjects in certain circumstances – described in shorthand in the table here as O_1 and C_1. It is then supposed that this initial configuration will be put to the test in the evaluation under the regime already described in Figure 2.1, identifying the many ensuing conditionalities, described above using the various subscripts $C_{1X}M_1O_{1X}$.

Table 2.1 Multiple CMOc propositions

Context	+	Mechanism	=	Outcomes
C_1	+	M_1	=	O_1
C_2	+	M_2	=	O_2
C_3	+	M_3	=	O_3
C_N	+	M_N	=	O_N

So much for row one – the first configuration. The table then proceeds through a range of other CMO hypotheses, mindful that programmes are rarely one-trick ponies. Let us suppose that the programme also offers advice and mentoring support (M_2). Hypotheses are then built around this second configuration $C_2M_2O_2$ in Table 2.1, which also assumes the ensuing discovery of a multiplicity of different responses to wise counselling in different situations ($C_{2X}M_2O_{2X}$). The process continues sequentially, considering the third, fourth and subsequent means through which the programme may work. Hypotheses multiply until the researcher reaches exhaustion or the limits of funding. This basic table can be elaborated in many ways and at various levels of detail. It can also be used to describe CMO findings as well as CMO hypotheses. But in all cases they are CMO configurations.

Alas, researchers have found another way to interpret and produce these tables. Given the endless complexity of programmes and the situations in which they are embedded, it is a task in itself to contemplate the very many ways in which change might be engendered, the multiple constituencies of stakeholders and their myriad responses. Several researchers have thus taken the realist task to be the enumeration of the explanatory ingredients. One can propel programme theory evaluation down the columns (especially if they are presented with gridlines). In so doing the explanatory elements become atomised and disconnected. CMOs become unconfigured and transform into C catalogues, M catalogues and O catalogues. I examine two examples, each providing illustrations of the drawbacks and their consequences.

My first sighting comes in a paper by Tolson and Schofield (2011) providing a 'realistic evaluation' of the benefits of a Scottish programme offering football-related reminiscences for men with dementia. Structuring 'remembrances' around an individual's life experiences is the core intervention, a therapy thought to be beneficial in building interests, identity and esteem in dementia sufferers. The authors explain that football is at the beating heart of Scottish popular culture. It was thus hypothesised that providing an intervention resourced by materials from the Scottish National Football Museum would provide a powerful focus for recalling former pleasures. Data, consisting of field notes and audio recordings, were collected by an experienced nurse researcher using non-participant observation. The analysis attempted to tease out the effective ingredients in this complex, adaptive intervention. It took the form of 'the identification and extraction of data pertaining to Context–Mechanism–Outcome configurations'. The findings from one locality are presented in a simplified form as Figure 2.2.

To make the critical analysis clearer, I place Figure 2. 2 cheek by jowl with Figure 2.3, the CMO table produced in another realist inquiry, Long's (2009) study of the efficacy of Shiatsu, a form of complementary and alternative medicine (CAM), in generating health and wellbeing. In this case, the thinking behind the table emanates from a particularly rich empirical study of key stakeholders. Long delves into the black box via a longitudinal study uncovering what clients hope to get from Shiatsu and in a survey of practitioners about what they considered essential in its delivery. I provide no details of the fine textured account of Shiatsu practice that emerges from these inquiries (noting, however, that this is Long's main objective) and concentrate on the CMO configuration as presented in Figure 2.3. The layout is instructive. As with the dementia study, both in the figures and the accompanying text, the narrative flows down the columns. The research task is understood as the provision of the right ingredients to populate the three columns.

There are two highly characteristic problems associated with this 'vertical' approach. The first is that the catalogues comprising each column, whilst already

Contexts	Mechanisms	Outcomes
Accessible, comfortable, congenial surroundings	Trained, experienced and flexible group facilitators	Increased sociability
		More talkative
Regular, reliable engagement	Empathy towards people with dementia	Increased confidence
Refreshments (breakfast, lunch or tea)		Takes on position as expert
An established 'host' organisation	Highly knowledgeable and passionate about football	Stimulation, fun and laughter
Male-focused activity	Access to a wide range of collections of images in addition to website images	Anticipation of future events
Provides support for related outside visits	Football used for specific interest but also as a trigger to other topics	

Figure 2.2 Unconfigured CMOs (version one)

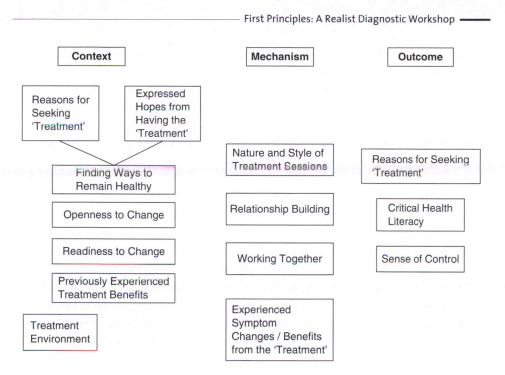

Figure 2.3 Unconfigured CMOs (version two)

substantial in our examples, are in actuality unstoppable. The predicament is evident if one scans the column 'context' across the two examples. Tolson and Schofield concentrate on aspects of the setting, the immediate locality of the intervention. Long (2009) concentrates on the characteristics of the individuals contemplating treatment (though there is an isolated, catch-all box referring to 'treatment environment'). Whilst entirely different, both are perfectly entitled to their contextual preferences. If one refers to Pawson and Tilley's (1997b) understanding of context, it includes the characteristics of: i) the individual players, ii) their interrelationships, iii) the institutional location, and iv) the surrounding infrastructure (see Chapter 3 for a fuller explanation). The upshot is that there is room for more, considerably more, in the cataloguing of context in our two exemplars.

Given that the potential content of each column is infinite, the consequence is that any particular effort to draw up a list will be arbitrary. One cannot tell which aspect of context will be important – just by looking and listing. For example, elsewhere in their text, Tolson and Schofield (2011: 4), describe further influential features of the locality, which appear to provide grounds for candidature in the complexity column but do not appear therein. For instance, we are told that the football facilitator is assisted by three attentive and encouraging volunteers, so might not an 'advantageous staffing ratio' provide another important backdrop to efficacy? Similarly we are told, insightfully I think, that the choice of a 'public location' (seaside hotel) rather than a dedicated healthcare setting may well provide contextual reinforcement for inclusion and normality. It is difficult to see, therefore, why details on the light refreshments rather than the public rendezvous should be selected for the context column. In short, the concepts in that column seem to make their way by fiat. At the risk of over-egging the problem, it is difficult to see why another pre-given aspect of provision, namely the 'trained, experienced and flexible group facilitators' are located in the mechanism column rather than under context.

This brings us to the second problem with such 'ingredient listing', one that has become a classic realist headache – the CMO lottery. Under which column do the hypothesised constructs belong? Let us turn to Figure 2.3 to examine the dilemma. Under 'context' Long's linked boxes concentrate on the client characteristics that mark them out as suitable cases for CAM treatment; they are seekers not sufferers. There is also the separate box for 'treatment environment', the characteristically interactive atmosphere that pervades CAM therapy. All of these features are well within the broad ambit of what realists refer to as context.

Next we move down the mechanism column and things become murkier. The first box is labelled 'nature and style of treatment sessions'. There is no sign of client reasoning here, one of the defining features of a programme mechanism. Indeed, taken in isolation it reads very much like the aforementioned context, the pre-existing 'treatment environment' in which the intervention occurs. Next we have two boxes explaining how the treatment is taken on board – mechanisms to be sure. Then comes another perplexing box, 'benefits from the treatment', a phrase perhaps more redolent of outcomes. Turning to outcomes proper, there are two boxes which interestingly point to a crucial idea that CAM clients pursue ends somewhat different from the norm. Confusingly, there is a further outcome box sharing exactly the same label as one of the initial contexts, 'reasons for seeking treatment'. Possibly the intention here is that initial expectations about the purpose of treatment are reinforced in the journey. It is impossible to say.

A similar exercise can be run on the football CMOs. The nature of mechanisms is much discussed in the literature (Astbury and Leeuw, 2010) but for present purposes I retain Pawson and Tilley's (1997b: 65) core notion that programme mechanisms capture the way in which the programme's resources impinge on the stakeholders' reasoning. By contrast, in their mechanism column, Tolson and Schofield choose to list only the resources. Moving to the right of Figure 2.2, 'stimulation, fun and laughter' appear to be regarded as significant outcomes of the intervention. Arguably these are key mechanisms which trigger the real outcomes of building confidence, identity and esteem in dementia sufferers. I will labour the point no further, for the authors themselves come to the crucial point: 'Our experience with CMO configurations has taught us that the elements of contexts and mechanisms are not always clear cut' and go on to suggest the need for ever tighter operational definitions of each term (Tolson and Schofield, 2011: 4).

I take a different lesson away from these examples. Programmes do not come in pre-ordained chunks called contexts, mechanisms and outcomes. Rather, these terms take their meaning from their function in explanation and their role in testing those explanations. If this function is ignored and the exercise becomes one of identifying, labelling and enumerating disconnected aspects of an intervention then it will always be unfinished and arbitrary. As intended, CMOs are configurations, specific propositions that tie specific Cs and specific Ms and specific Os together (recall Figure 2.1 and Table 2.1). If research hypotheses are set up this way, rather than as a fishing expedition, then the fuzzy boundaries disappear. A realist investigation of these two interventions should interrogate the proposition that the specific treatment modalities (M) are effective for specific clients in specific situations (C) so producing specific contributions to wellbeing (O). One item leads to another and, so to speak, defines the others.

Conclusions

These summary remarks offer a brief recapitulation of the main methodological arguments before returning to the very idea of a 'diagnostic review'. The chapter's first conclusion is that the phrase 'theory-driven' means what it says and that designs that attempt to utilise the realist explanatory apparatus without a prior grounding in programme theory will end with explanations that are ad hoc and piecemeal. A second tenet is discovered in realism's penchant for sitting in the middle, between process and outcome evaluation, between qualitative and quantitative research and so on. It should be stressed, however, that in the realm of research evidence, one obtains the best of both worlds by operating in both worlds. Process research cannot masquerade as outcome research and qualitative utterances cannot chart quantitative differences. The final conclusion advises that programmes do not come with pre-determined ingredients called contexts, mechanisms and outcomes. Rather these terms take their meaning from their function in explanation. As wise mothers often insist – it is not the ingredients that make the dish but how they are brought together in the cooking process.

Some final caveats are now in order. The first is to reaffirm as strongly as possible that these four studies do *not* constitute a realist rogues' gallery. To repeat, there is no such thing as a perfect empirical study, realist or otherwise. A part of our pragmatic art is to apply compromises and cut the funding cloth as far as it will stretch. The immediate priorities of evaluation research are to respond to the research brief, to deal with the given substantive issue, and to contribute to policy development – rather than to aim for methodological purity. In the longer term, however, it is collective scrutiny of method that drives method forward. And it is in this activity that joins the ethereal ambitions of Chapter 1 with the picky pronouncements made here. Let me repeat Campbell's (1988: 303) telling phrase: 'Organized distrust produces trustworthy reports.' In other words, methodological advance comes from a close scrutiny of each other's work and the ensuing debate.

It is with this in mind that I have named this chapter a 'diagnostic workshop'. This is one of several instalments, in which a revolving list of realist concepts and realist evaluations and realist syntheses will come under scrutiny. A previous version of this paper, with a different case study, has appeared in journal form (Pawson and Manzano, 2012). It will also be published as a feature paper in the

SAGE website www.methodspace.com. This offers a forum for reply, debate and discussion – an electronic version of 'organised distrust'. When it comes to methodology there is no such thing as the last word. All of the points made above are open to rebuttal and refinement. Whilst it might be conceded that theory should be prioritised in realist research designs, there are further issues about how programme theory should be sourced and selected (Weiss, 2000). Whilst the battle cry that 'evidence should be a blend' might be conceded, its exact balance still remains an enigma (Greene et al., 1989). Whilst it might also be conceded that CMOs are configurational propositions, the matter of where to begin their construction is still open for discussion (e.g. are they really MCOs?). The answers to these further questions are already 'out there' – it is simply a matter of reeling them in to discussion and debate.

Curiously, the requisite close scrutiny rarely happens in the evaluation literature (see also Gargani, 2010). There are, of course, very many examples of cut and thrust as paradigm wars make their periodic appearance in the journals. What I have in mind is something less vituperative – less about wrecking other methodologies and more about refining a preferred one. The idea is to take on studies in their own terms, over which task a commentator might spend several pages of close scrutiny, and in response to which the commented upon might yield here but defend there, and as a result of which the research community might find 'improved validity'.

PART 2

The Challenge of Complexity: Drowning or Waving?

The central problem of our age is how to act decisively in the absence of certainty.

Bertrand Russell, *An Inquiry into Meaning and Truth* (1950).

What can be uttered in a word but contemplated forever? What do fools ignore and pragmatists suffer? What is evaluation's greatest challenge? These questions present no riddle, no mystery, and no conundrum. The answers are: complexity, complexity and complexity. Every attempt to conduct an evaluation is beset with the impossibility of covering every angle; every attempt to conduct a review is faced with the impracticability of chasing down every single issue. So, too, have the evaluation paradigms floundered in the face of complexity: experimentalists struggle to maintain control over every event, variable, whistle and bell; constructivists ply constructions on the co-constructions of an endless supply of stakeholders; formative evaluators excavate to discover there are processes within processes within processes. And so whether evaluation seeks to judge, describe, inspire or explain, there is an ever-present predicament in claiming to have achieved closure in covering all eventualities.

This part of the book confronts the challenge, seeking to discover whether evaluation drowns under complexity's menace or comes up waving. The allusion here is to Stevie Smith's poem describing a distressed man whose thrashing in the sea causes onlookers to believe that he is waving happily to them. The following three chapters describes the efforts of another distressed man as he attempts to refine the realist response to complexity. Realist evaluation trades in a rather different currency to the other perspectives – preferring to pose the question, 'what works for whom in what circumstances and in what respects?' But this objective offers no hiding place from complexity. There is no disguising the fact that the ideas driving an intervention are often multitudinous and compelling, no concealing the reality that the same intervention can trigger change in myriad ways, and no way of camouflaging the truth that the different contexts in which programmes are implemented are as wide as society is wide.

For the group that I perceive, ungraciously, as 'old readers', it is worth setting down the realist track-record on complexity. *Realist Evaluation* busied itself in accelerating complexity into the research act. In cajoling evaluators into looking at why programmes worked, it interjected into research design the then new conceptual scheme of 'mechanisms, contexts and outcomes' – all of which elements are potentially multitudinous. For example, Tilley and I were able to show that even a fixed, deaf, dumb, colour-blind and partially-sighted CCTV camera could 'work' to reduce crime in surprisingly different ways – by detection, by deterrence, by improving staff deployment, by reducing the time for crime, by encouraging more usage of the monitored area and thus increasing natural surveillance, by changing the balance of usage of that space towards the law abiding, and by inspiring additional crime reduction efforts from the latter. Even a decoy camera (minus the electronics) could still work through repute and publicity (Pawson and Tilley, 1997b: 78–82). However, apart from the useful insight that apparently simple interventions can be devilishly intricate, that book devotes no designated space to complexity.

A decade later and perhaps because the distressed man had, by that stage, had many lung-filling encounters with many sea-tossed interventions, *Evidence-Based Policy* devotes a half-chapter to describing a basic 'anatomy of programme complexity' (Pawson, 2006a: 26–37). The message was plain, since it is impossible to be all embracing we must learn how to prioritise. Further pragmatic urgings followed in the paper 'Simple Principles for Evaluating Complex Programmes' using a monster urban regeneration initiative as its inspiration (Pawson, 2006b). And this brings us more or less up to date and the current counsel I utter at the start of every lecture, presentation and advisory group meeting – namely, look before you leap.

At the commencement of any realist evaluation or realist synthesis, the research team should locate the intervention under research within the dynamic policy and social systems that surround it and within the dynamic cognitive and behavioural systems that underpin it. There should be an attempt to 'map' complexity. This will leave the group feeling queasy since it will be clear that their investigation, or indeed any assemblage of investigations, cannot possibly cover everything. Having looked it is necessary to leap. At this point all research confronts a choice, deciding upon those sub-systems that will fall under empirical scrutiny. Note again there is no other choice, only a finite number of programme theories can be interrogated. New ground is sighted. Other potential territory is left uncharted. This, I beg to suggest, is the real complexity conundrum for it provides the debating point for this part of the book. What is the status and what is the utility of the partial understanding so created? At issue, in policy terms, is the question posed in the section epigraph, Russell's challenge: how to act decisively in the absence of certainty.

The book now moves timorously forward to face these issues. Chapter 3 provides an overview, a reconstruction of the task of mapping complexity – what are its dimensions, what are its dynamics, what are its systems and sub-systems? On offer is a simple checklist of core issues that evaluators might use to build such a map (whilst being fully aware, of course, of the parrot sitting on my shoulder explaining that infinite complexity cannot be reduced to a fixed set of determinants). Chapter 4 goes on to compare this portrait of complexity to those interpretations that have emerged in other schools of evaluation and social research. In perusing the complexity bazaar, we encounter several quite different expositions and responses. I will leave the various schools of thought unnamed at this point but, as a foretaste, it can be said that they provide a fine range of alternatives to drowning and waving. Complexity is dealt with by: ignoring it, mystifying it, lording over it and, I suppose, learning to love it. After probing these perspectives in more detail and finding them wanting, Chapter 5 gathers together the realist solution in detail and considers the implications of evaluating and policy making in the perpetual estate of partial knowledge.

THREE

A Complexity Checklist

A century ago the Swiss historian Jacob Burckhardt foresaw that ours would be the age of 'the great simplifiers' and that the essence of tyranny was the denial of complexity .... What we need are the great complexifiers, men who dare not only to understand what they are about, but who will dare to share that understanding with those for whom they act.

Daniel Moynihan – farewell speech to US President's Cabinet in 1970.

What makes a programme complex? What brings intricacy to interventions? Providing answers to such questions is, by default, an infinite task. But this effort, being a realistic perspective, takes up the challenge by offering a checklist. A basic assumption of realist evaluation is that programmes are complex interventions introduced into complex social systems. So what are the basic dynamics of these systems within systems? In attempting to answer this question, the chapter sets down a potential starting point for all evaluative inquiry. Note well that it should be considered a point of embarkation. These are the seas that the researcher should chart, long before crews are impressed and sails are set. I observe a custom about checklists by sticking to the magic number and presenting the key characteristics of programme complexity under an acronym – VICTORE (Volitions, Implementation, Contexts, Time, Outcomes, Rivalry, and Emergence). I illustrate each of the seven features by drawing on examples from all across the policy waterfront. But note a significant claim here – namely, that all of them are characteristics of all programmes. Evaluators, systematic reviewers and policy analysts should think through how each issue applies to the intervention or family of interventions that they are about to investigate. Each question is never ending. The point is to begin the mapping of these contours of complexity as a prelude to deciding where empirical research is needed. The seven items are explored in turn with a summary (Box 3.1) at the end.

1. Volitions

It is always useful to begin by considering those on the receiving end of programmes and policies. Realist evaluation has a little motto in this respect – interventions do not work, it is the interpretations of their subjects that produce results. Programmes subjects are active agents, not passive recipients. Evaluation research needs to discover, and thus may usefully begin, with some expectations about the volitions of programme subjects. How will they respond to the policy? Interventions seek to open up new choices – but will they be chosen?

To begin to answer this question, we need to investigate what has been usefully termed the 'choice architecture' addressed by an intervention (Thaler and Sunstein, 2008: 3). If one thinks of the most commonplace of interventions – the classroom – then every teacher knows that success will depend on the aspirations of the taught. These range from outright hostility to downright enchantment. All readers have sat in school and thus can begin to complete a list of the dispositions that fall in between – the urge to disrupt, incomprehension, feigned boredom, real boredom, time serving, grade chasing, plucky resilience, genuine effort, great expectations, true devotion and so on. This balance of volitions plays a vital role in determining whether the lesson or the year's work will work. And so it is with all programmes, regardless of the policy objective and regardless of the means pursued to realise those objectives. They will succeed or fail according to the range and stability of the participants' worldviews. Whilst this balance is never indiscriminate it is never entirely predictable. The more innovative the programme and the less well visited the target population, the less we tend to know about this balance. Volatile volitions thus represent one of the great imponderables of evaluation research and thus mark the first root cause of complexity.

Programmes seek to change minds. The likelihood of this happening depends not only on pre-existing mindsets, as described above, but on the process whereby minds are changed. Programmes do not work through Pauline conversions and divine deliverance. On the whole they persuade people to reconsider their options and such cogitation tends to occur gradually. Dozens of choices are made along the way. Gas guzzlers do not become pushbike users overnight. Food guzzlers do not become diet conscious in an instant. The list of potential sinners and saints is infinite and, again, readers will be able to add their own – tax dodgers to net contributors, garbage throwers to green recyclers, and so on. The key point is that the choice architecture of programmes needs to accommodate and manage a whole series of volitions as programmes subjects ponder an entire journey: whether they wish to be on a programme in the first place; whether to make the first hesitant steps in enrolment; whether to suck, see and to hang around; whether to play a more positive part; whether to see the process to finish and graduate; whether to exit, stay converted and proselytise for the programme. This, the pace and pathway of participant choice, is never uniform and another significant element of programme complexity.

The most successful and somewhat rare programmes are ones that can accommo- date both high-flyers and plodders, people who assume success and those accustomed to failure. In the absence of a sophisticated system to support allcomers along all points in the chain, interventions may progress or fail at any point from enrolment to exit. Subjects respond under different motives and at a different tempo. Choice architecture is multi-dimensional. It is our first source of programme complexity.

———— 2. Implementation ————

The object of evaluation carries several names – treatments, interventions, pro- grammes, schemes, services, legislation, policies and so on and so forth. It is, of course, possible to make useful distinctions between them but it is what they have in common that is of interest here. The common thread is the time they take to build and execute and this, the length of their implementation chains, is our next source of complexity.

Terminology can be misleading in this respect. One might say that Lord Noswap's 'intervention' in the Upper House was decisive or that little Raymond went to the school 'treatment' room for a sticking plaster. These are both short-and-sharp practices. Indeed, the idea that medical treatment is singular, well-defined and eas- ily distinguished from non-treatment still lies at the heart of much trial methodol- ogy. But this is misleading, for implementation chains are always long and long in several different respects.

They are long in the personnel and institutions needed to design and deliver them. Take for instance healthcare interventions such as improving blood pres- sure management or reducing waiting-list times. Such innovations often begin life in policy and media chatter but let us concentrate on the implementation chain proper. In the UK it might well begin with political calculations in Westminster, which are then passed over to civil servants in Whitehall for initial financial and feasibility estimates. The policy might then head south to the Department of Health on Waterloo Road where a different group of civil servants add deci- sions about delivery and responsibility chains. We have now reached the National Health Service (NHS). I've yet to fathom the management structure in this beast of an institution, the point being that the implementation chain is now spread- ing though Strategic Health Authorities, Primary Care Trusts and Acute Trusts. Each layer of management therein adds specificity to the policy, detailing finan- cial flows and divisions of labour in, but also deciding upon, the key modifica- tions in practice that must follow to meet the key objectives. We now arrive in hospitals, wards, surgeries, and so on, where a different group, the practitioners (themselves internally divided into hierarchies of doctors, nurses and ancillaries) move to detailed, day-to-day implementation. Only now do we reach the patient, strapped to blood pressure monitor or opening her appointment letter.

Implementation chains are also long in terms of what is delivered. Consider a subject progressing though an intervention – what does she confront? Let us stay in the realm of medical treatments and follow a typical patient pathway (still in the UK, my apologies). Mrs Long feels unwell and then falls ill. She tries to figure out what is wrong and decides to consult her GP (general practitioner). He conducts a preliminary investigation of symptoms, considers potential diagnoses and decides to send her for further tests. A second consultation occurs to discuss the result of the test and a decision is made to refer the case on to a specialist. After further consultations and tests, the consultant deliberates over the findings and, for example, may then advise Mrs Long that surgery is the best option. The story continues. Mrs Long ponders and awaits the knife and its outcome.

Complexity is endless here. I've made dozens of simplifications. There are microprocesses within each of these processes. Having a test requires Mrs Long to return home to deliver a specimen or make an appointment with the practice sister or test centre. Investigations, ranging from angiograms to X-rays are conducted. Results are interpreted, checked, dispatched to the physician and relayed back to Mrs Long – who then rejoins the implementation chain. Even here, I've made omissions – most noticeably the many tedious, fretful hours in waiting rooms and on waiting lists (themselves open to change under the ministrations of the aforementioned policy makers and practitioners).

The point is made I trust, a point which is captured in many forms of evaluation research, via logic models, outcome mapping, theories of change diagrams, etc. All evaluators using these approaches tend to make the same discovery, namely that passing a programme through many hands does not lend itself to uniformity. Whether they describe the movement of ideas, institutions, personnel or subjects, implementation chains are prone to inconsistency and reinterpretation, blockages, delays and unintended consequences. They are often sites for contestation and sometimes they are thrown into reverse as one responsible group chooses to ignore or countermand the expectations of their predecessors in the chain. Sometimes procrastination is a deliberate goal as when policy dictates that there should be 'user-input' or 'bottom-up' decision making (e.g. patients' charters in health services under slogans like, 'no decision about me without me'). Implementation inconsistency is a way of life. Complexity is designed in.

3. Contexts

The context of an intervention, the circumstances in which it is played out, constitutes another endless source of complexity. The realist approach to evaluation can take a little of the credit, I believe, for the growing appreciation that the success of an intervention depends crucially upon its location in an appropriate context. Context, we have gradually learnt, is not unwelcome noise, not a confounding variable to be controlled for – but an integral part of a programme (Davidoff, 2009).

The concept of context has been described in considerable detail in previous publications, illustrated diagrammatically as a large set of concentric ovals surrounding the programme mechanism and described metaphorically as the onion skins composition of programmes. An *aide memoir*, the four I's, has also been provided, listing some familiar contextual layers:

i *Individuals* – the characteristics and capacities of the various stakeholders in the programme.
ii *Interpersonal relations* – the stakeholder relationships that carry the programme.
iii *Institutional settings* – the rules, norms and customs local to the programme.
iv *Infrastructure* – the wider social, economic and cultural setting of the programme.

Little more needs to be said about the complex contours of the concept context – other than perhaps to offer another, hopefully persuasive example. Consider programmes targeted at disadvantaged, dispossessed youth (in the UK these are often described under the acronym NEETs – those 'not in education employment or training'). Many interventions (Education Maintenance Allowances, Learning Agreements, Mentoring Plus, etc.) have tried to open these three doors, with mixed success. Here's why:

i Individuals are NEET for a smorgasbord of reasons – some distinctly unappetising (drugs, learned helplessness), some more digestible (family responsibilities, job closures);
ii Interpersonal relations with programme staff vary with the latter having various backgrounds – youth workers, social workers, career advisors, volunteers, former offenders, school staff – some of whom are seen by some clients as a continuation of the problem rather than its solution;
iii Institutional providers vary between, for instance, Further Education Colleges with experienced, highly trained staff but offering only inflexible, long-term provision and private providers who can offer a tailor made service but often deliver in makeshift premises and with hastily assembled staff;
iv Infrastructural conditions govern the chances of escaping the NEET net and vary markedly with recession and growth, dip, recovery and double dip.

I have just scratched the surface here with these pocket descriptions. The contextual layers are infinitely complicated, intertwined and in motion. Sometimes the programme will face an admixture that is malleable; sometimes the contextual configuration will provide a brick wall. We discovered in the previous discussion on implementation complexity that interventions are never enacted in the same way twice, to which we now add that nor are they ever implemented in exactly the same circumstances.

4. Time

When one thinks of context a rather long list of locals and localities, as above, come to mind. Yet we operate in both space and time. Variation in the latter is just as important as a source of complexity. Intervention history and timing are vital, as any experienced evaluator and gnarled practitioner will be able to relate. Several trade terms express this message. For instance, the 'showcasing effect' often troubles the interpretation of pilot programmes. Enthusiasm is infectious and the first trial of a brand spanking new idea will attract enthusiasts both to run the intervention and, perhaps, to take part, should subjects be able to volunteer. Enthusiasm creates winners. Enthusiasm, alas, is also time bound. It often begins to wane as intervention activities become routinised and less capable of inspiring change. I've rather lived off a little joke spun to me in this respect, as when a much disappointed and particularly gnarled community police officer announced his reworking of the acronym (NDC) of a prestigious, then new regeneration programme, the 'New Deal for Communities'. His version became the less inspiring 'No Discernible Change'.

This illustration recounts a familiar enough tale when repeated ineffectuality of a series of programmes in the face of particularly tough challenges prompts disillusion on the part of some stakeholders. Another example of the same ilk takes us back to the plethora of programmes aimed at getting unemployed young people off benefits and back into education, training or work. Some unfortunates trail from one such scheme to another and there comes a point when entry into a new variant becomes counterproductive. Again to rely on personal anecdote, I recall interviewing a young man about his experience on such a UK scheme called *Connexions*. Although he had participated for several weeks, he had no idea that he was on this particular programme, let alone what it was trying to achieve – 'some bloke just told me to come here, and I did'. Empirical research, alas, indicates that several of his compatriots have experienced similar programmes in similar ways (Colley, 2003).

Cynicism and somnolence are, however, not the only reactions to repeated programme failure. If one considers the diet industry, then previous failures become the spur to try the new programme variant. There is even a much used temporal slogan, 'you've tried the rest, now try the best' and on this basis thousands of willing horses are busy on nosebags containing low-fat, cabbage, 32-chew, F-plan, macrobiotic and Martini diets. Unable to resist the temptation to cry, I'll drink to that, I return to the paradox of high failure rates. One review notes that the majority of research on commercial weight loss programmes omits to examine drop-out rates and in the few that do, attrition figures ranged from 18 to 67% in the first year (Tsai and Wadden, 2005). Much, apparently, depends on the felt need for the programme goal. In this case the overwhelming desire for the trim figure sustains the pursuit of the smallest hope.

With examples such as these in mind, policy makers have become much more aware of the importance of the timing of policies and the sequencing of programmes. Let me call an end to time travel with a positive example. Consider legislation banning smoking in public places. Rather against some expectations that disobedience might follow because addiction was strong and that enforcement would be weak, these laws have begun to work. One reason is a temporal trick known as denormalisation theory (Chapman, 2007). Bans are introduced in stages (on public transport, followed by office and indoor workplace restrictions, followed by smoke-free restaurants and then bars, pubs, and gambling venues) in a kind of 'domino theory', and it is this incrementalism that is the key to changing behaviour. Smokers grow used to being pushed around.

The puzzling effects of history, time and sequencing confront the evaluator with yet more complexity. Trying, trying and trying again is sometimes a winning strategy and sometimes counterproductive.

5. Outcomes

Those were the days. Measuring the impact of a programme used to be simple, clinically simple. Having identified the variable that the initiative was designed to change, the investigator undertook its measurement 'before' and 'after' the intervention was applied. This pre-test/post-test difference became the outcome touchstone, made more secure in its significance if the researcher was able to apply the same measure to an untreated control group. Here then is the elegant origin – one yardstick applied twice.

Nowadays outcome mapping has a structure that is decidedly inelegant. To help secure causal inferences most commentators recommend comprehensive monitoring systems, charting progress through the 'black box' of the intervention. There are many such measurement models; a relatively simple one adapted from Earl et al. (2001) is reproduced as Figure 3.1.

Such models provide useful reminders that evaluators are well advised to check that the planned activities under the programme really have occurred and are being delivered in appropriate quantities at the right time to the right subjects and so forth. I omit all technical details here, highlighting just one feature of such models, namely that each link in the chain is a plural. Multiple measures are now the norm. It is obvious, for instance, that inputs into a programme are considerable (budget, design, choice of partners, location, timing, etc.) and indeed crucial (skimpy budget, scant impact). More interesting, perhaps, is the contemporary growth in ambitions for programme outcomes. Consider, for instance, a youth mentoring programme. Outcome measures will map progress, or otherwise, in school behaviour and attendance, exam performance, drug and alcohol misuse, family and peer relationships, and so on (Grossman and Tierney, 1998). Shifting to the collective level, a community development scheme will have designs on housing infrastructure, crime and incivility reduction, unemployment rates, public health, environmental improvement, etc. (www.communities.gov.uk/). Again, my aim here is to merely tot up complexities rather than to address technicalities. Thus I note only in passing that any item in the above can produce measurement migraines: consider, for instance, the problems of measuring highly camouflaged outcomes such as teenagers' usage of drugs, cigarettes and alcohol (Magura and Kang, 1996).

Figure 3.1 Outcome mapping

The complexity plot really thickens, however, as we turn to the next challenge. Outcome measures do not speak for themselves and their interpretation is often contested. These mutterings grow loudest whenever evaluators involve themselves in comparing outcome across institutions. I'm thinking here of the various 'league tables', 'report cards', and 'star ratings' on which schools, hospitals and even individual surgeons are rated (Snelling, 2003). As all evaluators and some policy makers know, raw outcome data can be highly misleading because they do not take into account the abilities of children at intake, the depth of the disease of the patient on the operating table, and so on. Technical resolutions are to hand, of course, in the form of value-added measures, risk-adjusted outcomes, etc. But the interpretation problem is never easily solved. Riskier cases have been accepted for surgery, but is this acceptable? Value added measures may be published but will parents only have eyes for the raw scores? Measurement itself has intervened and subtly changed the problem.

And this brings us to the muddy, murky climax of outcome measurement. Where there is policy there is politics, and performance measurement (a crueller term for outcome measurement) is always heavily politicised. The obvious examples here are the programmes, nay the crusades, of recent UK governments to bring down waiting times for treatment in the NHS. The measurement of the routine activity of thumb twiddling is, sadly, beset with a great methodological challenge, namely – when does the clock start ticking? To postpone that moment it is often possible to modify booking systems, to increase the number of referral points, to introduce triage and guidelines to damp down demand (Bevan and Hood, 2006). Whether these manoeuvres constitute service improvement is a moot point. The measure looks healthier but is the performance? Complexity bubbles up again. The first objective of evaluation is to measure change but we discover that the act of measurement is multitudinous and may itself change the behaviour under evaluation.

——— 6. Rivalry ————————————————————————————

Where are interventions dispensed? It would make life easier for the evaluator if the answer were – a vacuum. Alas, we have already described a mêlée of contexts, times, histories and localities that condition the action of all interventions. But there is a further category that deserves particular mention. Interventions are always dispensed into a world of existing interventions. These adjoin and inter-communicate. How an intervention sits alongside its policy neighbours is another key determinant of its fortunes.

Acquaintance with two particularly crowded neighbourhoods throws light on the ensuing complexities. The first is the UK's NHS, which I have already singled out as an embodiment of long, winding and branching implementation chains. Making matters more complex is the co-existence along that road of scores upon scores of other interventions, large and small. Three quotations separated by a dozen years help me to make the point with respect to the former:

The NHS is 50 years old. Alongside remarkable stability in the espoused pur-pose of the NHS there has been almost constant structural change ... There is a paper mountain of advice on reforms, restructuring and managing change. (Plamping, 1998)

The NHS is suffering from reform overload with too many rushed, uncon-tested and untested reforms, redesigns and reconfigurations. (Royal College of Nurses, 2007)

Over the past 30 years, governments have reached repeatedly for structural reorganisations. ... They have created, merged, and abolished health bodies and distributed service, functional, and geographical responsibilities in dif-ferent ways ... with at least 15 identifiable major structural changes in three decades, or one every two years or so. (Walshe, 2010)

Another jostling policy location is the 'sink community'. I use the disparaging label to make the point that no one really wants to be seen therein, with the exception of interventions. Please allow me a further anecdote in this respect about a pilot visit to the aforementioned New Deal for Communities. The offices of a particular NDC scheme (not the one with the sceptical sergeant) were to be found in a half-empty row of shops, provided with the assistance of the local authority. Next door were the offices of Sure Start, another new heavyweight government scheme aimed at early-years' development. Next to that was a more established premises of the Citizen's Advice Bureau and across the street was a doctors' surgery proudly refurbished as a Community Health Centre. Cheek by jowl one has government, local authority and third sector programmes. And on top of these community-focused interventions, almost every individual in the neighbourhood was eligible for schemes aimed at them by dint of age, disability, single parenthood, unemployment and so on.

Readers will see the point coming, which applies to both examples, namely that it is ferociously difficult to evaluate the impact of a particular programme, when all around revolve other schemes aimed at similar outcomes and common improve-ments. In short we encounter the 'attribution problem' writ large. This is no place to discuss the technicalities of how one might solve it, for we are yet to plumb the depths of the problem. Programme contiguity will have dynamics of its own. Sometimes it will embody policy contradiction. Complex policy systems combine many objectives, each potentially worthy in its own right, but which collectively may clash. A health system like the NHS that is 'free at the point of delivery' faces constant financial pressure and so has spawned a range of rules and strategies for demand reduction. But then, having intervened to restrict the flow, another worthy intervention comes along offering patients the right to 'choose and book' the time and location of treatment. The evaluator may try to keep her nose on a particular programme grindstone but often ends up chasing different political philosophies.

We are yet to finish with policy clamour. Life in the intervention metrop-olis is not all rivalry and turf wars but also about cooperation and collusion. Programmes provide employment. The considerable body of programme managers and practitioners is faced with a perpetual and jostling stream of schemes (so-called 'interventionitis'). They react, not as docile intermediaries, but by claiming some control over the implementation process. For instance, large national programmes often hold annual conferences to 'share and shape best practice' (the 9th UK Sure Start event is taking place at the time of writing). Professionalisation also takes a hold. For example, if one works in 'multi-agency, early-years settings' a NPQICL (National Professional Qualifications in Integrated Care Leadership) might give an edge to your input. As well as these particular lines of control, the 'continuous quality improvement' ethos is encouraged informally in the direction of most large scale services as is the demand for better 'joining up' of delivery. In short, programmes do not stand in pristine purity awaiting evaluation. Programme theories are begged, stolen and borrowed and these generic management adaptations always infiltrate and redirect programmes. In this policy saturated world it is increasingly difficult to see where one programme starts and another one ends.

———— 7. Emergence ————————————————————————

We come to the complexity's final and most devilish twist, the concept of emergence. In broad terms this refers to the ideas that components in a system will often combine to produce novel components, thus continually changing the composition of the system under investigation (Corning, 2002). In social science this phenomenon is rooted in the remarkable sensitivity of people to their place in the world. We interpret situations and those collective interpretations have causal powers. Sometimes what emerges is continuity; we choose to stick with institutions and systems that we collectively favour. Sometimes these interpretations lead to change and produce new institutions and systems. And sometimes these interpretations generate unintentional, unwanted changes to institutions and systems. A pocket illustration lies in the consequences of casting a vote, which may: i) reaffirm and consolidate the democratic system, and/or ii) lead to a change of government, and/or iii) lead to a coalition government that very few will have voted for.

What is the relevance of all this for evaluation? Programme and policies seek to change peoples' sensitivity to their place in the world. One set of agents seeks to change the choices of another set. This may result in any of the outcomes described above: no change, change, unintended change. What the phenomenon of emergence tells us is that we have imperfect control over the three outcomes. The reason is that programmes not only work to change behaviour but they may also change the conditions that make the programme work in the first place.

Examples are legion but the really rapid fire of emergence comes in the field of situational crime prevention. Let us pick up the example of crime reduction due to the powers of those unintelligent bits of glass, metal and circuitry known as CCTV cameras. On introduction some thirty years ago the relatively few machines met with some success often because of their unseen presence and unknown capabilities, which led respectively to the arrest of the inattentive criminals or the temporary displacement of activities of the more cautious. Today, police estimate CCTV numbers in the UK at 1,853,681. This translates to one camera for every 32 UK citizens. The London Underground network alone has over 10,000 cameras. The growth of the scheme has changed the context that enabled them to work. Nowadays, no self-respecting criminal would go off to 'work' without the assumption that a camera may lurk. The wisest of them have expertise in camera angles and resolution quality. This is the emergent property. As with all situational crime prevention efforts, effects wear off as criminals wise up, adapt and await the next smart idea. Even more dramatically, the law abiding now find themselves in an emergent property know as the 'surveillance society', leading to increasing public calls for proper legal regulation and more proportionate use of CCTV (Armstrong and Norris, 1999).

The most notorious and most disputed emergent property in the world of social policy is the potential for welfare provision to become welfare dependency. As I heard a radio pundit claim this morning in a discussion of 2011 UK inner city riots, 'the welfare state started as a safety net, it then became a hammock, and now it is a noose'. One does not have to assent to this simplistic picture of a feral, welfare-scrounging underclass to appreciate the methodological point. Successful programmes attract. The more successful the programme the more adherents and the more adherents the more mixed their motivations. One powerful motivation may be to stay on the programme, should its benefits be perceived as outweighing those of leaving. For practical purposes this requires programme designs to pay due attention to 'weaning off' rather than just 'weaning on'. But in terms of complexity the example tells us that programmes make and remake society as well as affecting individuals.

In summary, I have suggested that all evaluators, systematic reviewers and policy analysts should step back, before they commence research design, before they enter the field, and they should attempt an initial mapping of these contours of complexity as they envelop the intervention(s) under study. Box 3.1 provides a handy version of the checklist:

Box 3.1

A complexity checklist

1 Volitions. Map the choice architecture of the programme. What choices do subjects have to make to achieve the ambitions of the programme? These choices will vary significantly across the totality of subjects, so the map should cover the full range and balance of volitions. Minds tend to be changed slowly so the volition map should also sketch the pathways of persuasion, the sequence of choices a subject has to make in moving from outsider to insider status.

2 Implementation. Map the implementation chains of the programme. Programmes come to life over many months and years and a great diversity of 'traffic' flows

(Continued)

(Continued)

through them. Implementation maps might begin to chart: flows of resources; chains of responsibilities (individuals and institutions); reception and transmission points for subjects; as well as the different theories of change that lie behind each stage, strategy and tactic.

3 Contexts. Map the pre-existing contexts in which the programme is embedded. Consider for whom and in what circumstances the programme might work. Contexts vary from the micro to the macro, so the map might include profiles of: stakeholders and their characteristics; the interpersonal exchanges through which the programme is delivered; the organisational settings in which it takes place; the wider societal location of the programme.

4 Time. Map the history of the family of programmes of which the intervention under study is a member. What has happened previously will shape what happens next. Temporal mapping might include: previous experiences of programme subjects and communities on similar interventions; previous experiences of stakeholders in delivering similar interventions; the successes and failures of previous attempts, of whatever kind, to address the given policy objective.

5 Outcomes. Map the monitoring systems that are likely to be applied and have been applied to programmes like the one under study. Consider which measures are likely to be contested, how stakeholders might differ in their interpretations, and whether behaviour might change as a result of being monitored rather than as a result of the intended action of the programme.

6 Rivalry. Map the pre-existing policy landscape in which the programme is embedded. Other, contiguous programmes and policies may share or oppose the ambitions of the intervention under study and can override the actions of stakeholders and subjects under study. Consider how generic implementation strategies such as 'continuous improvement' will continue to modify the delivery of the programme.

7 Emergence. Map the potential emergent effects, long-term adaptations, societal changes and unintended consequences associated with the programme. Consider whether the spread and duplication of the programme might blunt its effectiveness. How will the programme be able to maintain a balance between recruitment, retention and exit?

Let me clarify a little further some expectations about this mapping exercise. First, consider again the use of the classification system. It is a rare set of categories that is totally inclusive and mutually exclusive and this is inevitably true of a complexity map. I have built the VICTORE categories using illustrations from a range of different programmes. It goes without saying that the complexities facing, say, national legislation on alcohol pricing are not the same as those confronting, say, classroom-based sex education programmes. Close inspection of any single programme may reveal additional intricacies under some of the above headings and quieter waters in some others. But I am in no doubt that the categories drawn up here are spelt out at a level of abstraction that will enable them to be located in all programmes. The point is to stress their ubiquity rather than paint them into corners.

A second clarification concerns my use of the term 'map'. Do I foresee researchers sharpening their pencils and sketching arrays of implementation arrows, policy networks, contextual surrounds, temporal graphs, organisational blockages and so on? Indeed I do. Books are a rather poor medium for reproducing doodles and diagrams and so I have relied here on an acronym and pen pictures to build the portrait of programme complexity. Programme portrayal, whether termed logic mapping or concept mapping, is quite familiar in evaluation research and many of the conventions can be borrowed (Kane and Trochim, 2006; Funnell and Rogers, 2011).

On the basis of the arguments so far it should be obvious that there is no correct way to map complexity. However, for readers interested in the craft of visualisation, a brief mention of two further resources may be useful. The website www. visualcomplexity.com is a cornucopia of complexity maps used across a variety of disciplines. It contains the famous 'obesity system influence diagram' compiled by Vandenbroeck and colleagues. This huge plate of spaghetti shows the interconnections between the multiplicity of factors contributing to the obesity epidemic: 108 variables are depicted, unearthed in a review of studies ranging in perspectives from individual psychology, physiology, food production economics, dietary cultures, food consumption habits and attitudes, physical activity, built environment and so on. It serves as a useful reminder that the many pet schemes promoting 'healthy eating' are but a scratch on the surface of the problem. Vast as it is, it should be noted that the map's concern is essentially with the activities of individuals and with the systems in which they are located. In short, it covers only the 'V' and the 'C' in VICTORE.

Another stunning set of maps (www.stanford.edu/~rhorn/) emanate from Horn's work on 'visual analytics for public policy'. One interesting sub-type carries the name 'mess maps'. Their 'look' is different, with sector blobs and information nuggets, but the function is the same – 'behold complexity'. They are designed to illustrate the functioning of whole services and the dilemmas and problems associated with implementation and delivery. Their main concern might be said to be the 'I' and the 'R' in VICTORE. Horn claims an important evaluation function for such large scale murals – they provide an immediate mental map of a service and its problems. 'Seeing' the issues, he claims, generates instant stakeholder involvement and is far more valuable to practitioners than the typical 60-page formal report.

We arrive at the terminus of our tour of complexity. If I may be allowed a call-to-arms, the recommendation for practitioners of evidence-based policy is simple. Whilst the complex system that embodies and surrounds your programme can never be fully described, mapped and visualised – you should still go ahead and try it. What does VICTORE spell out for your programme? Such an exercise always needs doing, and doing before the headlong rush in which most evaluators reach out for new evidence on whether a new programme is working. There is an undeniable case that these seven major themes matter when it comes to programme effectiveness; the balance of fortunes is foretold here. Indeed, my view is that these essentials of programme architecture make the task of evidence-based policy more realistic, for in telling us what *could be* researched, they immediately remind us that any specific evaluation or review will only take a limited and specific cut at the issues. They reveal what has and what has not been envisaged in empirical research. In passing, I note that 'reviews' possess the nap hand over 'evaluations' in terms of their capacity for capturing evidence across this broad terrain. But the conclusion is the same, even if we pile evaluation on evaluation, review upon review, we can never obtain perfect knowledge of all of the dynamics of policies and programmes. The end point is a vanishing point. VICTORE cannot be vanquished.

Battling with it can, however, be remarkably useful and in the third chapter of this part of the book, I will return to the positive story of researching in the midst of ignorance and uncertainty. Since nescience is not the usual rallying cry for scientific inquiry, it is worth a careful detour to consider how others have responded to the chaos of complexity.

FOUR

Contested Complexity

Having compiled a basic realist model of programme complexity, this chapter goes on to compare notes. Dealing with complexity has become an obsession across many schools and all disciplines of social science. Indeed, there is equal observance in the hard sciences of biology and physics (Mazzocchi, 2008; Ellis, 2008). As one travels the complexity paradigms it becomes clear that there is no agreement on either its nature or in the resolutions to its challenge. The purpose of this chapter is to create some elbow room, casting a critical eye on the rival perspectives. Given the vastness of the complexity literature I do not claim to produce a comprehensive overview here. Four broad approaches to complexity are perused:

- The augmented trials perspective
- The systems perspective
- The critical realist perspective
- The pragmatist perspective.

For each perspective I identify the core understanding of complexity, the favoured resolution, and examples of the remedies in action. It will become apparent that each approach embodies quite different tactics in attempting to appease or to slay the complexity monster. A detailed critique of each strategy is presented. The first three approaches are declared counterproductive for evaluation science: the first simply underestimates the problem of complexity; the second works at a level of abstraction too remote from evaluation's practical ambitions; the third uses philosophical smoke and mirrors to bluff its way to an ideological solution. The fourth perspective offers pragmatic solutions in the battle with programme complexity. Whilst a heavy dose of practicality is essential in the conduct of evaluation, the problem with pragmatism, almost by definition, is that its solutions to complexity are plural, piecemeal and contested. It lacks a unifying philosophy. It awaits a realist foundation, which is pursued in the next chapter.

The augmented trials perspective

One major impulse in the literature is to admit complexity but to conceive it in a sufficiently truncated form so that it can be dealt with within the traditional mainstream of evaluation approaches. The most influential of these strategies is the UK Medical Research Council (MRC) guidance on 'Developing and Evaluating Complex Intervention'. This first appeared in 2000, with revisions leading to a more comprehensive and authoritative (MRC, 2008) version: www.mrc.ac.uk/ complexinterventionsguidance. The report contains fourteen 'cases', which exemplify the empirical capture of complexity and there is also a summary in the *British Medical Journal* (BMJ) (Craig et al., 2008). Note well that this is advice from the MRC, home to clinical orthodoxy and to denizens of the randomised controlled trial (RCT). Given this pedigree, one must welcome the admittance of a range of social science methods into the medical heartlands. There is support for the role of theory in understanding how outcomes are shaped, there is room for the incorporation of process evaluations (provided they do not replace the study of outcomes), there is advice on using multiple outcome measures, and there is development of new modes of trial methodology going well beyond the simple programme-on/programme-off comparison.

Along with the gains, alas, there are shortcomings and these can be located in the MRC's basic understanding of complexity. Its key features are conveniently described in a summary box, which is reproduced here as Box 4.1.

Box 4.1

The MRC Typology

What makes an intervention complex?

- Number of interacting components within the experimental and control interventions;
- Number and difficulty of behaviours required by those delivering or receiving the intervention;
- Number of groups or organisational levels targeted by the intervention;
- Number and variability of outcomes;
- Degree of flexibility or tailoring of the intervention permitted.

Vital clues on the understanding of complexity lie in this immediate formulation. It is instructive to engage in a bullet-point by bullet-point comparison with the more varied contours of complexity identified in the realist model set down as Box 3.1. Let me identify three differences that hit the eye before elaborating on them in further discussion. First is the assumption, tacked oddly onto the end of the opening bullet point, that the intervention will be ultimately assessed within the parameters of an experimental trial. This is no slip of the pen. The method used to evaluate the intervention is not, of course, an aspect of its complexity and yet it finds its way into the rulebook. This is part of the automatic, habitual vocabulary of the trialist; interventions remain in some intrinsic, essential way those things that get tested by experiment and control. It is no surprise, then, when the MRC summary (Craig et al., 2008) comes around to asserting that expectation: 'experimental trials are preferred to observational designs in most circumstances'.

The second noticeable feature of the MRC framework is the explication of the complexity problem as a matter of 'numbers' (in four of the bullet points). The first item, for instance, refers to the fact that many modern programmes combine a number of different measures (a fitness promotion campaign might offer advice, fitness testing, apparatus, premises, a trainer and so on and so forth). Looking down Box 4.1, it is sheer magnitude, the number of inputs, the number of stake-holders, the number of institutional levels and the number of outputs that is said to make for complexity. Missing is any notion of emergence, of internal, adaptive, self-generated, or historical change. On the realist account what matters is not only numbers of this, that and the other. Complexity comes about because inputs, stakeholders, institutional features and outputs are all in a state of constant change, with or without the help of the programme.

Thirdly, consider bullet point five where this important issue of implementation drift does seem to be acknowledged. This is an important concession. But note the precise phrasing of the issue – the degree of implementation flexibility that is 'permitted'. Still uppermost, unerringly, is the mentality of control and the assumption that stakeholder interpretation is some kind of noise, a contaminating influence, there to be monitored and marshalled. For the realist programmes are carried by human activity. Intervention outcomes are realised through human interpretation. The participants are the programme. No one 'permits' them to interpret what is going on.

Let us move to discuss these issues in more detail. The realist perspective has always rejected the gold standard methodological status afforded to the RCT (Pawson and Tilley, 1997b: chapter 2; Pawson, 2006a: chapter 3) and a complexity perspective drives home that case. To appreciate the shortcomings of the RCT, it is useful to review its core concepts and revisit them in the light of what we have learned about complexity. Think again of the basic structure of experimental logic – to create a situation in which the only difference between the experimental group and the control group is the application of the intervention and, this achieved, it follows that the intervention must be responsible for observed difference in outcomes. For the logic to apply one must think of the experimental and control groups as stable and identical conditions and one must conceive the intervention as singular and stable. The whole thrust of the decades of debate on complexity is that the uniformity demanded in this scenario cannot be realised in social interventions. What experimental logic treats as a singular and stable treatment is actually a long and ceaselessly changing implementation process. What experimental logic treats as stable and identical experimental and control conditions are actually complex and ceaselessly changing social systems.

If we look back momentarily at what we learned from the VICTORE typology, we see that implementation of the so-called treatment is in the hands of many choice-makers (policy makers, managers, practitioners, subjects). Significant parts of their lives are bound up in the intervention and they cannot be forbidden from choosing and remaking its course. Then if we consider the so-called experimental 'condition' in which the treatment is applied, our previous discussion tells us that this is not just the group of individuals on the receiving end of a programme but a system with many levels (individuals, interactions, institutions, infrastructures). That system, moreover, always takes on a varied character because of its history, culture, location and policy neighbours and as a result the experimental condition is always in flux. Now consider 'control' conditions. These are not dormitories of repose. They are complex social situations with their own stakeholders, histories, environments and polities. They are not open to closure. So whether the subject sits in the experimental or control arm, the world will transform around them independently of the programme and regardless of the efforts of the researcher. Change is incessant, automatic and self-generated. In reality, the experimental and control comparison is one in which a complex and changing intervention 'A' is thrust into a complex and changing system 'B' and compared to a complex and changing system 'C'.

It may be objected that my objection here is to the most basic, pre-test, post-test, one-control group design. And here I come to specific critiques of the MRC guidance. The history of the development of the RCT is, of course, the history of anticipating 'threats to validity' and then bringing those threats under control via more sophisticated variations on the basic design. For instance, if a programme has a number of aims, the difficulty is dealt with comfortably by using multiple before and after measures. My point, however, is that most of the MRC 'threats' are pre-conceptualised in a way that can be accommodated into the RCT framework and that the underlying problems are effectively undersold. Moreover, the more advanced designs are purpose-built to deal with one threat at a time, with no design being capable of dealing with the totality of the complexity problem. Above all, it is impossible to devise a trial to follow the ceaseless, self-generated, emergent change that is a condition of all programmes. In short, one cannot design out complexity. Let us pick up these points with some examples.

Following tradition, the MRC guidance highlights some more advanced designs which it claims are more suited to evaluating complex interventions (Craig et al., 1998: 981). For example, there is the colossal and massively expensive 'stepped wedge design', formulated to deal with the delay between the implementation and evaluation of the pilot, the assessment of their findings, and the eventual decision to roll out a programme nationally. Policy problems are often pressing, experiments are sluggish. The stepped wedge design is said to solve this problem by combining rollout and trial design by the random addition of sub-populations to the trial. So, for instance, the evaluation of an immunisation programme may begin in one region and national coverage may be reached in the following months and years as other regions are added on a random basis. The 'wedge' in question is the growing profile of regions added to the experimental condition.

To my mind this approach solves an implementation dilemma by fudging the purpose of the outcome evaluation. What happens at iteration four or fourteen if outcomes swing significantly in favour of the control group? Should rollout cease at five or fifteen? It turns out that this is not anticipated in this design which has a particular strength 'in overcoming objections to randomised studies of interventions which have already been shown to do more good than harm' (MRC, 2008: 22). I cannot follow the logic here. Why is there a need to mount a fabulously long and expensive trial on something that has already proven its spurs? What is more, although implementation is subjected to random introduction, no investigation of its constituent processes and problems seems to be envisaged. One nugatory issue (rollout speed) is overcome only for others (impact thresholds and process variation) to be ignored. My only explanation is that randomisation, in and of itself, carries methodological status, regardless of whether it contributes to explanation. It has become a fetish.

Another novel design recommended in the guidance is the 'preference trial'. Experimental subjects, note the MRC, often have strong preferences to join a programme rather than to soldier on under the control condition that might come their way in the tough love of random allocation. The preference trial 'solution' is to break potential programme subjects into subgroups of those with and without such strong preferences. Thereafter, separate randomised experiments are run, at different levels of complexity (Cohort designs, Wennberg designs, Zelen designs and so on) on the two sub-groups. The basic gain is that experiments now monitor outcomes separately for willing horses and the herd at large. I put it like this to indicate that we are dealing with a feeble solution to a complex problem. The volitions of subjects do not come in two modes (keen versus not bothered). Real preferences have been described in the previous chapter (under V for volitions). They range along a huge continuum from hostility to apathy to ignorance to caution to stoicism to enthusiasm. Moreover, 'preferences' are not just exercised at one point. The programme encounter is a long one and choices are exercised all along the way – is the intervention on my radar? shall I investigate it? does it seem worthwhile? shall I enrol? shall I remain? shall I be active? shall I complete the programme? shall I continue with its lessons? Fetishism repeats itself. Complexity is dealt with by defining the problem in a way that can be accommodated by experimental variations and by secondary and tertiary randomisation. Subdividing trials into four or more rather than two groups is quite frankly an insult to the issue. Best, I think, to treat the problem of preferences on its real merits.

Let us move now to some of the positive strides in the MRC guidance, noting how they remain stunted because of the looming expectation that experiments remain the ultimate proving ground. Several perspicacious examples are highlighted in the report such as Case Study 10, in which a process evaluation solves the mystery of zero net impact in an RCT on computerised decision support systems (CDSS) for GP consultation on asthma and angina. Outcomes were unchanged because usage was low and usage was low because physicians considered they were already familiar with the content of the guidelines. Moreover, the qualitative data goes on to show that a range of other conditions – the patient's own preferences, the lack of incentive to change, the complications of referral management systems and so on – also intervened in decision making to thwart programme ambitions. So far so good – process data provides a useful explanation of the observed outcome.

The crucial question is how these routine interpretative processes are conceived. Basically what happens is that both interpretative process and pre-existing contextual constraints are recast as confounding variables, which need at some point to be brought under control. The Guidance spells out the MRC's understanding: 'Investigators need to be clear about how much change or adaptation they would consider permissible. Any variation in the intervention needs recording, whether or not it is intended, so that the fidelity can be assessed in relation to the degree of standardisation required by the study protocol' (MRC, 1998: 14). There could not be a clearer statement of the upside-down perception of what goes on in an intervention. This proposition requires the investigator to perceive the focal point of the inquiry as the execution of this pro-gramme called CDSS. From this vantage point, the GP's reasoning, the complexities of upward referral, the patients' preferences and so on are understood as potential sources of aberration which may lead to programme infidelity.

What is actually under investigation is the introduction of a complex system into a pre-existing complex system. What is actually under study is a routine inter-action that long predates CDSS, namely the consultation process, and what is actually observed is how GPs adapt to the incorporation of this new gizmo into their decision making. The complexities are not just a matter of an extraneous this, a contingent that, an infringing other. One cannot remove the history of doctor–patient relations from the encounter, one cannot control out the con-straints of NHS capacity, one cannot standardise patient preferences, one cannot fix trust in new technology, and so on. They pre-exist the intervention and are thus part of the intervention.

Dealing with complexity is not a matter of sorting through these contingent behav-iours and deciding whether they are 'permissible'. No one can prevent stakeholders from reflecting on their actions. Thinking about an intervention does not require the 'consent' of a protocol. It is this ceaseless reflection that makes programmes complex and leads them to develop internal change, feedback loops, emergent properties, unintended consequences and so on. To drive the point home, let me report on the reactions of a group of empirical researchers who have also struggled to make sense of the MRC guidelines (MacKenzie et al., 2010). Their programme, 'Keep Well', aimed to install improvements in the system of anticipatory care – identifying those at risk and introducing a new range of health checks and services.

> The MRC framework assumes that interventions that follow the guidance will reach a point of stability. However, complex organisational systems are character-ised by flux, contextual variation, and adaptive (or even maladaptive) learning rather than stability. In *Keep Well* learning between and during pilots led to prac-tices changing their approaches over time. Encouraged to operate as reflexive learning organisations, pilot practices met regularly to share learning about how to encourage health checks and make iterative changes to practice accordingly. This

kind of learning occurs independently of the evaluator, and the tension between stability and learning is found within almost all programmes that are evaluated in real life rather than within the bounded (and artificial) constraints of a randomised control trial. (MacKenzie et al., 2010: 340)

A concluding statement in the new MRC guidance must begin by recognising the step-change in methodology that resides within; particularly gratifying is the acknowledgement of importance of multi-method inquiry as demonstrated in the CDSS case study above. A fundamental problem resides in the limited conceptualisation of complexity. There is no understanding of life's universal backdrop of continuous, adaptive change and thus of the inevitability that interventions can only hope to introduce adaptations amidst other adaptations. The guidelines read as if they were written by a committee because they were written by a committee and this permits frequent returns to the mother ship of the RCT and the notion that one can evaluate a programme by isolating and dismantling its effects from those of the rest of the world. The penny has yet to drop that programmes embody that world.

The Systems Perspective ———

With this approach we come to an enormously wide-ranging group of thinkers, so taken with the notion of complexity that they consider its study worthy of a new and rather erudite perspective, often termed 'systems thinking' or 'systems theory' or 'complexity science'. Readers might like to consult Byrne (1998) for a sympathetic overview, written with applied social science in mind. There are so many varieties of system thinking that I hardly know where to start (an old complexity theory joke by the way). Varieties include general systems theory, holism, chaos theory, actor–network theory, diffusion models, complex adaptive systems theory, soft systems theory, agent based modelling, morphological analysis, and so on. There is no common intellectual foundation here and indeed tribal distinctions are inevitably drawn such as those between types of complexity (e.g. restricted and general) and types of system (e.g. dissipative and near to equilibrium). Accordingly, I will not attempt to follow the flight of the entire star-ship here and concentrate only on the attempts to inhabit the planet Evaluation. Evaluation research, evidence synthesis, policy analysis and so on are rather pragmatic arts – so the question for this sub-section is what, if anything, can be plundered from these cosmic perspectives and taken back to the world of policy and practice.

The first point to note is that since complexity is the domain issue here an inordinate amount of effort is put into the issue of defining the 'c' word. When do systems become complex? Our hunt for the formula begins with the pioneering paper by Glouberman and Zimmerman (2002) in which they developed a now widely-used distinction between 'simple', 'complicated' and 'complex' problems. The classification was illustrated by the beseeching examples of, respectively, 'baking a cake', 'sending a rocket to the moon' and 'raising a child'. And indeed the difference between these tasks is telling. In the former, one must follow the formula (the recipe) and plenty of previous experience is useful. In the second, formulae are exacting and vital but it is expertise rather than experience that gets you there. In the latter, formulae have limited application and, unless one has had many children, experience is likely to follow rather than precede the task. Each scenario bestows a different likelihood of success, respectively: an agreeable result every time; solid certainty if the formula is followed; uncertainty of outcome always lurks. Pleasing as it is, this exposition of the complexity in terms of the magnitude and uncertainty of the task confronted is of little help in evaluation research. We know that the tasks of social policy are never simple but helping a prisoner go straight, persuading motorists onto buses, improving public health, reducing energy consumption, and so on are all surrounded by uncertainty and all seem crowded in the complex category.

One can seek a little more traction on the issue by considering what is said to distinguish the complicated and the complex. Rogers (2008) has produced the most careful dissection in the evaluation field and readers are recommended to go to the small print. Basically, she suggests that complicated interventions are those with multiple strands – multiple sites, multiple ambitions, multiple stakehold-ers, and so on. For these, Rogers suggests that one can get by using conventional analytic methods that are able to prise apart the different contributions of the different combinations. Complex aspects of interventions are those that have a life of their own and thus may lead programmes to develop internal (endogenous) change, feedback loops, emergent properties, unintended consequences and so on. For these situations, Rogers suggests a switch to modes of 'non-linear' and 'emergent' evaluation, approaches that we are about to inspect in further detail.

Alas, whilst this complicatedness/complexity distinction (basically, magnitude versus internal intricacy) is clear conceptually, at the level of the intervention on the ground these states are indistinguishable. They go hand in hand – the more complicated the stakeholder structure the more likely are members to fall into dispute, the lengthier the implementation chain the more likely it is to fold back on itself, the murkier the history of a programme the more likely the new incarna-tion is to be troubled, the greater the ambitions of a programme the more likely they are to collide with those of rival interventions, and so on. In general it is true and therefore better to say that all social programmes and policy interventions are both complicated and complex, and since this is something of a mouthful I have preferred, and will continue, to stick to the latter.

Another means of defining complexity is to provide a taxonomy or checklist of its components. Since this was precisely my method in devising the VICTORE typology it is instructive to compare notes. Let us start with the obvious example from the complexity literature, the much reproduced ten characteristics of 'wicked problems' from the much celebrated paper by Rittel and Webber (1974). Wicked problems are wicked (rather than tame) because they are set in a sea of political and moral disputes, so generating the set of features reproduced as Box 4.2.

Much has been said by way of clarification and criticism of these criteria (Munro and Jeffrey, 2008). I am unable to resist the temptation to join in with some individual quibbles before I come to an overall criticism, which is about their ineffective sum total. Some of these criteria are deliberately perverse; with rule one getting us off to a decidedly wretched start, being rather like saying, 'we cannot be sure what we are talking about – but here goes'. What the rule actually means is that the elements of complexity are inexhaustible and one can never reach a totally inclusive description of the entire system. Some of the definitions are sensible if oddly worded; rule two about 'stopping rules' pointing mundanely to the fact that there are no final, complete and fully correct solutions to social problems. Some of them, such as rules five and seven, seem to embrace solipsism and deny that we can learn from inquiry to inquiry. This is perfect nonsense, a negation of the very possibility of evaluative inquiry. To be sure, no two programmes will be exactly alike but we would be unable to recognise them as programmes unless they contained common elements: resources, implementation chains, stakeholders, inputs, outputs and so on. We would be unable to understand that the problems confronted were indeed wicked without the pre-existing and chequered family history of attempts to overcome health inequalities, underdevelopment, drug abuse, crime victimisation, and so on. On balance, I prefer Mark Twain's starting point that history does not repeat itself, but it rhymes. Some of the criteria, such as rules seven and eight, contradict; if one can say that a unique problem has a detectable cause one is already detecting regularity and on one's way to understanding the problem is not unique. Some of the definitions simply tease; rule ten appears to require an omniscient policy maker but actually requires the planner to justify modest, selected, feasible improvements rather than final solutions.

| Box 4.2 |

The characteristics of wicked problems

1 There is no definite formulation of a wicked problem.
2 Wicked problems have no stopping rules.
3 Solutions to wicked problems are not true or false, but better or worse.
4 There is no immediate and no ultimate test of a solution to a wicked problem.
5 Every solution to a wicked problem is a 'one-shot operation' because there is no opportunity to learn from trial and error: every attempt counts significantly.
6 Wicked problems do not have an endurable (or an exhaustibly describable set of potential solutions, nor is there a set of permissible operations that may be incorporated into the plan.
7 Every wicked problem is essentially unique.
8 Every wicked problem can be considered to be a symptom of another [wicked] problem.
9 The causes of a wicked problem can be explained in numerous ways. The choice of explanation determines the nature of the problem's resolution.
10 With wicked problems the planner has no right to be wrong.

I must put an end to this petty wrangling, however, for what is crucially amiss with these criteria is at fault with each and every one of them, namely – the high level of abstraction used in expressing the issues. The definitions in Box 4.2 are reproduced as they are because they are intended to apply to systems in general. All social, political, economic, institutional and administrative systems, the argument goes, will generate and have to confront such wicked problems. Alas, the higher the level of abstraction of the conceptual system the less likely is the building of any consensus on how to put empirical inquiry to those concepts. If researchers know only that wicked problems are 'essentially unique' and have 'numerous explanations' and have 'no true or false solutions' and so on, they have no recognisable canvas on which to work. This is the decisive difference between my own typology and the one reproduced above (Boxes 3.1 and 4.2). VICTORE does not speak to problems that are any less 'wicked' but uses a recognisable vocabulary of intervention building to describe their intractability. This brings us to my first critique of complexity science, whilst recognising, of course, that I am not the first to spot it. Let me pass over to one of its most trenchant critics: 'The ideas of complexity theory function more as a descriptive conceptualisation of the backdrop to action and one which at times seems very wordy and taxonomically over elaborate' (Pollitt, 2009: 229).

To hammer home Pollitt's point, let me make it clear that my examples above emanate only from the lower slopes of abstraction. For twenty-first century levels of abstruseness I can think of no finer example than Andriani and McKelvey's (2009) 'scale-free theories of nature': i) Exogenous energy impositions cause autocatalytic interaction effects such that new interaction groups form; ii) Heterogeneous agents seeking out other agents to copy/learn from so as to improve fitness generate networks; with positive feedback, some networks become groups, and some groups become larger groups and hierarchies; iii) Multiple exponential or log normal distributions or increased complexity of components (subtasks, processes) set up, which results in a power law distribution; iv) Surfaces absorbing energy grow by the square, but organisms grow by the cube, resulting in an imbalance; fractals emerge to balance surface/volume ratios. Readers may be pleased to know that I have saved them from another eight, scale-free, pearls of wisdom.

Following its definitional work, complexity science turns to solutions, the fresh modes of policy analysis required to face the new conceptual challenges. Immediately apparent in this literature is the powerful echo of high abstraction; the ambiguous formulations of the nature of the complexity 'problem' have a habit of finding their way forward into the 'solutions'. This results in recommendations for analysis that are mere incantations. The goal is to 'rethink' the whole process of evaluation, public administration, policy analysis, organisational studies, management science, etc. What is required is a new Zeitgeist, a new research mentality. Consider, for instance, Clarke and Stewart's (2003: 279) advice on dealing with 'wicked programmes' of contemporary public policy: 'The style is ... that of an explorer who has a sense of direction but no clear route. Search and exploration, watching out for possibilities and interrelationships, however unlikely they may seem, are part of the approach.'

There is advice that goes beyond such sloganeering but the level of abstraction remains high. So, for instance, Clarke and Stewart go on to recommend: 'holistic not partial and linear thinking, capable of encompassing the interaction of a wide variety of activities, habits and behaviours' (2003: 275). This is reminiscent of calls for 'whole systems thinking' made ever since the coinage of the idea of wicked problems. Going back to an earlier, very influential paper there is a similar plea, to 'accommodate multiple alternative perspectives rather than prescribe single solutions', to 'function through group interaction and iteration rather than back-office calculations', and to 'generate ownership of the problem through transparency' (Rosenhead, 1996). To this day 'holist' or 'whole systems' perspective carries considerable weight with the same sentiments being found as the basis for the analysis of every conceivable problem in health service delivery – obesity, mental health, chronic disease management, clinical commissioning and so on (Dattée and Barlow, 2010).

Whole system thinking, alas, meets its nemesis when systems become infinitely large. In the previous chapter I have argued that interventions are complex systems thrust into complex systems. Programmes are complex because they have human subjects and thus have to connect with the full range of human reasoning and because they are implemented in long and dense administrative thickets and because they are implemented in different contexts with different admixtures of stakeholders operating to different rules and traditions and because they are located at specific points in history with what has happened before influencing what happens now and because they seek to address different outcomes whose interpretation is likely to be contested and because they are implemented in crowded policy landscapes with many other interventions vying for the attention of the subjects and because their enactment has emergent effects and thus may change the original conditions that enabled them to work in the first place. I cram all of that into one, breathless sentence to re-emphasise the conclusion of the previous chapter, namely that one cannot gain a simultaneous empirical grip of the infinite considerations that make a programme complex. One cannot conduct inquiry into the entirety of a system in any meaningful sense.

This conclusion is borne out if one inspects what is actually done in the name of 'whole systems' inquiry. Nowhere to be seen is that intrepid explorer with a keen sense of direction, grasping everything. Rather, the tag is mostly used to describe collaborative learning between stakeholders. The methods put to use are actually rather narrowly based and rooted in the long tradition of co-participatory inquiry, action research and developmental evaluation. Likewise, the policy issue under investigation is usually quite specific – assisting stakeholders to work more closely together in an aspect of the co-design, co-production or co-delivery of services. An example is the design for a Four Level Healthcare System produced by the US National Academy of Engineering and the Institute of Medicine (Proctor et al., 2005), which seeks to join up the needs of: i) patients, ii) health care teams, iii) organisations and iv) the regulatory and market environment. There is no need to comment upon the success or otherwise of this exercise here. The point to note is that whilst the goal sounds impressively lofty, it only stretches to developing ICT tools to connect selected stakeholders in these four portals. As ever and oxymoronically, 'whole systems' approaches always boil down to 'partial system' inquiries.

Although holism is one of its buzz words, many readers with a systems back-ground will have sat impatiently through the previous paragraphs, given that myriad complexity theorists are quite dismissive of attempting a grand amalgamation of the components of a system, because 'one of the most important things about the approach is precisely its rejection of analytical structures in which things are reducible to the sum of its parts' (Byrne, 1998: 14). Here, for many, is the true stamp of complexity science and here, perhaps, lie the important implications for evaluation science. The crucial point is that systems have properties of their own and since evaluation deals with systems inserted into systems this powerful intuition must be incorporated. Concepts like 'emergence', 'non-linear effects', 'tipping points', 'unintended consequences', 'endogenous change', 'feedback loops', 'boundary decisions' and so on are true systems concepts. They describe the behaviour of all systems and, inevitably, are making their way into the evaluation argot (Williams and Hummelbrunner, 2010). Let us now attempt to gain a measure of their significance.

Attentive readers will note that I have already used the most general and all embracing of systems theory ideas, the notion of 'emergence' as part, but only one part, of my typology of complexity (Box 3.1). I first came across the idea in historical sociology under rather attractive metaphors about coal picks transforming into typewriters. This provocative image is not about the wondrous transmogrification of material objects but about the transformation of a system, the capitalist system. The argument is that labour power, such as in Arkwright's coalmine, creates the wealth to enable the growth of the commercial sector, such as in the typing pool in Acme Ltd. Commercial transactions themselves become a source of profit and the system as a whole continues to change – to a point a couple of years ago where the computer screens at MegaBucks Bank were considered the very seat of wealth creation. Evaluation research will be so much the poorer unless the possibility of such systems level transformation is accommodated. In the previous chapter I have already given examples of how surveillance apparatus became the surveillance society and how welfare benefits begat welfare dependency. Knowledge of the impact of a particular CCTV camera or particular disability benefit cannot be assessed without some knowledge of the state of play in these wider systems. But what is the overall significance of such systems concepts on evaluative inquiry?

Let us follow the consequences through with another system concept, that of non-linear effects, best known from its popular treatment in *The Tipping Point* (Gladwell, 2000). The basic idea is that system change is often slow and gradual, but sometimes it may be sudden and, indeed, exponential. These sudden spikes occur, the argument goes, because of a system-level attribute know as the tipping point. In epidemics, disease spread really begins to multiply at the point when a particular proportion of the population becomes infected so that opportunities for contagion become commonplace. Another system dynamic responsible for local epidemics occurs when there is a 'super infector', for instance a particularly promiscuous individual who becomes the epicentre for the transmission of a sexually transmitted disease.

Gladwell argues that the same system parameters can be detected in a whole range of social transactions and trends. The 'flat line followed by boom' profile can be observed in the sales of sportswear and popular novels, in the viewing figures of children's educational programmes and even in suicide cults. In the expectation that some underlying dynamic of social change had been uncovered, tipping point ideas entered the basic vocabulary of programme building and evaluation. For instance, the 'broken windows' programme theory argues that encouraging agencies to act immediately on minor environmental degradation is a crucial crime prevention scheme (Wilson and Kelling, 2003). It will 'cap the spike' whereby incivility booms and becomes the norm and will negate any subsequent need for a full-scale assault on established crime. Analogues for the super infector also abound, as when programmes attempt to utilise intervention 'champions' to infiltrate a system or a service for positive ends. Evaluators too have brought some of these systems ideas to the monitoring of outcomes. Effects are now monitored not only for their size but their profile; are there 'quick wins'? are there 'take-off points'?

To be sure evaluators should and have begun to anticipate non-linear change but the lesson that emerges from this brief example is that system concepts are important for evaluation research but they are not master concepts. They add to rather than underpin the evaluation landscape. Indeed, it can be argued that 'systems thinking' multiplies rather that solves the complexity burden. The reason why many complexity theorists have thought otherwise can be located in a key principle. The nub of the issue lies with the vital axiom that 'systems are not reducible to the sum of their parts'. I rather suspect that many complexity theories perceive this as the more powerful invective that systems are 'greater than the sum of their parts'. I prefer to defend a more analytic principle that one cannot understand system properties without a working knowledge of their parts.

To appreciate the idea let us go back to the tipping point thesis. Its starting point is the striking similarity of the sudden change profiles in many systems and the explanation for it does indeed involve system-level properties such as the 'connectivity' of the agents. However, as soon as one tries to apply the idea, whether it is for a commercial application, such as how to achieve exponential growth in the sales of my sports shoes, or a programme application, such as how to apply the broken widows thesis to my community, one has also to come to an understanding of individual agents and their particular ideas, and an appreciation of specific communities and their cultures and histories.

Unsurprisingly, it turns out that the broken windows thesis has both succeeded and failed in dealing with spikes of incivility (Hope and Mocan, 2005). Much depends on the area chosen for preventative action and the extent to which the community has learned to tolerate incivility and disrepair. Much depends on the implementation of the programme and whether appropriate targets for vandalism are covered. Much depends on whether the intended subjects bother to take note of the programme and this in turn depends on who holds power within the community. Moreover, if one looks at Gladwell's thesis as a whole, it is populated by non-system concepts such as the 'Law of the Few', the 'Stickiness Factor' and 'The Power of Context'. These concepts sound newfangled and redolent with complexity but again note that they are about intervention specifics: the role and actions of key stakeholders, the captivating power of specific ideas, and the influence of immediate social and cultural environments.

In conclusion one can say that in order to generate any explanatory power in programme evaluation one has to have theories that link these wider interpretations of system dynamics to mundane activities of stakeholders. Complexity theory has had much to teach us about the controlling and enabling power of large-scale systems but that remains only a part of the practice and policy equations. To reinforce the point I close this section with the perceptions of two acute observers of policy systems who have encountered the same problem.

> Accounting for change at the whole system level is highly complex. Theories which engage with complexity at a system level ... give prominence to the behaviour of organisations, networks or collectives as the basic unit of analysis. This fits well with analysis at a macro level but does little to assist the understanding of the everyday micro-level components of clinical practice. Indeed, one result of the application of complexity theory may be paralysing uncertainty about the unpredictable consequences of intervening in complex systems. (May, 2006: 3)

> All of this raises the possibility that 'the jam will be spread rather thin', i.e. that complexity theory may have a little to say about many things but not much to say about particular and specific things ... what remains is a set of impersonal processes working themselves out over extended periods of time and on a large scale ... these elements do not yet amount to a theory of complexity in public administration, in the sense of a propositional explanation of actions and outcomes ... [Its] elements need careful testing in particular applications/contexts. Not all sectors' policies and issues are likely to be characterised by this combination of volatile elements. Indeed, some areas of public policy and management are remarkably stable and predictable. (Pollitt, 2009: 215)

Whilst systems theory can rightly be charged with conceptual overdressing (exogenous energy impositions, autocatalytic interaction effects and all the rest) the main conclusion here is that it embellishes rather than deals with the burden of complexity in evaluation research. It demands more elaborate programme theories, greater subtlety in the measurement of outcomes, ceaseless vigilance in the study of implementation, and, above all, the idea that the fortunes of an intervention are deeply embedded in contextual layers that are themselves subject to change. The issues remain endless.

The critical realist perspective ——

The chapter now moves on to contemplate a third and very different solution to the problem of investigating complex systems. Its roots are not to be found in evaluation research or applied social research or any school of thought therein; rather it is a philosophical solution. It is of crucial concern here because the approach goes by the name of 'critical realism' and, perforce, its roots intertwine with the realist approach presented in this volume. Indeed, this book begins with some common ground, Chapter 1 identifying important fundamentals to be found in Bhaskar (1978). Here, Bhaskar asserts correctly that experimental science does not rest on the observation and measurement of the relationship between variables. Rather we explain nature's uniformities by unearthing the underlying mechanisms that give rise to them. To achieve this requires theory and it is generative theories that allow us to both know how to manipulate the experiment and explain the results we then observe. These remain important lessons in the face of the powerful residual forces who wish evaluation research to march to a fixed set of techniques, designs and protocols.

It is Bhaskar's side step into social science that I want to eschew, particularly the treatment of how we should approach the matter of explanation in complex systems. Bhaskar arrives at his model of social explanation in a convoluted set of metatheoretical thrusts and parries. I begin by presenting the argument in miniature (Box 4.3) in order to show how he gets to the 'critical' in critical realism.

Box 4.3

Seven (Bhaskarian) steps to critical realist inquiry

1 Physical and social systems are ordered but infinitely complex. No amount of observation and measurement will allow us to understand how they are organised. Theory is needed to guide inquiry, to raise hypotheses about what might provide order within these complex systems.

2 Physical science and social science share the same explanatory structure in that both attempt to explain the complex and sometimes confusing everyday flux of events with reference to some persisting, underlying mechanisms.

3 However, physical science and social science are different in that societies, being shaped by human volition, are in a permanent state of self-transformation. People choose. Electrical circuits do not.

4 This difference goes on to determine the nature of and potential for empirical inquiry in the two domains. Laboratory experiments enable the researcher to neutralise external forces and so isolate conditions in which the laws of nature are revealed. Social science cannot contrive closed systems and empirical observation alone will only produce endless, partial descriptions of an ever-changing social world.

(Continued)

(Continued)

5   The fact that the laws of nature are only produced in artificial closed systems does not mean that they are in any way under human control. Laws are laws but their sphere of operations is at an underlying level, they endure whilst not acting in the open environment.

6   Although the social world transforms ceaselessly, this does mean it is endlessly chaotic. Social institutions change but not into blue cheese. There are corresponding social mechanisms that govern and limit social transformations. These too are located in the deep, underlying structures of society.

7   In social sciences, experimental closure not being possible, an iterative spiral of theoretical inquiry and philosophical critique can take us a long way to explanatory adequacy. Abstraction and conceptual clarification become the analogues for experimental inquiry. The objects of social science inquiries include ideas. Soundly based theoretical ideas may be used as the basis of criticism of false beliefs.

This is a long, long propositional chain and in the remainder of this section I ponder each step in more detail. But to cut to the quick, all goes awry, in my view, at Step 4. Bhaskar's account of the nature of laboratory control is deficient. Experimental science is a much more speculative, contested and prolonged affair than in his account of the crushing, neutralising power of closed laboratory systems. Laboratory systems only ever achieve partial closure and they do so gradually, building and rebuilding experiments over long periods of time. It is this collective, iterative, synthetic process of investigation to which the science of evaluation can aspire, with its enormous repertoire of methods to follow systems through time and to compare and contrast their evolution in different contexts. Correcting Bhaskar's view of the might of the laboratory experiment and rectifying his ignorance of the coverage of social inquiry absolves us of the need to follow Steps 5, 6 and 7, and the descent into the arms of politicised inquiry. It enables us to offer an alternative, corrigible, realist view of the conduct of evaluation research, which is articulated in detail in the following chapter. Let us now examine critical realist metaphysics one step at a time, resuming with the points of agreement, briefly considered.

Proposition one. Realism begins with the notion that scientific inquiry is much more than the systematic compilation of carefully measured 'facts'. The starting point is an assumption about complexity. The physical world contains an infinite number of properties and the social world is made up of an infinite number of events. Simply to describe such worlds would commit us to an everlasting task and so scientific inquiry needs something to direct our gaze and we find that direction in 'theory'. Theory tells us where to look but also what to look for. Theory provides explanations and so directs us to vital explanatory components within the world, their interrelationships and the things that bring about those interrelationships. In order to validate these theories we need complex observation systems to interrogate each aspect of the explanatory system.

If social science is to imitate physical science, if evaluation is to follow natural science, they too need to be theory-driven.

Proposition two. Realism, as noted, assumes that the natural and social worlds are patterned; some physical properties are related uniformly and some social events unfold in regular sequences. These regularities are not discovered through observational routines and the mechanical application of measuring instruments. Correlation is not causation. Uniformities occur because of some underlying order in the world which is to be discovered at the level of the generative mechanism. Physicists explain causal relationships such as the gas laws through knowledge of the kinetics of molecular action. The attributes of compounds, such as gelignite's capacity to explode, is explained by their underlying chemical composition. Biologists explain evolutionary change through the mechanism of natural selection. In medicine the 'mechanism of action' of a drug is what enables it to attack viruses, kill cancerous cells, heal bacterial infections, and so on and so forth.

If it is to follow a scientific method, then social science too must use a model of generative causation. If sociologists discover a significant correlation between socio-economic background and educational attainment in a population, they do not suppose that the former has caused the latter but that there is a class system in place, an underlying distributive mechanism that bestows advantage to the well positioned. Likewise in the world of interventions, realist evaluators do not suppose that we can discover whether a programme has worked without pursuing some theory of why it has worked. It is thus a crude oversimplification to say that interventions change behaviour; they work by providing some resource that persuades the subject to change and this is the underlying generative mechanism around which inquiry is constructed.

Proposition three. Whilst all investigation is surrounded in complexity there are obvious differences between physical and social systems. Much rests here because it is the nature of this difference which, for critical realism, is said to determine the amount of empirical purchase that the researcher can apply in investigation. It transpires that Bhaskar's impeccably correct but absolutely mundane criterion of demarcation is rooted in the 'transformational character of social systems' (Bhaskar, 1979: 165). This refers to the idea that people 'both create and are created by society' (Bhaskar, 1979: 45). This is a venerable idea caught by dozens of aphorisms such as Marx's (1852), 'men make history ... but under circumstances already existing and transmitted from the past' and Felson's (1986) 'people make choices but they cannot choose the choices available to them'. It is also the basis of Archer's (1995: 165) famous sociological riddle, 'what is it that depends on action but never corresponds to the actions of even the most powerful?' Her answer, of course, is 'society' but note that the underlying dynamic applies exactly and unequivocally to social programmes. Interventions attempt to change history but never in conditions over which they have control. Programmes work through human actions but their outcomes never conform to any particular stakeholder's actions, even the most powerful. So, for the moment, I am still with Bhaskar.

Realist evaluation and critical realism are at one assuming that collective, constrained choices permeate social life and thus social programmes.

Proposition four. It is the empirical upshot of this ever-changing society that marks the point of contention between the two realisms. According to Bhaskar, the physical sciences are able to come to an empirical mastery of the complexity of the physical realm by manufacturing closed experimental systems, whereas empirical research in social science, can only ever follow and describe the surface, fleeting, ever-emergent texture of history.

> For in the absence of spontaneously occurring, and given the impossibility of artificially creating, closed systems, the human sciences must confront the problem of the direct scientific study of phenomena that only ever manifest themselves in open systems – for which orthodox philosophy of science, with its tacit presupposition of closure, is literally useless. (Bhaskar, 1979: 27)

What does Bhaskar mean by a closed system? We are in for a bit of a disappointment if we begin with his formal definition: 'I will define a "closed system" simply as one in which a constant conjunction of events obtains; i.e. in which an event of type 'a' is invariably accompanied by an event of type 'b'. In other words it is a physical system within which its components are perfectly correlated' (Bhaskar: 1978: 70). And how does one go about creating such a system? This is a matter of laboratory control, explained thus: 'A closure thus depends on either the actual isolation of a system from external influences or the constancy of those influences' (1978, 74), and embellished somewhat later in this fashion: 'an attempt to trigger or unleash a single mechanism or process in relative isolation, free from the interfering flux of the open world, so as to observe its detailed workings or record its characteristic mode of effect and/or to test some hypothesis about it' (Bhaskar, 1986: 35).

In short, Bhaskar affirms (for physical science) an 'isolation' model of experimental control; complexity is managed by cleansing from the investigatory apparatus all other confounding influence thus allowing the physical law to unfold. This is reminiscent of a school textbook idea of the sterile laboratory kept at constant temperature, free from extraneous electromagnet forces, shielded from over reactive instrumentation, on guard against the ham-fisted experimenter. This model is depicted on the left in Figure 4.1, the oval representing the protective barrier of the experiment, the physical wall deflecting the interfering flux of open-word forces and thus safeguarding the closed system in which a single mechanism generates the perfect correlation of 'a' with 'b'.

The problem with the 'deflector' model is this. How does the scientist know which extraneous forces to control? In an infinitely complex world there are countless forces to be reckoned with. Science cannot know them all in advance or it would already be complete and we would have an entire state description of all the laws of physics. So the fallible scientist has to depend on a bit of guesswork, some judgement, and a developing, collective understanding of what seems to

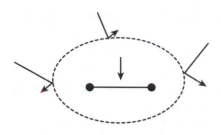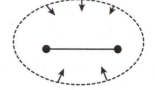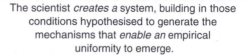

| The scientist *controls* a system, which deflects all other forces *isolating* the single mechanism that generates the invariable empirical uniformity. | The scientist *creates a* system, building in those conditions hypothesised to generate the mechanisms that *enable an* empirical uniformity to emerge. |

Figure 4.1 'Isolation' and 'enablement' models of the experiment

be important in these 'sorts of systems'. In other words the controls put in place are based on hypotheses. And what the experimental scientist actually attempts to design and create is a system in which many forces are manipulated so that 'a' invariably follows 'b'. Experimental apparatuses, on this second account, are manufactured by trial and error until we create an entire system that enables the regularity to unfold, a scenario depicted on the right in Figure 4.1.

This idea that experimental manipulation is achieved in an iterative series of conjectures may be witnessed in the history of any of the fêted experimental laws of physics. Ohm's law crops up a few times in Bhaskar's account of the experiment as does a little quip about how schoolboy versions of the experiment have a habit of going wrong. Here's why. The experimental apparatus used to contrive Ohm's law was decades in the making and was the making of many research teams. Ohm's experimental labours took two years (1825–26) and were published in *Die Galvanische Kette, Mathemtish Bearbit* in 1827. Before this, in 1781 Cavendish conducted early experiments on the electrical resistance. His apparatus was somewhat primitive, consisting of jars of varying diameters and length filled with salt solution through which a 'degree of electrification' (voltage) was applied. Cavendish anticipated that the 'electrical velocity' (current) produced would vary jar by jar, which he measured by noting the strength of the shock as he completed the circuit with his body.

Ohm had rather more sophisticated apparatus at his disposal including, blessedly, a galvanometer to measure current. The laboratory years, however, were spent making and remaking the apparatus. For instance, the experiment requires a constant voltage source and, following some inconsistent results, he substituted a thermocouple for his original choice of voltaic piles. After further manipulations his apparatus produced the proportionality between current (C), voltage (V) and resistance (R) that he and several others in the scientific community had hypothesised. But note that such regularities, here and elsewhere, are always specific to the apparatus used to manufacture them. Ohm, as noted earlier, published his results with the subtitle *Mathemtish Bearbit* (investigated mathematically). Thus Ohm's law, as first conceived, was not C = V/R, as we learn as schoolboys and schoolgirls, but x = a/ b + l, where 'x' is the reading from the galvanometer, 'a' is voltage as controlled by thermocouple temperature and 'l' is the length of the wire used to vary resistance in the circuit. This result and this piece of apparatus provided the elementary rendition of what we now call Ohm's law.

Since these investigations a range of other contingencies have been added to the understanding of electrical resistance. Ohm varied electrical resistance by adjusting the length of the conducting wire. The resistivity of materials is, however, temperature dependent. Putting a current through a resistor can increase its temperature and so the basic 1825 experiment 'works' only because they were conducted with limited modifications in this key variable (hence the room for schoolboy errors). Ohm, thanks to knowledge of Joule's work on heating conducting bodies, found a set of conditions to make the uniformity manifest but we had to await Maxwell's work in 1876, which mastered a more complex algebraic rendition of the law as it applies under different heating conditions. Further experimental adaptations continued over the centuries adding more and more contingencies to Ohm's 'law'. Most significantly, it turns out that many modern electrical components do not obey the law; current does not increase linearly with the applied voltage but follows a chordal (curved) shape. Only a subset of conducting material turns out to be 'ohmic'.

I have spent an inordinate amount of time in the physics lab but these details provide vital clues for realist inquiry. We see that Ohm's experiment was literally strung together and has since been restrung in dozens of combinations. Nowhere in this history do we encounter anything remotely like a Bhaskarian closed system in which the key properties are examined 'free from the interfering flux of the open world'. Rather the scientific community comes to understand the law and the partial closure achieved in experiment after experiment as stepping stones in the understanding of electrical conductivity. Different contingencies are encountered, understood and incorporated. Moreover, the law itself is accepted as valid only, to coin an evaluator's phrase, in particular circumstances and in particular respects (for average currents in ordinary resistive materials).

Note, crucially, that the law found acceptance without the ability to understand or manipulate experimentally a 'single underlying generative mechanism'. To be sure, generative thinking underlies all the work but it took over a century to grope towards an understanding of its nature. Right from the start, the uniformities of electrical resistance are assumed to be generated because of some propensity of the conducting materials. But precisely what it was about the structure of these materials that generated resistance was not initially known. The early experiments used concepts like 'electrical velocity', understanding resistance as something that restricted its speed. Thereafter, the hydraulic analogy came into favour with the flow of water in pipes being used as a simple model (water pressure as voltage, aperture as resistance, current as flow), with 'flow restriction' being understood as the basic mechanism of electrical resistance. We now know that the resistance of materials is ultimately a matter of their atomic structure, though it was not until 1900 that Drude produced a mathematical model mapping the collisions of electrons (the charge carriers) bouncing through ions (the structure of the materials) which agreed closely with the relationship uncovered in the empirical work on Ohm's law.

By following this history, which by the way is to be found in Shedd and Hershey (1913) and Schagrin (1963), we reach the crucial methodological point. Nowhere in this account, nowhere in a century of scientific endeavour, do we see the production of a closed system to control the action of a single generative mechanism. There is no crucial experiment. The system, its outcomes, its contingencies, its underlying mechanisms and the contexts in which they operate are understood as a result of continuous empirical and theoretical labour.

Here then is the significant result. If we aspire to social science, if we hanker after a science of evaluation, it is better to pursue the correct model. Contra Bhaskar, experimental work does not achieve and does not require closed systems. There is no need for social scientists to turn their heads to alternative strategies because of the impossibility of achieving closure. Uniformities in the behaviour of properties are suspected, explanations of the underlying mechanisms responsible for the uniformities are hypothesised, experiments are performed to create a system that generates the regularity, under close scrutiny the regularity turns out to be partial and imperfect, scientists come up with different reasons for the anomalies and build further experimental systems to test these subsidiary theories, these in turn meet with partial success leading to the reworking of a fresh set of theories and experiments, and so on, and so on, and so on. Science only makes slow, partial progress gathering knowledge of the complex contingencies that influence physical systems. Business is always unfinished – but the journey is the thing. This account of progressive, unfinished closure is entirely consistent with the logic of scientific discovery, the model of conjectures and refutations, found in mainstream philosophy of science (Popper, 1963: Lakatos, 1978). It is this realist vision to which evaluation can aspire and it is this model of partial closure that I will build upon in the next chapter.

Proposition five. Having identified our crucial point of departure from Bhaskar, we continue on his journey, revealing why it is a cul-de-sac. The next crucial assumption of Bhaskarian science is known as depth realism. At issue here is the question of ontology – how is the world composed and where in this world should we locate the depository of knowledge that we need to explain it. Realism, in all of its brands and in relation to both the physical and social world, uses the notion of causal powers or underlying generative mechanisms as the seat of action and as the axis of explanation. The propensity of gunpowder to explode is not only explained by its encounters with a lighted match but by its unstable and underlying chemical composition – the capacity of nitrate, sulphur and charcoal to produce exothermic reactions. And of the social world, to use one of Bhaskar's pet examples, the batsman's ability to stroke the ball to the boundary depends on his physique and accumulated skill. These underlying powers remain, regardless of the fact that he may be sitting in the pavilion or whether a fielder intercepts a particular shot. Whether a mechanism is fired depends on its context. In critical realism, especially, this idea of underlying, unrealised and often unobserved powers lies at the heart of its understanding of reality.

In the previous paragraph, and in a way that is entirely consistent with critical realism, I have used the adjective 'underlying' on four occasions to describe the action of generative mechanisms. Nature's underlying mechanisms lay permanently installed even though they may be unexercised and unrealised at any moment. And here we reach the core of critical realist ontology, variously named the transfactual, the normic, the intransitive, and the transcendental. At this level reside the structural essences of nature, which possess ultimate, if not everyday, control of surface appearances.

Enormous explanatory power is invested in these essences. According to 'depth realism' (Figure 4.2), the world consists of three domains: i) the empirical, ii) the actual and iii) the real. As a first approximation, we can say that the empirical domain consists of our experiences of the world, the observations and perceptions that clamour for our attention (fireworks exploding). The actual domain is realised at the level of pattern, when we see that our experiences are patterned in sequences of events (in the presence of a flame, fireworks explode). The final and supreme level, the real, is discovered when we penetrate to an understanding of the subterranean mechanism that creates regular patterns of events (fireworks explode in the presence of a flame because of the chemical composition of gunpowder).

What is Bhaskar's purpose here? Quite appropriately, he disputes the once dominant empiricist notion of science, where the 'empirical world' was seen as real and the subject of study, where direct experience or observation was the means of studying it, and where concepts, being stuff one cannot see, are not real. As most philosophy now acknowledges, although biologists cannot directly observe 'natural selection', and although virologists cannot discern 'viruses' with the naked eye, and although physicists have still to penetrate the full depth of 'atomic structures', all of these things are key to understanding how the world is organised and are therefore real.

But note the extent of Bhaskar's reversal of the old order. Regard closely the first column of the table. Things become real – the domain of the real is actualised – only when the three levels are fused. Events and experiences only become real when they are subsumed under the action of their underlying mechanism. They are only real within the totalising, transcendental system. Otherwise, they flip to columns two and three and are not to be considered real. Why? Bhaskar's answer

	Domain of Real	Domain of Actual	Domain of Empirical
Mechanisms	☑		
Events	☑	☑	
Experiences	☑	☑	☑

Figure 4.2 Depth realism

is that when they are made outside the strict confines of the closed experimental systems, our observations might well be misapprehensions and our perceptions of relationships between events might well be spurious. Only under total laboratory control are experiences and events brought into line with reality.

Figure 4.2 is much reproduced in the literature, with little acknowledgement that it is preposterous. We cannot wait upon experimental closure to reveal transcendental reality because there is no such thing as the closed experiment. What was clear in our brief history of Ohm's Law and is true of the episodic nature of all empirical work is that the explanation confederates only very slowly. We did not have to wait for the Drude model, and we do not have to await knowledge of the underlying, immutable subatomic mechanisms to make splendid progress in the understanding of electrical conductivity. All of the empirical work may be considered limited, partial in scope, contaminated by other systems and so on. There is no closed, crucial experiment that lifts an underlying causal reality into view. But all of the partially closed experiments reveal useful, partial truths. All of them, and rather rapidly to boot, had practical electrical engineering applications. It is a perfect nonsense to declare that this intricate set of conditions and contingencies and of events and experiences are not yet *real*. Going right back to the beginning I would deem Cavendish's electric shock real enough even though he had yet to figure out its generative roots. The appropriate language to be used of all of the findings throughout this episode, as in all science, is about their limited 'reliability', 'replicability', 'validity' and 'generalisability' – rather than supposing that their 'reality', or lack of it, is under question.

An issue keeps struggling to the surface here. Why is Bhaskar placing such emphasis on these transfactual, nomic, structural essences? Why does reality only show its face in these constricted domains? The answer, perhaps surprisingly, is that all of this labour through natural science is done with social science in mind. To demarcate something is essential and real and, moreover, being able to separate it off from other, endless, peripheral states of being is to grant it privileged explanatory power. And many social scientists, as we are about to see, have been extremely pleased that one can overlook empirical complexity in the name of science.

Proposition six. Briefly, and for completeness's sake, we follow Bhaskar's journey. It now reaches a crucial cross-road – the possibility of naturalism, the idea that nature and society can be studied in the same manner:

> Moreover, because the mode of application of laws is the same in open and closed systems alike, there is no reason to suppose that the mode of application of social laws will be any different from natural ones ... if a social scientific theory or hypothesis has been independently verified (on explanatory grounds) then one is in principle just as warranted in applying it transfactually as a natural science one. (Bhaskar, 1979: 58)

The argument faces in two ways at this point – social systems can never be experimentally closed and yet they too are underpinned by enduring, underlying mechanisms. The paradox is resolved in his understanding of the 'transformational model of society'. As we noted at Step 3, society is in a permanent state of self transformation. In Bhaskar's words: 'Society is both the ever present condition (material cause) of human action and the continually reproduced outcome of human agency' (Bhaskar, 1979: 34). The added complexity of agency means we can never isolate society from the play of human choice, we can never predict what agents will choose to change and how they will do so. However, on the other side of the argument Bhaskar (1979: 47) reminds us that though people choose and that change is unceasing, this does not mean that our choices are free and unconstrained or that social change is random and haphazard. Real choices require conditions and resources to actualise them, so what the choice makers are doing is 'self-consciously transform the conditions of existence (social structures) so as to maximise the possibilities for the development and spontaneous exercise of their natural species powers'.

And with this bound Bhaskar is free. What is real about society is the totality – the pre-existing structure as well as the limited, emerging relations that can follow under human interpretation. Change is incessant, mutations and transformations occur all the time but they occur 'within relatively enduring social forms and social structures' (1979: 52). Social structures are thus made up of what Bhaskar (1979: 51) calls 'slots' or 'tendencies' or 'relations' into which active subjects must slip in order to reproduce them. And with this decidedly slippery chain of reasoning we arrive, supposedly, in society's transfactual domain and so glimpse the possibility of naturalism. It is the slowly mutating totality that is real. These evolutionary tendencies, decrees Bhaskar, are society's generative mechanisms and this is where the laws of social science may be found (1979: 68).

Proposition seven. The remaining, daunting and defining question for critical realism, of course, is how does social science go about the discovery of its transfactual truths and law-producing mechanisms? We already know that Bhaskar rules out closed system inquiry. We cannot control and empirically isolate the underlying structures for they are transforming under human agency. We cannot rely on empirical social inquiry, since for Bhaskar it will only reveal the 'mish-mash nature of social reality' (1979: 63). We already know that he has ignored, at Step 4, the possibility of naturalism in quite another form, namely the slow confederation of evidence drawn from partially closed systems. So how do we get at these deeply-hidden, underlying structures?

Eventually he reveals his famous 'compensator' for experimental activity (1979: 59–69). Redemption, it transpires, takes the form of intense, abstract, theoretical work. Because of the added complexity of agency, 'more theoretical work needs to be done to set up and test explanatory power in open systems' (Collier, 1994; 166) and, moreover, it needs to come first. 'Thus in social science attempts at real definitions will in general precede rather than follow successful causal hypothesis' (Bhaskar, 1979: 63). The conquering strategy for social science thus boils down to the production and celebration of *a priori* reasoning. As Bhaskar puts it, 'Now the substantive employment of essentially apodeictic argument should occasion no surprise' (1979: 64).

I have to say that when I first discovered that apodeictic means 'clearly established' or 'beyond dispute' (*Oxford Dictionary of English*), I was surprised enough to fall off my chair. It is now brutally clear to see where critical realism is heading. Indisputable experiments are replaced by indisputable theories. 'It has always been the special claim of Marxism to be able to grasp social life as a totality' (Bhaskar, 1979: 55). 'The power of abstraction, as Marx said, must replace chemical reagents' (Collier, 1994: 166). 'Capital may most plausibly be viewed as an attempt to establish what must be the case for the experiences grasped by the phenomenological forms of capitalist life to be possible; setting out, as it were, a pure scheme for the understanding of economic phenomenon under capitalism, specifying the categories that must be employed in any concrete investigation' (Bhaskar, 1979: 65).

As promised, we reach the final flourish, the critical in critical realism. Followers of Bhaskar's method, being capable of generating pure schemes for understanding what must be the case for social forms to exist, are also in a position to criticise ideas generated outside the fold. The explanatory method is also a method of explanatory critique. Woe betide anyone, for instance, who might consider individual actions such as the fecklessness of the underclass as a reason for unemployment or the recklessness of short sellers as a reason for economic crisis, when we already know that the real causes lie in the institutions and market forces of the capitalist system (Collier, 1994: 171). Complexity is introduced into social science with the recognition of the relentless play of human choice and is then dealt with by deciding *a priori* which choices are truly human and which bear the marks of false consciousness.

Bhaskarian critical realism is a parody of science and yet another grab for the totalising explanatory systems for which vainglorious social science has an insatiable appetite (McLennan, 2009). The ability 'to grasp life as a totality' belongs to idealism and it is not surprising that Bhaskar's further journeys in search of these powers have ended in the heavens (Bhaskar, 2002). It is a strategy for lording over complexity rather than analysing it. It is a strategy with no use whatsoever in applied social inquiry. The science of evaluation starts by recognising that the fate of social policy lies in the real choices of choice makers and its task is to explain the distribution and consequences of those choices rather than to condemn them.

The pragmatic perspective

Our inspection of the quartet of complexity perspectives ends with one that is to be reckoned with – namely, the pragmatic perspective. I term it thus because it emanates from the labour of evaluation practitioners rather than an abstract, preconceived model of complexity. It has developed as follows. In the midst of a study, the evaluator will encounter some unforeseen complexity. There is an endless list to choose from: newly-appointed managers driving the programme in a fresh direction, the supply of subjects drying up, practitioners falling out, a replication of a successful pilot programme heading for dismal failure in a new context, another programme turning up to turn the heads of those under investigation, etc, etc.

As a result the evaluator adopts some remedial adaptations to the planned design and, if all goes well, the unanticipated dynamic is tracked and harnessed. This is, of course, a familiar story and over time the corrective is drawn into the standard repertoire of evaluation methods. Indeed it is such a familiar story that we now have textbooks providing practical, off the shelf remedies to combat the headaches of evaluating complex programmes (Morrell, 2010; Patton, 2011).

This approach to complexity has much to recommend it. It has led to some ingenious designs that capture the unforeseen and unintended in policy making. But let me hint at the problem. Solutions are arrived at piecemeal. The field researcher is always best placed to spot the latest intricacy, the first to herald complexity's newest twist. They will draft up a methodological solution which, if it shows promise, will be imitated by other evaluators. One splendid idea after another is added to the evaluation toolbox – but with what result? Methodological pragmatism bursts evaluation at its seams. The toolbox requires a truck to transport it. No evaluation study can encompass all of its contents. Any single evaluation will always fall a crucial spanner or two short.

I will explore the thwarted ambitions of pragmatism in three manifestations. The first lies in a series of contributions by Hawe and colleagues, chosen because they are amongst the most influential in the complexity literature (Hawe et al., 2004, 2009a, 2009b). As can be seen from one of the titles here, *Theorising Interventions as Events in Systems*, the authors are fully *au fait* with *complexité* of complexity. Secondly, I review an emerging approach known as 'developmental evaluation' (Gamble, 2008; Patton, 2011). This has beginnings in ethereal complexity theory but is chock full of practical applications as can be seen from Patton's pragmatic sub-title – '*Applying Complexity Concepts to Enhance Innovation and Use*'. Thirdly, I call into service a survey by Sridharan and colleagues (forthcoming). They attempt an 'overview' of key practitioners' ideas on how to tackle complexity. And a compendious overview is what results – endless answers to never-ending problems.

1. Events in systems

Let us commence scrutiny of this approach with an example of a particularly thorny problem and an ingenious pragmatic solution. I am referring to item (I) in the VICTORE typology and the issue, to quote myself, that 'implementation inconsistency is a way of life'. This problem is fielded in a telling example on school community health interventions in the aforementioned papers by Hawe and colleagues. Being healthcare interventions, these programmes are often dogged by expectations about the 'fidelity' of the programme – namely, that in order to conduct trials on their effectiveness they should be implemented in a standardised form, replicable across every site. Our attention is drawn to the issue via an empirical study of fidelity, which embodies all the woes of that concept (Dusenbury et al., 2005). A research team monitored the implementation of a school, drug abuse prevention programme, assessing it on: 'adherence' to the curriculum; teacher 'attitudes' towards and 'understanding' of the programme; and the 'valence' of adaptation. The overall result was that 63% of the teachers adapted the programme in ways that in the observers' opinion were negative. Hawe and colleagues read the situation perfectly: 'Presumably, however, the teachers thought the opposite; otherwise they would not have made the adaptation. Whose knowledge and insight matters most?' (Hawe et al., 2009a).

Their real world answer is that nothing can stop adaptation and their pragmatic solution is thus to move investigation onto the issue of what becomes of adaptation: 'the ultimate determinant of whether a change was adaptive in a positive sense would be determined objectively in outcome evaluation' (2009a: 95). To put this into practice the team recommends that 'in complex interventions the function and the process of the intervention should be standardised not the components themselves' (Hawe et al., 2004: 1563). How does one standardise function rather than form? Their answer is to 'build capacity'. For example, in a health promotion campaign, instead of distributing identical information, all sites should be tasked with devising materials tailored to local literacy, language, culture and learning styles. Similarly, workshops, rather than following a prescribed frequency and content, should be tailored to local venues and schedules.

An exemplification and evaluation of the capacity building strategy may be found in the *Gatehouse Project* (Bond et al., 2004). This was a 'healthy attachments' programme run in schools aiming to improve students' emotional wellbeing, sense of security and positive regard, thereby reducing health risk behaviours associated with the use of tobacco, alcohol and illicit drugs. The intervention was perceived in terms of function rather than form; school based 'action teams', with the mission to build mental health capacity in ways appropriate to local conditions, were dispatched to 12 intervention schools, with 14 others acting as control sites. Hawe and colleagues set great store by the results:

> The evaluation of the Gatehouse Project intervention showed substantial reductions in adolescent students' risk of smoking, drinking and drug use … they were far greater than interventions by other investigators who have used conventional means of standardising the intervention across sites and conventional ways of measuring implementation quality …. In other words the intervention was effective whilst being adapted widely to context. (Hawe, 2009a: 95)

So, all victory to adaptability and capacity building? Let us look more carefully at the design and the findings. Consider first the original summary of the Gatehouse trial:

> A comparatively consistent 3% to 5% difference was found between intervention and control students for any drinking, any and regular drinking, any regular smoking, and friends' alcohol and tobacco use … the largest effect was a reduction in the reporting of regular smoking by those in the intervention group … there were no significant effects of the intervention on depressive symptoms and social and school relationships. (Bond et al., 2004: 997)

To my eyes this seems like an entirely typical, mixed bag of rather modest changes. The problem, which is entirely symptomatic of the pragmatic approach, is that one can modify a design to accommodate one arm of complexity only for its other limbs to trip up the inquiry. In this instance, findings are generated in trial mode providing us with batteries of before and after measures (three follow up waves of self-administered questionnaires) on which to compare experimental and control behaviour. In short, it is basically black-box analysis with many further and unexplored aspects of complexity, three of which are briefly noted here.

The first point to note is that although implementation is allowed its head, there is no specific investigation into how each action team went about improving wellbeing. All that is observed is a null change in psychological dispositions and social relationships. Bond et al. describe this as 'disappointing' (2004: 1002). However, given that the programme theory was based on the development of wellbeing, security and emotional trust it seems curious that such capacity building is completely absent from the pupils' perspective. It is also disappointing, for instance, that there are no recorded reductions in reported victimisation and bullying. The significance of this lacuna also occurs to the authors who seek to safeguard the core theory by meandering further from the data in the following ad hoc speculation: 'three years of implementation may not have been sufficient to significantly have an impact on school climate to the extent of affecting the experience of social relations and emotional climate' (Bond et al., 2004: 1002). Possibly the authors are correct, possibly not. The point is that providing the answer lies beyond the scope of the particular inquiry.

Let us move to the more positive findings. What accounts for the decrease in reported usage of tobacco, drugs and alcohol? The programme also has elements, suitably tailored to local conditions, aimed to alert pupils to such risk factors. Have these 'individual skill components' made the crucial difference? Possibly, possibly not. In the realist roll call on complexity the social and political pressures on outcome measurement were identified as another, ever-present challenge. The outcome measures in this instance are collected by self-administered questionnaires using school laptops. A rather obvious counter hypothesis stares us in the face – is not the improvement a matter of the 'social desirability effect'? Given, for this group, that smoking, drinking and drug use are illegal and, moreover, are being highlighted in the programme as risk factors for adolescent mental health, is it not better for smart students to side with the angels and to input indications of improvement into the laptop?

Unsurprisingly, the researcher team has also considered this possibility and reckon it covered in another clever aspects of the design – namely, that this is a cluster trial with randomisation carried out at the level of the district and then the school rather than by classroom or by individual, with the intervention, moreover, being woven into the normal curriculum. They argue, therefore, that it is 'unlikely that the subjects were aware of being subject to an intervention' (Bond et al., 2004: 1003). It might be suggested, by contrast, that subjects were hardly unaware of being tested – being asked to respond no less than four times to the unfamiliar demands of a computer assisted questionnaire. Moreover, in the midst of these measures, the experimental group encountered a curriculum that had alerted them simultaneously with a risk agenda and a moral solution. Despite the legendary levels of innumeracy in today's youth, it is not too difficult to imagine them putting two and two together and answering, if not acting, in a way that favours the intervention. Is this the correct interpretation? Possibly. Possibly not. The point is that complexity still has the upper hand and that to choose decisively between the two interpretations would require a further excursion in data collection using some of the intricate measures to detect questionnaire response bias, themselves fallible, or applying a sledgehammer to crack this nut in the form of urine or hair follicle measures for substance traces (Magura and Kang, 1996).

Another one of complexity's challenges to this particular design comes in the third element of the VICTORE typology, namely the shaping force of context on outcomes. In this instance the researchers operate in the experimental paradigm and so seek to obliterate context from the equation by randomisation. The specifics of context remain uninvestigated, despite the core idea of the programme being about influencing context, namely – installing a school ethic, hopefully in less than three years, which will nurture wellbeing and influence behaviour change. That programme theory is bound to meet with varying success according to the type of school in which it is attempted. Some schools, no doubt, would claim that building a sense of wellbeing and trust was already at the core of their provision; other schools, perhaps more results oriented, would start with a more competitive ethos; other schools, perhaps more unfortunate in their intake, would place emphasis on discipline and control. School climatology watchers can no doubt extend this list of prevailing atmospheres. Bundling all contexts together across the two trial conditions nullifies a key policy challenge, fathoming out where such interventions have a better chance of working. This particular omission could, of course, be potentially addressed in a further investigation, examining implementation and outcomes across different school sub-groups. The conundrum is repeated. No evaluation can cover all eventualities and in any one-off investigation complexity remains firmly in control.

I have probed three sore points in this particular investigation and discussion reveals a pattern. One problem is foreseen, a design is put in place to cover it, but this begets a further design weakness, and a fresh solution emerges … and so on. Pragmatic solutions, even wise pragmatic solutions, would appear to leave us with an infinite regress of research tasks.

2. Developmental evaluation

A similar conclusion beckons if one follows the progress of any one of the evaluation paradigms as it rolls up its sleeves to tackle complexity. The previous example considers how evaluation's 'outcome' or 'summative' traditions approached the task. There is also a considerable body of literature on complexity emanating from the family variously identified with 'qualitative', 'formative', 'process', 'action' and 'utilisation-focused' perspectives. The latest rebranding occurs in the form of 'developmental evaluation'. Here, I examine two key contributions by Gamble (2008) and Patton (2011), noting in passing that they share some ancestry. Both authors commence in beholding the vastness of complexity challenge. Familiar themes are borrowed from the complexity theorists and the systems thinkers. So, for instance, Patton, the Douglas Adams of evaluation, provides a hitchhiker's guide to the difference between simple, complicated and complex programmes. He also evokes the wicked questions that should accompany the investigation of wicked problems. Above all, he provides an admirable pocket description (2011: 150–51) of the characteristics of complex systems: i) they produce non-linear change, ii) they involve internal, self-generated, emergent change, iii) they adapt ceaselessly to a changing environment, iv) they operate on the basis of uncertainty as well as creating uncertainty, v) not only do the constituent parts of the system change, their relation to each other is also dynamic, and vi) the evaluation of the system is part of the system and thus must co-evolve with system change.

Developmental evaluation is a quintessentially pragmatic venture and, wisely, does not suppose it can pursue all of these processes in all types of programmes and policies. It gains its identity by locating the scenario, the exact niche where one of these issues, namely uncertainty, is considered to loom largest. An organisation is in need of developmental evaluation if it has: 'no known solutions to priority problems; no certain way forward and multiple pathways possible; a need for innovation, exploration and social experimentation'. It covers, so to speak, the pre-programme niche (deciding which directions to take rather than have an existing programme to improve formatively and test summatively) and the post-programme scenario (anticipating the needs for improvements to follow the one about to be put in place). Here, perforce, is the first limitation of the method. Whilst these are indeed prime institutional locations for innovation and ingenuity, it is perfectly clear that the complexities explored within these two niches do correspond to all of the disobedient forces in complex systems. Happily, we begin on a point of agreement. In his introduction Patton, twice and in italics, makes plain that: *development evaluation is not appropriate for every situation* (2011: 15 and 16).

The operative question thus becomes – how does one evaluate decision-making in these particular niches? Gamble's *Primer* (2008: section 2.3) outlines the core approaches: network mapping, revised and emergent modelling, simulations and rapid reconnaissance, appreciative inquiry and visual language. Network analysis allows us to investigate the reach and spread of ideas, the points of resistance and the super infectors. Revised and emergent modelling requires a more sophisticated but still common use of logic models, catering for flows, blockages and feedback loops. Simulation is team-based 'what if?' analysis. Reconnaissance is monitoring. Appreciative inquiry is the development of trust between client and evaluator. And visuals have already been commended in Chapter 3 for their capacity to reveal the many tacit, unspoken ideas on which a programme is based.

Again, we see the entirely worthy pragmatic preference for a blend of methods – but we are left with a question that has troubled us from the start – why this mix of methods as opposed to any other blend? The MRC framework offered a set of recipes, Hawe and colleagues offered an alternative menu, and here is a further concoction cocktail, and here is another. The evaluation toolbox is gargantuan, so why enter the field with this particular sub-set in one's belt? Why is there no document analysis? What has happened to the once beloved focus groups? And perhaps even more telling why no mention of methods espoused by a fellow traveller in development evaluation, such as repeat interviews, bellwether surveys, twitter tracking, media monitoring (Patton, 2011: 335). There is no need to argue the toss here for, happily, we come upon further agreement. Patton in the *post-primer*, declares that 'Development evaluation does not rely on or advocate any particular evaluation method, design or tool'.

He goes on to list other core principles that really define the strategy:

> The process of engagement between the intended user (social innovators) and the developmental evaluator is as much the method of developmental evaluation as any particular design, methods, and data-collection tools …. Whatever methods are used or data are collected, rapid feedback is essential. Speed matters …. Methods can be emergent and flexible; designs can be dynamic …. Developmental evaluators need to be agile, open, interactive, flexible, observant, and have a high tolerance for ambiguity …. Reasoning is at the heart of developmental evaluation, synthesis, interpretation, and shared meaning making with the innovation team members. (Patton, 2011: 333–5)

Do these maxims meet the challenge of complexity? There are worrying signs. The reader might be forgiven for thinking that this is: a) evaluation-by-adjective, and b) evaluation-by-personality. I would be the last to decry the need for timely inquiry and effective rapport in any form of social research. The point is that these principles paint Patton into a tiny corner of the complexity puzzle. So, to be instructed, for instance, that 'speed matters' could perchance contradict mother's advice about 'more haste, less speed'. There is no choosing between proverbs. Perhaps more to the point, it contradicts much that we have learned in the 'decisions' literature about the perils of short-term innovation. Agility and the need for speed propelled thousands of financial lemmings into the foaming sea of bad debt. Recall that I, too, have included the time factor as one key source of complexity in Chapter 3 but under the argument that the previous history of a programme, the period in which it is implemented, the order and sequencing of interventions, the uneven pace of implementation, the stakeholder's experience of previous programmes all count in understanding how intervention works. This mixture of long and short waves, rather than the need for evaluation urgency, marks the temporal challenge of complexity.

Even more limiting is Patton's focus on the key co-participants in developmental evaluation – 'clients', 'social innovators', 'team members', and those with a 'hunger for learning'. To be sure, I have argued previously that stakeholder complexity provides evaluation with one of its major challenges. But these stakeholders may well include those individuals who created the conditions in which the programme operates and within these may number the long-dead, with whom it will be difficult to engage in 'shared meaning making'. Also crucial to the fortunes of an intervention, but in the difficult to engage category, include opposition lobbyists, recalcitrant subjects and programme rivals. All might hanker after learning but not necessarily be prepared to undertake the developmental lessons on offer.

So where do we stand? What is developmental evaluation? If one has the perseverance to read to page 303, all becomes clear:

> This chapter has offered a hodgepodge of ideas, approaches, examples, and rants to stimulate your thinking about the possibilities of engaging in developmental evaluation. I won't pretend that the chapter is particularly coherent or well integrated. It is messy like complexity and real world evaluation. That is why I chose the metaphor of *bricolage*. I have scoured my developmental evaluation experiences and encounters picking out and sharing odds and ends that can be used to illustrate possibilities and pitfalls. (Patton, 2011)

In short, developmental evaluation is pragmatism incarnate. As I have said from the start, this is a strategy to be reckoned with. Rather than choosing off the peg strategies, it is better to approach the problem as a *bricoleur*, adapting methods to upcoming challenge after upcoming challenge. This is how to get the job done. But there is no reason, having done so, to suppose that one has dealt with 'complexity'. The problem is that pragmatic evaluation is atomised into a million discrete inquiries and set on an infinitely repeated hunt to find the right combination. On this conundrum, and in Patton's spirit, I offer the following cautionary tale of the agility and flexibility of one of the world's foremost *bricoleurs*:

> There was an old lady who swallowed a cow.
>
> I don't know how she swallowed a cow!
>
> She swallowed the cow to catch the goat...
>
> She swallowed the goat to catch the dog...
>
> She swallowed the dog to catch the cat...
>
> She swallowed the cat to catch the bird ...
>
> She swallowed the bird to catch the spider
>
> That wiggled and wiggled and tickled inside her.
>
> She swallowed the spider to catch the fly.
>
> But I dunno why she swallowed that fly
>
> Perhaps she'll die.

3. An agglomeration of answers

Perhaps the best way to appreciate the dilemmas of the pragmatic paradigm is to capture the collective reasoning of evaluation practitioners. A study by Sridharan and colleagues (forthcoming) enables us to follow their logic in detail. An email survey was conducted in the UK, US and Canada with a sample comprising of evaluation theorists and evaluation journal editors as well as a more specific sub-set of public health researchers, a field deemed beset with complexity issues. The survey chose not to provide a definition of a complex intervention; the plan was to probe the modern complexity zeitgeist, the broad set of ideas through which such interventions could be interrogated. The authors write that their purpose was not to generate an innovative 'list of methods'. I rather suspect, however, that that is precisely what was encountered. I reproduce the authors' typology of the strategic responses to complexity as Box 4.4, with a tiny sample of suggestions received.

I rest my case at this point with a reminder that I favour the pragmatic perspective – up to a point. It is an approach that works perfectly well in the context of a specific evaluation in which an unforeseen challenge arises. The evaluator will have already chosen an approach which concentrates on a particular sub-set of programme processes. Complexity is understood as the arrival of a particular sub-set of unforeseen challenges, in response to which the evaluator adapts a method to encompass the immediate threats to validity. So far, so good.

This adaptive, pragmatic perspective, however, does not constitute an answer to the overall challenge of programme complexity. In acknowledging that interventions are complex systems propelled into complex systems, evaluation can draw upon any solution from any mode of inquiry into any sort of social system. Evaluation research's problems become sociological research's problems and psychological research's problems and economic research's problems, and so on. Evaluation research's problems become data collection problems, data processing problems, data analysis problems and so on. Evaluation research becomes social science method – a babel of techniques never quite keeping pace with the noise and confusion of an ever-changing world.

| Box 4.4

Never ending responses to complexity

- **No need for new methods and approaches:**

'Apply the methods we already have – standard methods of outcome evaluation' ... 'the scope for using time series data has not been fully exploited.'

(Continued)

(Continued)

- **Combining existing methods in innovative ways:**

'... *network analysis ... system dynamics ... both have still much to offer evaluation, bringing the two together will be very powerful.*'

- **Applications of existing frameworks:**

'*In the UK as far as I'm aware most people have been using the MRC's complexity framework.*'

- **Using programme theory to integrate evaluation with implementation:**

'*time to shift the balance of what we see as quality from an exclusive focus on empirical method to one that embraces theory.*'

- **Methods to explicate programme theory over time:**

'*Concept mapping to develop a comprehensive conceptual map ... integrating process methodology with multivariate statistical methods.*'

- **Innovative methods to discover hidden populations**

'*Techniques such as Doug Heckathorn's respondent-driven sampling and Mackeller's time–space sampling approaches are taking centre stage.*'

- **Impacts of multiple interventions and systems of outcomes:**

'*... the growing relevance of computer simulation methods for studying the dynamic of multiple interventions.*'

- **Paying attention to the sequencing of programme activities:**

'*sequential and adaptive trials ... dynamic treatment regimes are time-varying treatments that individualize sequences of treatment to the patient.*'

- **Other approaches:**

'*... propensity scoring methods, multi-level modelling ... measurement innovations such as phrase completion and item response theory*'.

This is the hard, evident truth from the medley of tactics espoused by the 35 eminent respondents to Sridharan et al.'s survey. Their solution to the complexity problem might be paraphrased as follows: The pragmatic collective of evaluators recommends that complexity be tackled by following an approach which combines formative, process, experimental, outcome, theory-driven, realist, developmental and appreciative designs, and incorporates the use of network analysis, in-house ethnography, propensity scoring, multi-level modelling, step-wedge, sequential and adaptive trials, computer simulation, what-if thought experiments, concept mapping, system dynamics, time-series data, panarchy loops, and function standardisation, as well as insights from Doug, Daisy and Doris (and many others) – all done, of course, at high speed.

FIVE

Informed Guesswork: The Realist Response to Complexity

'We do not know: we can only guess.'

Karl Popper (1992: 275)

This chapter completes our exploration of complexity. Chapter 3 interrogated its fine texture, providing an overview, a summary (Box 3.1) and an acronym (VICTORE) in an attempt to convey what it is that makes policies and programmes complex and so difficult to evaluate. I will not rehearse again all of the different and intersecting dimensions of programme complexity, sufficient enough to remind readers of the predicament by using Morrell's (2010: 22) extension of the old metaphor about the difficulty of herding cats. Implementing a programme, he says, is more like herding invisible cats in a boundless terrain. I reckon that this renders evaluation as the task of monitoring the herding of these indiscernible creatures across infinitude. Not an easy undertaking.

Undaunted, Chapter 4 sought to classify the efforts of the various cat herders and their evaluators. I will not repeat the typology again, though a rough categorisation is useful in order to appreciate the direction of travel of my argument. So we have seen: perspectives that admit to limited outbursts of complexity and seek to bring these untoward processes under experimental control; perspectives that fully admit complexity and so transmutate the issue into one of 'systems thinking' and thereby risk losing any practical purchase on policy implementation; perspectives that fully admit complexity and abandon analysis for ideology; perspectives that fully admit complexity and seek urgent, pragmatic solutions that turn out to be piecemeal and partial. The invisible cat is variously cornered, turned into a butterfly, devil-worshipped and pursued breathlessly.

This chapter presents an alternative, realist resolution. Because every science is besieged by complexity and because, for some of these sciences that battle has become a comfortable, everyday backdrop rather than an oppressive, pervasive confrontation, I am going to presume to name the way ahead – 'evaluation science'. Whether this represents preposterous conceit, inane optimism, or a workable manifesto – only time will tell. I am quite clear, however, that it is a realist response to complexity because it is built on the foundational ideas established in Chapter 1. I should probably add, given the previous discussions of its soup-like varieties, that it is a manifesto for 'some kinds of realism'. Accordingly, I am going to focus on and develop some of the Campbell varieties – 'hypothetical realism', 'corrigible realism' and 'critical realism' (remembering, of course, that for Campbell the latter means the ceaseless, cross-examination athwart the scientific community). There are two broad thrusts to the argument – one about the need for evaluation science to pioneer forth, covering collectively as much of complexity's terrain as possible; the second to acknowledge the inevitable incompleteness of that task and to come to terms with the perpetual state of partial knowledge that accrues in the journey. Let me introduce these two principal motifs a little further before proceeding, in the core of the chapter, to their practical manifestations.

The first issue is this – evaluation research as currently practised starts each inquiry from scratch. And each inquiry comes away crestfallen having bitten off more that it can chew. The reason for the disappointment (of which, incidentally, it is in the interests of most stakeholders to disguise) is rooted in the commissioning structure of evaluative inquiry. Large amounts of public, private or charitable investment is put into the making of a new programme and, quite reasonably, the first evaluative instinct is to want to know whether it worked, whether it was indeed a good investment. Accordingly, the one-off intervention has always been the atom of evaluative inquiry. Evaluation methodology is constructed on the assumption that the latest programme off the assembly line, whatever the poor thing happens to be, constitutes the task in hand. This arrangement lands us slap, bang, wallop in the complexity problem. Every programme is a complex system inserted into a complex system and it is quite unreasonable to expect each newly-assembled research team, however agile, however experienced, to reach into its every corner.

The result is that any one-off evaluation will always fall short and be open to criticism. If it concentrates on outcomes, process aficionados will find it wanting; if it concentrates on process, outcome folk will want to know why; if it concentrates on programme theory 1, supporters of programme theory 2 will be up in arms; if it is propelled by the ideas of stakeholders A, stakeholders B will feel excluded; if it is based in the US, UK policy makers may consider it irrelevant, ...; ...; .... There is no need for me to continue the list other than with a summary item – if it attempts to cover everything, it cannot. No inquiry can cover everything about every V) stakeholder volition, I) implementation decision, C) contextual constraint, T) temporal change, O) output and outcome difference, R) rival programme influence, and E) emergent effect, as they apply to the programme in hand. As I've put it before, VICTORE cannot be vanquished.

Accordingly, the most obvious strategy for enlarging the reach of evaluation research is to move from the tree to the forest. I have long advocated this idea of decoupling evaluation research from its single anchor into 'the programme' and the preliminary task here is to spell out the strategy in more detail. It is useful to think of the potential enlargement in scope in two different modes. The first is from the one to the many; the second is from the one to the generic.

The strategy of systematic review embodies the first expansion. There are important, undeniable gains to be made in a shift in focus from the prospective examination of the next programme off the assembly line to the retrospective review of previous inquiries into the 'same family of programmes'. The vital issue here is what is meant by that telling phrase. In meta-analysis it means, quite literally and with supreme optimism, the 'same programme' as carried out in different trials on different occasions in different populations. The analytic task is basically to sum the fortunes of this same intervention across its different trials in order to come to a net estimate of its impact. In realist synthesis, it is assumed that programmes are not reproducible and that the circumstances in which they are played out will always differ. They may carry the same name but they are never the 'same'. Thus what is reviewed is a set of programmes with, quite literally, a 'family resemblance'. The analytic task is to focus on some key programme theory and to test out its fortunes in the different implementation and contextual conditions of each application.

This focus on programme theory produces a significant enlargement of the scope of evaluative inquiry. Not only are more programmes available for analyses, there is considerably greater availability of requisite nuggets of evidence. Realist synthesis will, hypothetically speaking, make use of: outcome data from studies 1, 2 and 3; implementation findings from studies 4, 5 and 6; sub-group findings from studies 7, 8 and 9; participant interpretations from studies 10, 11 and 12; temporal variation from studies 13, 14 and 15; contextual comparisons using studies 16, 17 and 18; ... and so on.

Most readers of *Evidence-Based Policy* have understood the enlargement of scope of realist synthesis in this way – from the one programme to many programmes in the same family. This is understandable enough since the book examines the fortunes of Megan's Law across its different incarnations in several US States and it evaluates youth mentoring programmes against a sub-set of UK and US examples. In this spirit, most of the emerging examples of realist synthesis take on a given 'type' of programme – a review of hospital infection control programmes, a synthesis of peer-led drug education programmes and so on.

What I had intended by breaking the link between evaluation and the programme was an even bolder enlargement in scope, namely from the one to the generic. The basic notion is that the battle with complexity is fought by testing out policy ideas in an ever widening array of conditions. Programme theory is now the unit of analysis and programme theories are perfectly portable. For instance, interventions in every substantive domain of public policy offer incentives in seeking to change behaviour (loans for loft-insulation, fee-waivers to widen university participation, subsidies to employers to take on the unemployed, and so on). 'Incentivisation' is thus a generic programme mechanism and an evaluation science would do well to build a common understanding of its overall strengths and weaknesses. 'Behavioural change' is itself a generic policy ambition. Programmes aiming to wean subjects away from overindulgence in food, drugs, crime, alcohol, games consoles and so on will share dynamics and fickle fortunes. Common lessons are there to be learned and learning is best resourced by examining the thousands of interventions that have already attempted to do so. Another widely embraced policy instinct is to apply 'legal sanctions' to prohibit undesirable behaviour. Before starting from scratch on the next investigation of the latest legislative twist, whatever it may be, it would be useful to have a bank of knowledge about the general conditions under which prohibitions have been successful.

This little handful of examples is intended to give no more than a flavour of the potential 'generic platforms' for research that I am seeking to identify, and a later section of the chapter spells out the idea with rather more precision. The foundational idea, however, should be clear. There is nothing new under the sun. Policy problems and their solutions are never unique. Rather than starting from scratch each inquiry should begin where previous ones have left off. The basic antidote to complexity is for inquiry to be iterative. Evaluation science, if it is to be a science, requires whole programmes of research, programmes of research, moreover, that are co-ordinated, cumulative and mutually informative.

Before I become carried away with ambition and rhetoric, it is necessary to slam on the brakes and contemplate the other fundamental platform in the realist understanding of complexity. I am going to borrow some Popper/Campbell nomenclature in terming it 'corrigible realism'. Corrigible realists admit to a permanent state of partial knowledge. Popper considers this a perpetual condition of science and puts it most memorably and most teasingly as follows: 'we do not know: we can only guess' (1992: 275).The fundamental texts in Chapter 1 establish why realist social science is corrigible. Recall Archer (1995: 165) on its subject matter – 'society is that which no one wants for it is an unintended consequence'. The attempt to come to any definitive understanding of how society is structured is always thwarted because of the issue of emergence; society will always produce one further twist. We have also rehearsed the reasons why the findings of evaluation research are corrigible. The same inevitable, perpetual twist is ever present – programmes change the conditions that make them work in the first place.

It is important to note that the ambition to widen the scope of evaluation by addressing generic issues in policy making does not absolve us from corrigible understanding. Generic policy ambitions are still realised on the ground and thus are played out in a spiral of ever-changing social conditions. Bigger questions gain more ground on complexity but they do not allow for final answers. The realist way ahead, nevertheless, is to be braver in following the widest array of programme twists and intervention turns as possible – even though it is impossible to track them all. And the circle is squared by having a keen awareness of the limitations, but also the value, of partial knowledge. In short, the aim to raise evaluation science's game by contemplating co-ordinated, cumulative programmes of research must always be balanced by some acute modesty about what is obtained. Programme effects fire off in all directions. The intrepid evaluator chases complexity's tail, making visible and bringing understanding to certain of the changes, outputs and outcomes that follow. Designs may be put into place to bring understanding to one concomitant process after another. However, the coverage of the research is always partial and the understanding of any intervention is always imperfect, impermanent and thus corrigible. One issue after another may be grasped but with each discovery other imponderables are unearthed and the chase continues – permanently.

The second broad challenge of the chapter is to follow the dynamics of that pursuit and to explain what, precisely, is obtained and what is left unattained in the prosecution of evidence. As Smithson (1989: 1) has argued, we face a problem with developing such a perspective in that much of 'western intellectual culture has been preoccupied with the pursuit of certain knowledge or, barring that, the nearest possible approximations to it'. The randomised control trial can be said to be paean to that principle. The result, Smithson goes on to argue, is a tendency to think of uncertainty as non-knowledge and this propels him to remedy the situation by undertaking some pioneering work in the 'philosophy of ignorance'. No such grand ambitions are harboured here; rather the attempt is to come to a better understanding of the shades of grey that colour the evidence in evidence-based policy.

Many commentators have been surprised by Popper's characterisation of a science that does not know but only guesses. Few would deny, however, that the phrase is a fine characterisation of policy making and programme building. There is common ground here and this chapter may be thought of as an exploration and a celebration of the potential of informed guesswork. In particular, it follows Campbell's (1988: 519) idea of the trust–doubt ratio. What any scientific inquiry must do, he argues, is open up a percentage of its field to doubt, whilst for the time being leaving another proportion untested and down to trust. The second intimidating task confronting this chapter is to contemplate how these proportions apply in evaluation science.

We now careen to the core of the chapter, confronting the conundrum of complexity by charting the creed of comprehensive but corrigible realism. To strike the delicate balance between pursuing an ever extending set of questions and the need to achieve closure in any particular inquiry requires a new set of organising principles. We need to move from evaluation research to evaluation science. Just as the old saying teaches us that it takes a whole village to raise a child, it might indeed require an entire scientific discipline to evaluate complex programmes. Seven foundational ideas are discussed, tied together in the acronym TARMATO, and presented with an initial summary in Box 5.1:

Box 5.1

The organising principles of evaluation science

i **Theory.** Programme theories (rather than programmes) act as the unit of analysis of evaluation and the gathering point for cumulative inquiry.

ii **Abstraction.** Conceptual abstraction provides the means of establishing a common language to draw out the similarities between different interventions and to provide the bridgehead to link their evaluations.

iii **Reusable conceptual platforms.** Rather than starting each inquiry from scratch, a stock of recyclable conceptual frameworks is created to distinguish different classes of interventions and to set out their component theories. All evaluations then operate within a common set of programme theories, each inquiry being capable of adding to and refining that framework.

iv **Model building.** The conceptual platforms develop with each contributory evaluation providing a new set of contingencies to test the component theories. Refinements are added in a process of model building, providing a growing set of propositions specifying the conditions in which each programme theory applies.

v **Adjudication.** There are always contrasting expectations on whether a programme might work and alternative explanations of why it may do so. Adjudicating between rival hypotheses is the engine of progress in evaluation science. It is the main means of bettering programme theories and the basic strategy of model building.

vi **Trust.** Given the infinite number of potential influences on programme outcomes and the infinite array of theories to account for them, inquiry proceeds by taking some features on trust and by focusing inquiry on certain others – a difficult estimate known as the trust–doubt ratio.

vii **Organised scepticism.** All of the above steps demand judgement on the part of the evaluator. Discretionary components are unavoidable in science and rendering the judgements sound depends on continuing close scrutiny of each other's work. Organised scepticism is the superintending force.

It should be re-emphasised that this is a blueprint for a whole mode of inquiry. All of the elements are borrowed, and proudly so, from the ideas of the realist founding scholars. Many facets are established as part of the existing repertoire of evaluation. Other elements are somewhat hidden and need better articulation in the methodological literature and in the field. Other elements are barely present and call for a repositioning of the discipline. Note, however, it is the joint application of all elements that supplies the realist response to complexity.

—— 1. Theory

Realist evaluation has always numbered itself in the ranks of the 'theory driven' or 'theory based' schools of evaluation. The arguments for starting an investigation in programme theory are well established. I offer a quick recapitulation here, focusing on the implications for complexity. The basic idea is rooted in post empiricist-philosophy of science and the rejection of the notion that science commences with and builds upon careful observation and painstaking measurement. By contrast, Popper teaches us that: 'Observation is always selective … It needs a chosen object, a definite task, an interest, a point of view, a problem' (1992: 61). Parvin (2010: 41) elaborates this metaphysical principle in a proposition that speaks particularly well to evaluation research: 'Scientists cannot merely look (or listen or hear or feel), they need to know what they are looking for. Similarly, they cannot merely create, they need some context of ends (some problem requiring a solution) which can guide them'. The real starting point of science thus lies in 'theory', our ideas on the nature of the problem and on the nature of its solution. As Popper puts it, 'Theory … dominates experimental work from its initial planning up to the finishing touches in the laboratory' (1992: 90).

This idea carries directly into evaluation research. Interventions always begin as theories. They spark into life in the heads of the policy architects, pass into the hands of practitioners and then hopefully into the minds of programme subjects. The journey is an 'if–then' proposition (Pawson and Sridharan, 2010). The preliminary idea, ambition, expectation, hypothesis or 'programme theory' is that if certain resources (sometimes material, sometimes social, and sometimes cognitive) are provided then they will insinuate subjects' reasoning, generating a change in collective behaviour. Such propositions also provide evaluation research with its starting point. Indeed, there is nowhere else to start. Other strategies of evaluation research have advised upon different modes of ignition. To paraphrase Parvin, they have encouraged us to look at or listen to or hear from or share feelings with the intervention. But the same point always holds. Researchers need to know something about what it is they are measuring, communicating with or emancipating in order to meet those objectives. It is the same for programme architects, planners and builders. They cannot merely plan; they need to start with some understanding of ends (problems requiring solutions). Theory dominates evaluation from its initial planning up to the finishing touches in the field.

The modus operandi of evaluation must, therefore, follow the logic of scientific discovery. This is often depicted, following Wallace (1971) as the permanently rotating 'wheel of science' (Figure 5.1). Theories prompt research questions, which are cast as hypotheses, which are explored in research designs, which organise the gathering and analysis of empirical data, which allow tests of the working hypotheses and revision in the originating theories … all of which are then put to further refinement in continuing rotations of the wheel.

Applied to evaluation, the starting point is with the programme theory – ideas about what makes an intervention work. These are then cast as hypotheses specifying the conditions where the theory is expected to apply. Empirical work is then conducted to test out these propositions and the findings prompt revisions to the original theory. In the figure, the initial expectation is that the theory will apply in circumstances A, B and C. Research then confirms some of these expectations and confounds others, indicating that conditions A, B, D, E and F seem more conducive to programme expectations. The investigatory wheel turns, the next iteration uncovering a more subtle configuration of sub-conditions, let us say A_1, A_2, B, D_1, D_2, F_1, F_2 and F_3, to capture the domain of the programme theory.

In terms of complexity, there is a telling advantage of beginning inquiry in the realm of theory. Programme theories are immediately portable, whereas programmes are not. Instead of starting each inquiry from scratch, an evaluation science that starts with theories forces us to ponder recurrence – recurring policy ideas meeting recurring practical problems. Theory is the great connector, propelling inquiry around the wheel of science. Note, however, that the rotating routine of theory testing provides no resolution to the problem of complexity. Programme theories are nothing more than ideas on how and why interventions might work and we have seen in Chapter 3 that these considerations are endless. Figure 5.1 represents no more than a starting point (theories being what programmes have in common) and a collecting point (theories always being open to better specification). It shows us where the learning occurs but it leaves us with an infinite number of learning cycles. We need further strategies to optimise and guide that learning.

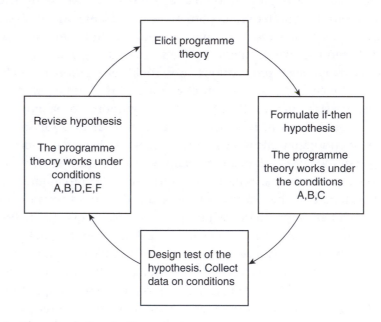

Figure 5.1 The wheel of evaluation science

——— **2. Abstraction** ———

Although rarely highlighted in treatise or textbook as a notable feature of inquiry, the role of abstraction is a key research function. It provides us with the language to connect up inquiries and to place boundaries around them. Abstraction receives relatively little methodological discussion, partly as a result of its mundane role in everyday life. If I arrive at the estate agents (or realtor), I fully expect to be introduced to a range of 'properties' and I know, of course, that this abstract term covers a lot of ground. It might include houses and apartments and every conceivable sub-type within them (mansions to maisonettes, semis to studios). I also know *not* to expect to discuss chemical properties, property mistresses, intellectual property, and so on. Boundaries are created instantly: we begin to know what is on the agenda and what is not.

The best known call for abstraction in social science is Merton's attempt to capture an appropriate, middle-range terminology to guide social research. The aim is to find concepts that are: 'sufficiently abstract to deal with different spheres of social behaviour and social structure, so that they transcend sheer description or empirical generalisation' (Merton, 1967: 68). Any event or sequence of events is open to endless descriptions and countless conceptualisations. In explaining them, social scientists have to rely on abstraction. In their heads they try to extract out various significant components or influences and figure out how they combine and interact. With such a theory in place they return to the concrete event and make sense of it. Abstraction is thus the thinking process that allows us to understand an event as an instance of a more general class of happenings. Quite literally, the reasoning goes – 'here is a specific instance, which I can explain as a "case" that falls into a broader explanatory schema'. The prize here is that we have a tool that provides the basis for drawing transferable lessons. Fruitful middle-range concepts will harness together and elucidate many different empirical instances. The same explanation may be located and relocated, used and reused.

Merton celebrated abstraction for its ability to harvest together seemingly diverse forms of social behaviour. He aimed to jolt sociology out of its substantive silos, wherein sociologists of the family mapped conjugal relations, sociologists of crime documented gang life, sociologists of industry dwelt on the shop floor, sociologists of health examined illness and death, and so on. His theory of 'reference group behaviour' can be used as an example of middle-range concepts as harvesting machines. The basic idea is that people take the standards of 'significant others' as a basis of monitoring their own situations. If we discover the reference group in play then a whole set of disparate attitudes become explicable. Merton first used the theory to explain the sometimes surprising loyalties and jealousies of US servicemen drafted in the Second World War (Stouffer et al., 1949a, 1949b). Army conscripts felt contended or resentful by turn. Married soldiers compared themselves unfavourably to the unmarried recruits and to married civilians. If the soldier happened to be a non-combatant he often felt that the Army favoured the fighting forces. If the conscript happened to be black, he compared himself unfavourably to white recruits but favourably to his black counterparts in civvy-street. The core idea turned up again and again in explaining group loyalties and rivalries. In UK industrial sociology it explained why shipyard workers in the north of England measured their worth against local tradesmen rather than in comparison with, say, southern stockbrokers (Runciman, 1966). And onwards, the idea travelled into the sociology of health, with research into Parkinson's disease being able to explain why new victims often preferred to compare their plight to the worse off in the later stage of illness (Charlton and Barrow, 2002).

Evaluation research can make use of exactly the same strategy in order to harvest knowledge from its thousands of primary studies. Ground can be made on complexity by locating the common conceptual ground that confederates programmes. The idea is illustrated in Figure 5.2. At the top of the diagram we have the present picture – thousands of evaluations of the thousands of interventions aimed at thousands of immediate problems (each circle represents hundreds of studies). They are somewhat disorderly. By and large each evaluation will have started from scratch. If there is organisation, this will be arranged by policy domain, seven of which are illustrated in the middle section of the figure. A loose, tacit assemblage of evaluation know-how emerges with the same commissioners hiring the same evaluation teams to research similar programmes aimed to tackle similar problems. Then, of course, there are newly favoured systematic reviews, which have the express aim of connecting up inquiries. But even these cover limited ground, bringing together evidence from similar studies of the 'same' programme {illustrated in the curly parentheses in the figure}.

If, however, programme theory becomes the unit of analysis, then the spread of evaluation know-how has a different starting point and learning from evaluation has a different trajectory. The same programme theory repeats itself regularly and repeats itself across many policy domains. This is illustrated across the lower half of Figure 5.2. I begin on the left and return again to the oldest programme theory on the books. In a stupendous range of examples policy makers have puzzled upon

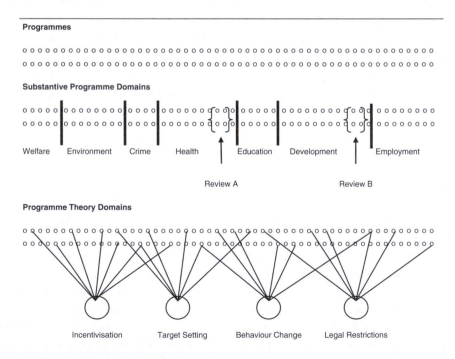

Figure 5.2   Confederating inquiry in evaluation research

ways of influencing behaviour and come up with the 'incentive' – the give-away, the grant, the subsidy, the loan, the allowance, the benefit, the premium, the reward, the gratuity, the bonus, the honorarium, the subvention and so on. Generically speaking, the working hypothesis is that the incentive offers deprived or recalcitrant subjects the wherewithal to partake in some activity beyond their normal means or outside their normal sphere of interest, which then prompts continued activity and thus long-term benefit to themselves or their community or their organisation.

One ubiquitous idea provides immediate breadth to evaluation science. Incentivisation, perforce, operates in all seven policy domains illustrated in Figure 5.2. Welfare systems, of course, offer payments as a basic 'safety net' but as soon as the objective transposes into welfare-to-work then allowances are manipulated, targeted and tapered so as to incentivise the move into employment. Environmental incentives include subsidies for bus travel, home insulation and solar panel installation. Crime busting incentives have included everything from free distribution of household bolts, bars and locks to cash payments to Afghan farmers to cease heroin production. Health service incentives include everything from low cost distribution of nicotine replacement patches to smokers to increased payments to GPs to work out of hours. Educational incentives include maintenance allowances to encourage poorer young people to remain in school and fee-waivers to encourage them on to university. In international development programmes, performance-dependent subsidies are offered for improving transport, construction, education, water and sanitation systems. Unemployment is tackled with the provision of free training and by offering subsidies to employers to take on the workless. The list could be easily extended but, hopefully, the point is already made, namely that a 'programme theory' orientation provides a stupendous opportunity for learning from one scheme to another.

The description of Figure 5.2 is completed by noting that abstraction offers evaluation science many different starting points for inquiry. The figure, quite randomly, identifies three more generic interventions: target setting, behaviour change, legal restrictions. The latter two have already received a brief mention and come under extended treatment in the third part of the book. The other example is a reminder of the remorseless borrowing of key ideas in intervention building. I will not list examples of targets set in different policy domains because you, dear reader, are undoubtedly working in a regime that deploys performance indicators. The example is, nonetheless, useful because it reveals immediately the opportunities in evaluating at this level. Theories gain their spurs by putting them to the test. The theory behind target setting meets a widespread challenge, reducible to the maxim that people often attend to the measure rather than the performance. Thus teachers may achieve exam targets by teaching the test, hospitals may meet waiting time targets by resetting the measurement parameters, and countries may meet environmental targets by trading rather than reducing emissions. But in many, many commercial examples productivity is raised by the desire to meet targets. An inquiry into the merits of the next performance indicator would undoubtedly gain from a panoramic understanding of previous winners and losers.

————3. Reusable conceptual platforms ——————————————————

Identifying a body of generic programme ideas is only the beginning of a cumulative programme of evaluation research. Programmes often begin life as one 'big idea' but the grand design always has sub-components. Programmes do not just incentivise, they select behaviours thought to respond to incentives, they choose subjects thought to respond to incentives, they pick incentive levels thought to shift behaviour, and so on. Programmes do not just set targets, they devise the means of measuring, administrating and publicising the targets, they pick subjects and behaviours thought to respond to target setting, and so on. There are always theories within theories and in order to test programme theories, in order to compare and contrast their fortunes, we need to be able to specify the essential components. Knitting together the findings of evaluation research requires more than a programme theory label (incentives, target setting, peer support, regeneration, etc.), we need to populate each theory with an understanding of the core sets of process that will occur in that class of programme. In realist terminology these are referred to as the 'internal' or 'necessary' relations of an object (Sayer, 1992: 89).

This is another feature of inquiry that receives relatively little methodological attention but also one that is quite familiar in everyday life. Let us return to my visit to the estate agent. As well as directing me to the correct location in the shopping mall, knowledge of the abstract term 'property' also provides me with a range of 'givens' about the 'property transaction' that may follow. Thus I also know that all such transactions will involve competing interests, mine as purchaser and the owner as seller. I also know that these interests will be mediated by the estate agent and, if I have been around the block, I know this mediation may be decidedly slippery. I further know, because 'property rights' have been organised in this manner, that the transaction has a legal basis and will involve deeds, surveys, leases, land registries, local authority searches as well as another slippery set of customers, the solicitors. With the exception of my gross asides on two fine sets of professionals, all of the above features can be considered internal or necessary features of the property transaction – without buyers there can be no sellers, without land there can be no buildings, etc.

Most institutional affairs are arranged in such agendas; they create boundaries on what is and what is not considered relevant. These boundaries set limits but do not cover everything that goes on within a transaction. For instance, the clincher in my house purchase might be some incidental feature, perhaps the fact that I really, really did like the wallpaper in that living room. In realist terminology these are referred to as 'external' or 'contingent' relations (Sayer, 1992: 89). I cannot expect minor aesthetics to be covered in deeds, surveys and land registry documentation.

Here then is our next desideratum for evaluative science. It needs a vocabulary of 'internal' or 'necessary' components to be investigated over and again as we pursue the fate of particular programme theories. We need conceptual platforms that can be recycled. How fares evaluation research against this principle?

Evaluation research is laced with abstract terms that allow us to move from one inquiry to the next. Whether I am investigating attempts to rehabilitate drug users or efforts to promote household waste recycling I am able to recognise them as 'programmes'. Once identified as such, I know to anticipate a range of internal and necessary features. I know that there will be 'stakeholders' and that it is likely that I will be able to distinguish 'practitioners' and 'subjects', as well perhaps as 'managers' and 'policy makers'. I also know that all programmes have to be 'implemented' and are put in place with certain objectives in mind, so as an evaluator I fully expect that I will be able to recognise 'inputs', 'outputs' and 'outcomes'. The items in this conceptual schema are already part of the set agenda of evaluative inquiry.

What evaluation has been less prepared to do is arrive at an abstract set of concepts that span its substantive or policy concerns. Evaluators arrive at the threshold of a new programme knowing all of the above and with an instant ability to apply all of the terms to the task in hand. But in terms of programme content or substantive programme theories they are more likely to start from scratch. It is a situation rather akin to ethnography, another discipline much troubled by a lack of mutual learning. Geertz (1973) captured the problem superbly in a famous phrase about the anthropological method. Ethnography, he claimed, assumed so little about the necessary constituents of the societies studied that successive inquiries amounted to 'just another country heard from'. What is to prevent evaluation research from being 'just another intervention heard from'?

The solution, following Sayer, is to utilise an abstract set of substantive concepts that describe the internal or necessary components of the programme. The goal is illustrated in Figure 5.3 and described with a brief example from my previous research (Pawson, 2006a: chapter 7). Let us suppose the intrepid investigator is set to research the effectiveness of Megan's Law, the US intervention designed to reduce predatory sex offences by identifying released, former offenders to the communities into which they settle. Like many interventions it might be regarded initially as an entirely novel idea – an unusual solution to a thankfully, rare problem. But from the point of view of programme theory we have been here before. In everyday parlance it is often described as a 'naming and shaming' intervention. More formally, the programme theory can be described as 'public disclosure', the idea of throwing the spotlight of publicity on some errant behaviour so that the forearmed public can act to control the named party.

There are many, many such interventions aimed at a large class of miscreants and poor performers. Amongst those subjected to public disclosure include failing schools, underperforming hospitals, polluting industries, prostitutes' johns, violent drunks, and people with all manner of payment arrears. And here we reach the point: each of these interventions has the same skeletal structure. In order to work, there are component processes that must be completed successfully: i) the performance or behaviour in question must be identified and measured reliably and without ambiguity or error; ii) that data/information needs to be disseminated clearly and efficiently to the appropriate public; iii) the public should act on the information by applying appropriate and commensurate sanctions; and iv) the named party should respond to those sanctions being shamed and constrained. These are the 'internal' and 'necessary' processes of public disclosure (the full circles in Figure 5.3).

Here is the point. The evaluator does not have to reinvent the programme theory wheel at the start of each investigation. An available conceptual platform is available if we pay more attention to the history of inquiry. Understanding accrued significantly by evaluating how Megan's Law stuttered through these standard conditions. To be sure, there are also many separate or contingent ideas that also merit inquiry in any evaluation (the dotted circles in Figure 5.3). For instance, in Megan's Law, the information on released offenders has to be dispatched to the appropriate 'community'. This raises the moot issue of how to define such localities and, more to the point, raises evaluative questions about the optimal boundaries into which to release the information. Scores of other such contingencies apply and in Chapter 8, I will provide a further extended example of the use of a different conceptual platform and discuss how to balance investigation of the necessary and the contingent.

Here, I simply want to stress the potential utility of recyclable conceptual platforms. Evaluators are generally faced with assessing the merits of a novel programme, born of fresh ideas, carried out in a new setting. But from the outset this ensemble is not and should not be regarded as chaotic, random, wicked or whatever. Programme ideas are begged, stolen and borrowed. There are always some standard, routine processes, as in the above example, which we know will pertain. Research should move automatically from the new, concrete situation to be studied and out to a familiar, abstract framework of necessary relationships and back to the then, not quite so new, concrete programme to be studied in more detail. This double movement, concrete to abstract to concrete, provides the glue, the bridgehead, the source of continuity between inquiries (Sayer, 1992: 87). And through it, we begin to regain some ground on complexity.

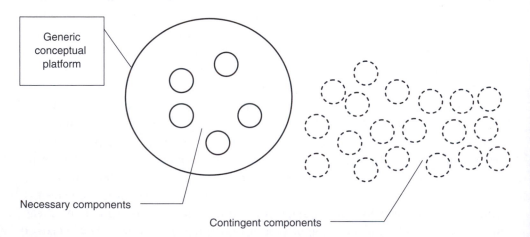

Figure 5.3   Necessary and contingent components of programme theories

Thus far in the realist march on complexity, I have stressed the use of programme theories as the focus of learning, the use of conceptual abstraction as a means of connecting inquiries, and the use of interconnected conceptual sets as the reusable platforms of inquiry. The function of these strategies is to provide evaluation with a unified starting point. Yet to be discussed is the means of extending the explanation. Programmes are complex in construction and complex in the footprint of their outcomes. Since we are now relying on theory to do the explanatory work, we now need a way of formulating theory so that it is extendable and has a gradual reach from the core and into as many peripheries as possible.

This is a standard requirement of the scientific method and achieved by a strategy known as 'proposition development', 'logical derivation' or just 'model building'. The core notion is represented symbolically in Figure 5.4. We commence in the previous Figure 5.3 with a conceptual platform specifying, say, three core ideas that make up the building blocks of the programme theory under research. Inquiry has progressed to the point where we know that a programme is more likely to have a particular outcome if the necessary components A, B and C (represented by the full circles) are in place and we have theories of why these elements are necessary (represented by the full arrows). These explanations are never complete and there are always other contingencies (represented by the dashed circles) that might be added to the explanation of the workings of the system. The growth of the understanding takes the form of theory building, the progressive development of knowledge of the components of the system and their interrelationships. Model building is represented by the addition of subsidiary hypotheses to the basic model (represented by the dashed arrows). Extending the theoretical model in this way draws more and more contingencies (D, E) into the explanatory system (represented by the interconnectors).

Capturing the growth of knowledge with a Microsoft palate being somewhat taxing, it is high time for an example of model building in programme theory. The following example, based on Pawson (2009b), uses Merton's theory

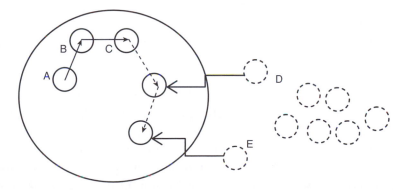

Figure 5.4 Building programme theories

of reference group behaviour to try to unlock the classic puzzle of programme evaluation, namely Rossi's Iron Law, that intervention success will generally be matched with intervention failure. Realist evaluation is much exercised in trying to specify the context in which a programme works. We know that interventions only work for certain individuals in certain circumstances but we do not suppose that winners and losers will be found at random. Evaluation science assumes that there will be some pattern to success and failure across interventions, and that we can build a model to explain it.

Model building begins by finding a level of abstraction to capture the explanatory dynamics and using Mertonian abstraction it can be argued that a great deal of public policy consists of attempts by 'ingroups' to influence the behaviour of 'outgroups'. Governments seek to persuade citizens, teachers attempt to inspire pupils, managers endeavour to shape the workforce, law enforcement officials try to control offenders, and so on. To do so they employ programmes deploying all manner of advice, overtures, restraints, and commands and all of them meet with mixed success. To understand a little more about these patterns requires that we delve a little closer into the relationships between the respective ingroups and outgroups.

We have already encountered Merton's idea of reference group theory under the idea that a group's attitudes follow according to its choice of comparison point. Sometimes an outgroup will change its behaviour under the influence of an ingroup: sometime outgroup loyalties will be hardened if the external reference point remains remote. Public policy often attempts to intervene in these choices, conspiring to change the subject's orientations from those of the outsider to those of the insider. A considerable prize awaits. If we can build a durable theory of how reference points are selected it should be possible to draw transferable lessons on the conditions under which a change of orientation is more or less likely. Merton began to unlock this puzzle via the typology reproduced as Table 5.1.

Table 5.1 Outsiders: a typology of contexts

Attitude toward membership	Eligible for membership	Ineligible for membership
Aspire to belong	1 Candidate for membership	2 Marginal member
Indifferent to affiliation	3 Potential member	4 Detached non-member
Motivated not to belong	5 Autonomous non-member	6 Antagonistic non-member

Source: Derived from Merton (1968: 344)

The table concentrates upon 'outsiders' and proposes there are some significant distinctions within such a station. First of all, it is feasible to differentiate between those who (by dint of some qualification or characteristic) are ineligible for the ingroup and those who are eligible but continue to remain unaffiliated. This simple contrast between entitlement and disqualification from ingroup membership is represented in the two columns to the right of the division in the table. The model also takes into consideration the question of attitude to group membership of these outsiders. Do they want to become involved with the ingroup? An initial threefold distinction is also drawn in this respect (aspiration, indifference, opposition) and is depicted in the three rows of the table.

Putting the two factors (eligibility and attitude) together then generates a repertoire of abstract propositions about different forms of reference group behaviour, according to the subject's membership of the six numbered cells in the table. In cell 1 we have non-members who both aspire to and are eligible for ingroup membership. Reference group theory posits that they are likely to choose that ingroup as a yardstick for their behaviour and to benefit from doing so. Cell 2 members, by contrast, may want to and attempt to copy the values and behaviours of the ingroup but the theory advises that they are likely to remain shunned and on its margins because of the lack of some crucial membership attribute. Cell 3 and cell 4 consists of people who are unconcerned with ingroup membership. 'They are entirely indifferent to its orbit. It constitutes no part of their reference group' (Merton, 1968: 345). Neither of these two groups is likely to reach out to or take cognisance of ingroup ideas. The main difference is that those in cell 3 may simply be more adjacent to its ambit; they are more likely to receive overtures from the ingroup. The bottom row identifies outsiders who actively oppose membership of an ingroup, but differentiates them according to whether they are eligible (cell 5) or non-eligible (cell 6) to join that group in the first place. Both regard the ingroup as a negative reference group. But the eligibility distinction raises the Simmelian hypothesis, that the qualified individuals who expressly reject membership are more likely to pose a threat to that group than are the antagonists automatically disbarred from membership. The members of cell 5's self-chosen autonomy provides the condition for effective hostility.

Simple as it is, Table 5.1 has all the attributes of model building. It is formulated in the abstract; no concrete social groups or identities being called upon. It is logically derived from elementary theories about human behaviour. It is formalised with a clear codification of its component elements. It is propositional in that it makes a range of predictions about how different groups will behave under an ingroup stimulus. Accordingly, it can function to make sense of a whole range of outgroup behaviours that have been observed in programme evaluation. I provide three very short examples here, noting that they are fully developed with full citations to the appropriate empirical evidence in Pawson (2009b).

First, let us return to public disclosure. The programme theory supposes that if the ingroup reveals publicly an official record of the poor or deviant performance of some outgroup, then the glare of publicity will shift their behaviour to ingroup norms. It is a simple idea that, as we have seen, has surfaced in dozens of sectors. The theory, of course, generates mixed outcomes; outcomes, moreover, that are tolerably well explained by Merton's model. Public disclosure of the non-payment of many arrears, taxes, child maintenance agreements and so on often fails to budge the identified subject and indeed may provoke renewed hostility. Outgroup members in this case have often taken up a long-term stance as outsiders and remain implacable being, in Merton's terms, 'antagonistic outsiders'. Quite a different reaction to negative publicity comes from 'aspirational eligibles'. Groups seeking to maintain or enhance their place in society are likely to jump to cover their less distinguished tracks. Many manufacturers, for instance, act quickly to preserve reputation in the face of negative publicity about the safety and durability of their products. In the middle, with the 'aspirational ineligibles', we find more complex manoeuvres. These marginal groups, says Merton, will want to comply with pressure to improve performance but lack the immediate wherewithal to do so. In this case what often follows is 'naming and gaming'. For instance, poorly performing schools identified in UK government 'league tables' employ a range of subterfuge and spin in removing their more difficult students for the next round of measures.

Moving to a different policy domain, we again detect the lingering presence of reference group affiliation. Mentoring programmes embody the idea that close personal involvement with a mature, caring adult can change the ambitions and behaviour of disaffected youth. The insider can mould the outsider. So much the better if, once upon a time, that insider also belonged on the other side of the tracks. The evidence shows, inevitably, that mentoring programmes meet with mixed success. Success follows approximately the locus of the mentee groups in the table of outsider conditions (cells 1 to 6), it being considerably easier to mentor those who have exhibited some talent and ambition. The record on mentoring 'antagonist outsiders' shows repeated falls from grace. The heroic mentor has to move on both axes, not only to turn around attitudes from hostility to acquiescence but to inspire some educational and training foundations on which the mentee can build. Not an easy undertaking for an individual.

For a third example we move to the domain of 'peer support', a class of interventions which is squarely built on a form of reference group theory – 'let's get hold of the hard to reach by using those already there'. Peer-to-peer mentoring has thus turned up to address a range of problems on drug abuse, school underperformance, sex education and so forth. An obvious problem lurks – how can an outsider inspire fellow outsiders to insider ambitions? The answer that emerges from the peer education literature suggests that all depends on the message that is exchanged. For instance in the area of sex education, adults rather than peers prove more convincing in explaining the 'mechanics' of pregnancy and sexually transmitted disease, whilst peers rather than adults were more successful in discussing everyday feelings around the sexual encounter. In short, peer education can share the predicament, adult mentoring can describe the risks. Reference group theory thus predicts that peer support can (only) move young people along the initial part of the ingroup journey – from isolation and detachment to less marginal positions, awaiting the next impulse.

These brief examples hopefully illustrate the enormous ground that can be covered with some basic model building. They exemplify the process depicted in Figure 5.4. A core conceptual framework is developed distinguishing some potential difference within the 'outsider' status. A model is developed showing how these positions will respond to 'insider' pressure. It is applied in quite different programme applications, bringing into its ambit the dispositions of subjects in a range of public disclosure, mentoring and peer-education programmes. It awaits the next application, slowly extending our understanding of who may (and may not) be controlled and cajoled in public policy. By building extendable models of the choice architecture of programmes we recover some ground on complexity.

5. Adjudication

Having shifted programme theory to the centre of evaluation attention we now move on to face a whole series of thorny philosophical challenges that have been raised about the process of theory testing. They are often captured in a phrase about the 'asymmetry of knowledge', namely that we can never prove theory but only probe causal hypotheses. A full account of this conundrum would require immersion in the entire philosophical thesaurus. Here, my aim is to demonstrate that this asymmetry is a fundamental problem in the evaluation of complex programmes and that a realist solution going by the name of 'theory adjudication' can serve us well.

The first challenge lies in Popper's seminal idea that empirical observations can never establish the truth of theories, though they do have the potential to falsify them. Whatever the weight of confirmatory data we can supply in support of a theory, there always lurks the possibility of a yet undiscovered disconfirmatory instance. The textbooks tell this cautionary tale against the hypothesis that 'all swans are white'. The fact that this generalisation might appear a solid law in a life-time's observations of ponds, lakes and estuaries does not rule out the possibility that another backwater might turn up with that black swan. We are actually rather comfortable with this axiom in the policy sciences for it is accepted that there are no universally successful interventions, no silver bullets, and no magic wands.

The second challenge is known as the underdetermination thesis. It purports to further weaken the idea that observation provides the testing ground for theory. It argues that for any body of observational evidence there will always be more than one theory that can account for it. In its strong versions this opens up the possibility of parallel truths. If the available data can support more than one theory, it would appear that we have to live with multiple explanations. Both Darwinism and Creationism are accounts of the ascent of mankind. Both the wave theory and the corpuscular theory can make sense of many aspects of the behaviour of light. Again, the basic dilemma is familiar in policy science. The difficulty of shifting a significant proportion of population out of long-term unemployment can be explained both in terms of the fecklessness of the underclass or by capitalism's tendency to create a reserve army of labour. The underdetermination challenge is, of course, endless. The above examples illustrate the idea in supposing there are two rival theories to account for a body of data. Alternatives, however, might be expected to line up in a much more complex fashion, including the possibility that there is always a, presently unconsidered, theory that will perform the explanatory task as well if not better than those presently tabled.

The third challenge is known as the Duhem/Quine thesis, which claims that it is never possible to test (to prove or indeed falsify) a theory in isolation because theories are made up of a whole series of propositions (http://plato.stanford.edu/entries/scientific-underdetermination/). The textbook example goes something like this. The fact that birds are not ripped asunder when they soar into the skies does not disprove the theory that the earth is moving with great velocity. The theory is protected because we also hold a series of background assumptions about the planetary motion and in particular one about the fixity of the atmosphere enclosing the earth. Whilst the reasoning within this little example might appear entirely sound, the strategy involved is argued to lead to a logical black hole. It has been taken to imply that there can be no crucial experiments, no decisive observations because it is always possible to protect a theory by modifying certain points in the many auxiliary and subsidiary hypotheses that make it up.

Whether physicists routinely go around finding reasons to protect a favoured theory is hotly disputed (Barnes, 1974; Toulmin, 1972). However, we can say that this business of ad hoc theory protection is rife in policy circles. Despite the miserable and palpable failure of the financial sector, UK bankers continue to advocate the theory that giant bonuses are crucial in incentivising their performance by invoking a sub-theory that the whole sector might up and leave the country should the regulation of remuneration be tightened. More generally, since complex policies impact at many levels and the success of any intervention may typically be measured by many indicators, the potential always remains open for proponents of theory A to protect it by picking one set of indicators, whilst advocates of theory B place their trust in others.

All of these fearsome ideas have changed the way that we think of the process of theory testing. They do not undermine the basic idea that theories stand or fall in the court of empirical evidence but they do destroy the notion that this transaction is a simple, one-off encounter. The defence, if that is the right word, of the empirical testing of theories is well established in 'post-empiricist' philosophy of science (Thomas, 1979). The meeting of theory and evidence is now generally conceived as a gradual, incremental process. Since there will always be competing theories, scientific inquiry is understood as the perpetual process of finding tests to adjudicate between rival explanations – a battle of the survival of the fittest. Such a notion is perfectly commonplace in physical science; theories are tested and improved over the decades (hopefully, this is demonstrated in my potted history of Ohm's Law in the previous chapter). By contrast, in evaluation research and, I suppose, in social science more generally, I have already noted the tendency to start each inquiry from scratch and to assemble evidence anew. The task here is thus to incorporate 'gradualism' into the account of how to evaluate complex policies and programmes.

The overall position that I want to defend here is known as 'corrigible realism' (Campbell, 1988: 444) and starts by acknowledging the above asymmetries in theory

testing. Thus it abandons the idea that theories (T) are simple A-causes-B propositions, which we test by recourse to the directly observable 'facts' about the co-
occurrence of A and B. Theories recount the action of some underlying processes
and it is these generative mechanisms that give rise to the observed uniformity
between A and B. So how does one test generative theories? The initial steps of the
theory testing process are illustrated in Figure 5.5 and we commence explanation in
the top section. We have formulated our generative theory (Theory 1), which predicts
uniformity in the relationship between A and B. Empirical work commences and it
turns out that A does indeed relate to B in the manner predicted. Is Theory 1 thus
correct? The answer is negative because we have not inspected any other generative theories that might have something to say about the relationship between A
and B. On the realist account, empirical work becomes the process of taking further
theories into account.

We cannot say that Theory 1 is correct but we can already say that it is better
than any other generative theory (Theory 2) which happens to predict no relationship or a different relationship between A and B, as at the top of the diagram.
We reach the crucial pivot in understanding the nature of theory testing. We can
never say that theory A is correct but we can say that it is better than (dashed)
theory B in a particular respect. The basic logic of theory testing changes from
'right versus wrong' to 'better versus worse'. I have always considered that this
vocabulary should have some instinctive appeal in the rumbustious field of evaluation because for every theory arguing why a programme will work there will be a
critical audience ready to explain why it will not.

We are still on the nursery slopes of theory adjudication, however. If they are
fruitful, generative explanations should be able to explain the whole footprint of

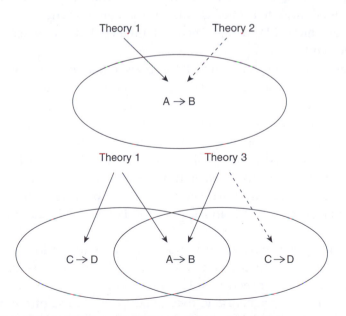

Figure 5.5 Empirical testing as adjudicating between rival theories

the relationship between the properties in a system. As explained in the previous section on model building, good generative explanations have the capacity to provide additional testable relationships – that C relates to D, that E gives rise to F, that G is correlated with H, and so on. To rely once again on a textbook physics example, the basic theory that matter consists of molecules in motion helps us explain the different properties of solids, liquids and gasses, as well as the Brownian motion of dust particles, as well as the interrelationship of properties such as the pressure, volume and temperature of gasses, and so on.

So how can model building be accommodated within a theory testing regime? We shift to the bottom section of Figure 5.5. Now, for any particular observation, the fertile imaginations of scientists will always provide alternative explanations. So it is quite possible, as the relativists teach us, there will be more than one account of why A relates to B. Theory 1 does the job but so too does Theory 3. Having two successful theories does not force us to remain in the world of parallel truths – for generative theories, as we have seen, will model multiple consequences. And if they are rival generative theories, they must have alternative consequences at some other point in the system; let us say in terms of properties C, D, E, or F.

The key to empirical testing in such situations is the process of finding 'lateral support' for explanations (Elster, 2007: 17). This process is illustrated in the second step in Figure 5.5, which commences with the successful prediction of a proposition from Theory 1 that A→B. The utility of such empirical corroboration may be challenged should there exist a rival Theory 3, which also provides an account for the same relationship between A and B. No amount of inspection of A and B will decide between two theories that agree that A→B. So we need to look elsewhere in the footprint of implications for another proposition on which to separate the theories. This is illustrated schematically in the figure by the lateral support for empirical outcome C→D, which Theory 1 predicts but for which Theory 3 is unable to account.

Here then is a simple rewriting of the basic function of the empirical test. Observational data cannot tell us that a theory is true, but it can say that one theory is preferable to another in particular respects. According to the model of corrigible realism this process continues indefinitely. Empirical testing is a perpetual process rather than a one-off event and a journey that takes us from theories T_1 to T_2 to T_3 to T_∞ and properties A to B to C to ∞. Disagreement can arise at any point in the journey. One set of rival explanations is settled only for another to fire up. The sequence perpetuates itself with empirical inquiry in science being thought of as a continuous process of trial and error – or as Popper (1963) has it, 'conjectures and refutations'

There is one further and crucial sub-principle of adjudicationism that I must table before we return to the consequences of all this for evaluation science, namely that the tests between rival explanations are run between what Popper and Campbell refer to as 'plausible rival hypotheses'. Those of a more relativist persuasion interpret the above processual model as fatally weak because it would

seem to imply, with Quine that scientific knowledge is fragile and impermanent amidst the possibility that a presently unknown rival theory may spring up at any time that will completely overturn the emerging lines of inquiry. Campbell provides the antidote: 'The mere possibility of some alternative explanation is not enough – it is only the *plausible* rival hypotheses that are invalidating' (1988: 264). In other words what the scientists do is to countenance and produce rival explanations and then test to see if they have more leverage that the ones currently in play. There is a survival of the fittest element. Theories can be wrong; they will contain errors. But each successive test does not overturn all that has gone before; it winnows down or refines interpretation.

The upshot of this particular principle has rather profound empirical implications. Instead of conducting each evaluation of each complex programme from scratch and in isolation, we should prioritise the confrontation of plausible hypothesis as the focus of empirical evaluation. It is something of an oddity that this is not already the case because rival hypotheses accumulate in antagonistic heaps in all phases of policy making. Let me provide an example, overheard on the radio this morning before writing duties commenced. The UK government has announced a new campaign to encourage us to eat more healthily. It comprises of three strands – wide public distribution of a set of healthy recipes, a deal with some supermarkets to discount the key health giving ingredients, and the use of a celebrity chef to promote the recipes. The idea is to perform the hat trick and to encapsulate in a single programme the idea that healthy food can be nutritious and cheap and glamorous.

The well-briefed presenter conducted the two-minute interview with the responsible minister by presenting a series of plausible rival hypotheses. Will the recipes be used, the problem being that unhealthy eaters don't use recipes and can't cook or won't cook in the first place? Will the supermarkets use this as free publicity and continue to line their shelves with whatever edible concoctions make the most profit? If one includes preparation time and costs, isn't the mass produced and microwaveable still cheaper? Might the celebrity chef be seen as an obnoxious little **** who would drive anyone to the nearest cheeseburger? This final question was never actually uttered but it did strike me as a plausible rival hypothesis. Both the economy and evaluation research is in a downturn so it is possible that this particular confection of programme theories will receive little formal research attention. But if it does, it is likely to be treated as a newly-minted, self-contained programme and net effect calculations will be attempted despite guaranteed problems of uneven implementation and the nightmare of attribution in the midst of a flurry of competing ideas on the nation's diet. Better to start, I think, with the well-worn theories that underpin it and better to start with some rival theories about their applicability.

This, of course, is a spur of the moment, top of the head example. But it does typify the state of play in all evaluation research, which treats programmes as unique, autonomous entities rather than temporary, malleable containers of old ideas. Proclamations and counter proclamations of plausible rival hypotheses

energise the policy debate and it is curious that this battle of ideas does not feature in evaluation research. Think of the standard antagonisms – should benefits be universal or means tested? should regeneration interventions be top-down or bottom-up? should education be selective or comprehensive? should we measure risk or settle for precaution? do health benefits accrue to the sick or the worried well? should blood donation be based on altruism or payment? should we treat drug abuse as crime or illness? I am not suggesting, for one moment, that evaluation research changes status and attempts to become the arbiter of the great normative debates in social welfare. By the standard realist argument, the resolution to these polarised debating positions is always that 'it depends'. The adjudication mentality is, nevertheless, the key to empirical testing and it should find its metier in relation to the smaller, more tightly focused debates that crop up perpetually about the targeting and tailoring of interventions.

6. The trust–doubt ratio

We now arrive at the point of principle that acknowledges and seeks to accommodate the harsh truth that evaluative knowledge is always partial knowledge. I have repeated, becoming blue in the face, that in all policy analysis the problems addressed and the solutions posited are endlessly complex. VICTORE can never be vanquished. Placing theory at the pivot of evaluative inquiry changes this not one jot. Programmes harbour all manner of activities and influences along their length and breadth. We will always have an excess of contending theories to explain the unfolding of an intervention. An evaluator might make some headway in refereeing between rival accounts of one aspect of the intervention. Collectively, the discipline might then go on to adjudicate between another pair of hypotheses and then go on to rule in or rule out several further explanations for programme outcomes. But, just as surely as day follows night, there will always be further hypotheses, and plausible ones to boot, waiting in the wings.

The way to deal with this predicament is to live with it. Whether the field is natural science or engineering or policy analysis or common sense, we inhabit a world of partial knowledge. Against expectations, we discover that molecular particles travel faster than light (seemingly), that cruise liners topple over, that programmes meet with patchy success, and that true love never runs smooth. Nescience is itself multi-faceted. Smithson's (1989) 'taxonomy of ignorance' runs through the subtle differences between error, irrelevance, untypicality, taboo, undecidability, distortion, incompleteness, confusion, inaccuracy, uncertainty, absence, vagueness, probability, ambiguity, fuzziness and nonspecificity. This list provides a horribly familiar characterisation of much policy discourse. Uncertainty is the norm and in all cases we learn to live with ignorance by reducing it rather than eliminating it.

This is Campbell's (1988: 318) solution to the complexity problem and his exposition of the idea carries several distinctly Campbellian labels, my favourite being the notion of 'squishy foundationalism', explained thus:

> There are no untouchable axioms: All are criticizable and revisable. Nor are there any foundational observations or facts. There are indeed at any historic period in time in any successful science a vast array of trusted facts, but none is immune from revision. For the atomistic ... foundationalism of the positivists we must substitute a holistic, squishy, quasi-foundationalism that I call the 99 to 1 trust–doubt ratio.

Translating this idea into evaluation research means that it is impossible to specify all the ideas that go to make up a complex intervention – let alone put them to empirical investigation. The only available tactic is to trust a sizeable proportion of the programme theory whilst putting certain of its facets to the test in the expectation that knowledge of them can be revised or improved. Campbell was probably unwise to quote a specific fraction for the trust–doubt ratio but the point holds that when a complex programme is under research or evaluation or inspection that its great bulk is left unobserved and empirical attention is and has to be focused. The crucial point is thus: where to focus attention.

Campbell was not the first to place trust in trust. He explains the idea in a paraphrase of a famous metaphor from Quine who in turn borrowed it from Von Neurath:

> We are like sailors who must repair a rotting ship at sea. We trust the great bulk of timbers while we replace a particularly weak plank. Each of the timbers we now trust we may in turn replace. The proportion of planks that we now trust we may in turn replace. The proportion of the planks we are replacing to those we treat as sound must always be small. (Campbell, 1988: 477)

As metaphors go, I much prefer a rival effort from Popper, already quoted in Chapter 1. The foundation depicted there, recall, was also distinctly squishy – the building of a pontoon bridge above a swamp. Inquiry never rests on the bedrock of hard, indisputable facts; rather the piles are driven down to the point where the empirical evidence seems firm enough to carry the particular inference being made. The bridge (and inquiry) then stretches forth adding further sections, which are also supported by empirical pontoons of tolerable strength. And so inquiry advances. Sometimes, we may be drawn back if the reliability of one of the pontoons is called into question. Rival reconsiderations are put to the test, after which we continue with the construction. More and more pontoons are added although we never reach firm ground. Or, to re-quote Popper: 'We simply stop when we are satisfied that they are firm enough to carry the structure, at least for the time being' (1992: 94).

I prefer this image because it bestows some directionality upon science. Inquiry never starts from scratch. All investigation has a history and a future. The edifice is constructed according to the blueprint outlined in this chapter. Theories are built connecting chains of abstract concepts. These models make hypotheses about how the world is ordered and we make progress by testing one prediction against another. A reasonably trustworthy bridge is built in the process of testing a series of plausible rival hypotheses, one after another. And it is here in mid-construction that each investigation actually starts. The next pontoon of inquiry, in the hands of a fresh group of bridge-builders, is planned in order to deal with the next unknown – a task executed, of course, by winnowing out yet further plausible rival hypotheses.

The absolute reliance of evidence-based policy on the trust–doubt ratio could not be exhibited more clearly than in the conduct of research synthesis. The whole exercise involves applying trust – again and again and again. The reviewer is tasked with understanding how, why and where an intervention works by locating the traces of evidence left behind in previous studies within that family of programmes. Only a selection of such programmes will have been evaluated and the reviewer takes on trust that the unresearched will mirror the evidence that is available. The same dissipation of evidence applies when we reach the level of the primary studies. Evaluations do not somehow 'reproduce' the intervention under study. Each evaluation is itself partial, applying particular research techniques to focus on particular features of that intervention, leaving all the rest on trust. The process of prosecuting the doubts and leaving the rest 'nolo contendere' continues as the reviewer moves on to probe the fine texture of the available findings.

Let us test the trust hypothesis by imagining a reviewer absorbing into a synthesis some evidence drawn from interview data. The totality of words spoken, the conduct of each question and of each prompt is likely to be lost in history and even if there are transcripts they most certainly will be hidden from the purview of the reviewer. A good review, nonetheless, might seek to doubt the reliability and validity of the data under the auspices of 'quality appraisal'. The point, again, is that appraisal can only go so far. For example, the reviewer may surmise findings might be distorted because the interview questions had been leading. This suspicion can be checked, up to a point, by close scrutiny of the interview schedule, which is likely to be reported or retrievable. But that is as far as doubt can travel. Thereafter, it is a case of conceding repeatedly to trust. The reviewer will have no perspective on the potential for errors stemming from inaccurate transcription or poor data coding. Nor will the reviewer be able to uncover information on uncertainties rooted in interviewer inexperience or lack of pay or training. Nor is it likely that any of the so-called subject effects on the interview will be available for appraisal, such as respondent disinterest or their capacity to dissemble.

These fragments are a mere overture to the huge list of potential factors that have to be taken on trust. For instance, it is a common cry among reviewers that information on the implementation of interventions and on the context in which they take place is sparse in the extreme in most published research – a tradition kept alive in RCT studies in which a disembodied intervention is compared to an incorporeal non-intervention. The solution, however, is not to produce, reproduce or inspect more data and yet more data. Describing the minute interchanges in the implementation process or enumerating the ever-widening contextual locations of a programme is an infinite task. A more feasible strategy is required – namely for the reviewer to probe those findings which appear most fragile and, in particular, to probe at points where doubt provides us with pressing rival theories to account for a particular finding, which we can then proceed to test.

We are led to a final question – what is that role of evaluative inquiry, once this inevitable use of the trust–doubt ratio is acknowledged? Given the ceaseless emergence of social problems and the perpetual shortfall of attempted solutions and, above all, the unremitting availability of alternative hypotheses to account for this schism, it should be quite clear that the evaluation's function can only ever take the form of 'decision support'. This notion that evidence-based policy ends in advice on the contingencies of programme-making, rather than the authoritative arithmetic on what will work, troubles only its residual, foolhardy, positivist wing. The upshot is that evaluation science should work with the trust–doubt ratio, and work to improve its balance rather than to labour in fear of the odds and in exasperation that they cannot be overcome.

7. Organised scepticism

The major lesson of the previous two sections should now be clear, namely that evaluation cannot hope for perfect objectivity but neither does this mean it should slump into rampant subjectivity. We cannot hope for absolute cleanliness but this does not require us to enjoy a daily roll in the manure. The alternative to these two termini is for evaluation to embrace the goal of being 'validity increasing'. It is of considerable interest to note that the realist justification of this mission includes an organisational as well as a methodological platform. Both Merton (1968: Chapter XVIII) and Campbell (1988: Part 6) produced sociologies of science as well as philosophies of science. In explaining what distinguishes science from other institutions, Merton used the acronym CUDOS to denote its guiding ethos – Communalism, Universalism, Disinterestedness, Originality and Skepticism. It is the latter feature, in its English spelling, that constitutes the final desideratum of evaluation science.

Organised scepticism means that any scientific claim must be exposed to critical scrutiny before it becomes accepted. My favourite rendition of the idea comes in another enigmatic phrase from Geertz, who readers may remember as the anthropologist who feared that his discipline merely wandered aimlessly from one descriptive case study to another. He too wished for organised scepticism, rendered as: 'the precision in which we vex each other' (1973: 25). Not only should studies cross-refer, each inquiry should seek to challenge, enlarge and refine the inferences drawn in a previous study. Note the key element – precision. Vexing each other is something policy makers and normative social 'scientists' do willy-nilly, what counts is the depth of critical scrutiny applied to the inferences drawn from any inquiry. And this level of attention depends, in turn, on the presence of a collegiate group of stakeholders and their willingness to put each other's work under the microscope.

We reach the $64,000 question for this section – how does one organise 'organised scepticism'? Judgemental, discretionary components are unavoidable in evaluation research. It is a long road from the commissioning of a piece of research, through its execution and on to its utilisation. It is interesting to ponder where and whether in that extended journey we find the application of precise, vexatious cross-examination. By and large it is the policy makers who make judgements on what problems should receive attention, what programmes should be funded and researched. They rejoin the fray at the end of the process with decisions on whether to use or ignore the research. Being highly politicised arenas, we can say that vexation is at a peak at these points, though such debate is not renowned for its precision. Another group, the practitioners, make endless judgements in the building of a programme and, depending on the chosen mode of evaluation, it is their implementation decisions that are likely to receive the closest scrutiny. But what about the third party? Who evaluates the evaluators? Who makes judgements about their judgements?

Not for the first time, Campbell puts his finger on the problem, which he terms 'the single evaluator model'. His (1988: 323) description of the 'one decision/one research' strategy still rings true. Programmes are funded by some central authority which also commissions a single research team to evaluate the first major manifestation of a programme. This tends to be organised on a once and for all basis and led by the ultimate question – does it work? Should the programme pass muster, its longer-term future is likely to remain unmolested by further calls for evidence. Under such an arrangement, the results of the evaluation are likely to be very heavily policed, its conduct far less so. However 'independent' the evaluator, sponsors always have control over the outputs and recommendations and, if all else fails, they can simply 'sit' on the results. By contrast, commissioners are likely to concede methodological expertise to the evaluators and the formal scrutiny of the research act is more likely to be confined to such matters as keeping to timetable, meeting agreed interview numbers, and dispatching interim reports appropriately. In short the standard commissioning structure induces a rather superficial 'performance management' approach to research scrutiny. As such it fails to interrogate any of the crucial issues that really bring science into evaluation – the distillation and exploration of programme theories, the promotion and adjudication of rival hypotheses, the decisions on what to trust and what to explore, etc.

There have been some significant changes in the structure of evaluation research since Campbell penned this gloomy prognostication. Methodological preferences have widened considerably, most notably the considerable increase in the repertoire of evaluation methods and the advent of systematic reviews and research syntheses. And then there is the sheer 'industrialisation' of evaluation, the arrival on the scene of more evaluators, more specialist evaluation journals, more professional evaluation associations, more published standards and protocol statements, and many, many more evaluation congresses and colloquia.

It would take a not insubstantial book to chart the consequences of these reconfigurations. I will attempt to cope with one paragraph. There are still reasons to doubt whether these changes have fostered competitive cross-validation. The expansion of any profession with roots in social science is apt to draw in its chaos of warrior paradigms. Whilst this might seem to provide a promising competitive infrastructure it also harbours a contrary impulse to organised subversion rather than organised scepticism. The vast growth in journals catering for policy evaluation allows many contrasting voices to be heard. Alas, it also comes close to assuring safe passage for all reportage; welcoming homes can be found for most methodological approaches, for most substantive conclusion and for most political preferences. The exponential growth in the number of journal papers submitted also means that the search for referees is tough and often ends in expedient choices from a paper's own reference list. Similar tribal loyalties may also underpin the choice of discussants, advisory group members and scientific committees, and so limit their role to providing succour rather than cross-examination. The role of standards, protocols and quality appraisal is to establish procedural uniformity and to vouchsafe only certain forms of evidence, more or less the opposite of the anti-authoritarian idea of focused disputation. Short papers, summaries, and poster presentations are increasingly favoured as the means of research dissemination, often leaving little opportunity for others to scrutinise what lies beneath. One casualty of the bullet point tendency is the virtual disappearance of the old-style critiques, replies and rejoinders in published literature. The proximity to the polity remains the great opportunity but also the ever-present curse of evaluation research. The political impulse to favour a particular approach and annihilate all opposition also obliterates any significant interest in adjudicating between rival hypotheses on some finer detail of a programme's implementation. Finally, there remains the old problem with our core business, namely – the business opportunities provided by the next programme. In the world of commissioned research, no one commissions the opportunity to collectively re-examine and rake over rival claims and counter claims about existing programmes when, coming over the horizon, there is an unmolested, unevaluated intervention.

I have presented a somewhat pessimistic view in my allotted paragraph, with the idea of painting the dark backdrop to the glimmers of hope. Before seeking the light, I should emphasise that I am not easily moved from the belief that the critical scrutiny of evaluation research tends either to the bloodthirsty or to the non-existent. Ideological and paradigmatic ire is easily provoked. But here is the key point. Nowhere in the expansion of evaluation has a function emerged in which one part of the discipline combs routinely over the fine texture of evaluation reports of their colleagues with the idea of considering whether its conclusions are firmly warranted in the evidence presented. In the world of contract research, no one is contracted to vex another's research.

Campbell, needless to say, had some bright ideas for 'getting mutual criticism and competitive replication into social experimentation and program evaluation'

(1998: 327). He prefaced his remarks by noting that none of them was practised in the United States at the time of writing. Here is an instant summary. Rather than evaluate only new programmes, research should be commissioned on mature or what he calls 'proud' interventions. Rather than awarding single contracts, research commissioners should let them as two or more independent studies – the beginnings of 'heteromethod' replication. There should be 'adversarial stakeholder participation' in the design of inquiries, so that alternative theories and feared unintentional outcomes will receive equal research attention to that placed upon promised benefits. There should be funded, competitive reanalysis of the major studies. Big studies produce big databases and it is a truism that only fragments of evidence are ever fully analysed. Finally and most dramatically, he encourages a form of 'whistle-blowing'. Closest of all to the data are the research teams that produce and analyse them. Since evidence is always multiply interpretable it is likely that there will be dissenting voices within the original team. Campbell's wish for organised scepticism extended to the desire to give every humble research assistant the right to publish independently. In terms of the formal commissioning of inquiries, I beg to suggest that these ideas are no nearer to the core mentality of evaluation research than they were in Campbell's day. However, there are glimmers of hope.

The first has already occurred and is signalled by the change in 'branding' of the entire exercise from evaluation research to evidence-based policy and the coming reliance on reviews of collectivities of evidence rather than the episodic, one question/one inquiry strategy. To be sure, there are paradigmatic wrangles here: no greeting cards being exchanged between, say, proponents of meta-analytic, meta-ethnographic and meta-narrative reviews. And indeed, there are also attempts to treat the act of synthesis as a technical exercise, closely bound by procedures and protocols. However, speaking of the approach to synthesis over which I can claim some acquaintance, a modest degree of vexing, hopefully of a precise kind, is incorporated.

No single study, primary study or review, can embody organised scepticism, it being a function of the efforts of a research community. Realist synthesis, nevertheless, aims to incorporate competitive cross-validation as its connecting thread. Each primary study incorporated in the review is subjected to critical scrutiny. This not a matter of favouring or disfavouring particular research designs but assessing whether the evidence brought forth supports adequately the inferences made. It is these inferences, the explanations for a programme's fortunes, that are the focus. Not only are dozens of programmes on show, but scores of competing hypotheses, inferences and theories are also there to behold. The very task of synthesis is about probing the clash of theories in order to seek their resolution. A first inquiry will contain some proto-explanation of why a programme performs as per the evidence constructed. The act of critical scrutiny lies in using a second study to qualify and adjust the inferences of the first. A third study is added to test the inference drawn from whatever emerged from the adjudication of the initial pair, a fourth inquiry is positioned to refine further the developing explanation, and so on. The repeated application of this process is synthesis. There is no final point. Other researchers and other reviewers will be able to refine, qualify and situate the developing understanding. It is the collective scrutiny of one inquiry from the perspective of another that keeps the process honest and thus may be said to be 'validity increasing'.

The second glimmer of hope lies in an arena previously painted in a rather negative light. Policy making at its political end, as everyone knows, is impatient with evidence. Although evaluation is increasingly acknowledged in these quarters, it is often hijacked in throwaway assertions about what the evidence 'shows', sometimes backed by a favoured illustration or two from a favoured study. But note, we are discussing political football here and the thing about football is that it has two sides per game and a league full of opinions overall. The political sphere is undeniably a hothouse for developing arguments about why an intervention will or will not work. The basic form of political reasoning is that subjects, being what they are, will respond to an intervention in a particular manner and that reaction will seal the fate of the intervention. Opponents will specify a different reaction and a different policy outcome. If one puts these propositions together, there is the beginning of some rival realist hypothesis about for whom and in what circumstances and why an intervention might work. In short and with modifications, the football match is capable of being refereed. The suggestion here, rather than to shun politics, is to incorporate its rival assumptions into the core of the method. Chapter 8 will provide an example of how realist synthesis can throw light into the heated politics of smoking control legislation. The idea is to organise scepticism by transforming normative posturing into competitive cross validation.

My third sighting of the rare beast of organised scepticism within evaluation is indeed a part of its social structure and a modern development to boot. Recall that what is sought is competitive debate and discussion on agreed grounds rather than under territorial banners. Such channels are much more likely to develop and to have meaning if mustered informally, thus carrying a degree of anti-authoritarianism. Merton's norm of universalism, access for all involved to have a say, is often captured in the backchannels of science. It is a form of social networking and evaluation has provided vehicles for such activity. I am not describing an Evaluation Facebook here. I am not claiming an Arab Spring of Evidence. Nevertheless, evaluation research has moved on from the splendid isolation of separate inquiries. Alongside the industrial growth there are many more cottage industries, informal spaces in which evaluators can listen and learn and swap advice. I am thinking, in the wider sphere, of such channels as *Evaltalk* (http://aea365.org/blog/?tag=evaltalk). In the particular domain of realist evaluation, there is also brisk discussion as exemplified in the two websites associated with this book (see preface).

Drowning or waving? ———

I conclude Part Two by returning to the question posed at its outset – under the challenge of complexity does evaluation research drown or come up waving? I am afraid I have had to report upon quite a few dead bodies washed upon the shore. As for the survivors, none of them have managed to surf the big wave and returned in harmony with the seething ocean (I believe the expression is 'stoked'). As best as I can understand it would seem that the survivors are still out there, continually driving down the bridge pontoons or fixing the raft on which their journey depends.

It has to be this way because complexity confronts evaluation with a never-ending challenge that cannot be completed. My first conclusion is thus to call on evaluation to begin an endless journey. It should probe, in investigation after investigation, at the boundaries of where programme theory 1 has applicability. The effort should be repeated in respect of where programme theory 2 holds good, where programme theory 3 finds its domain, and so on. The exploration of each new theory adds to the totality of understanding whilst at the same time circumscribing the reach of previous theories. Such a gradual, progressive, cumulative process of inquiry is difficult to maintain. It can just as easily go round in circles. My second conclusion suggests that maintaining this ever-shifting, mutually-improving, validity-increasing, middle ground can only be achieved collectively and through constant critical scrutiny of each other's work.

The end result will be partial knowledge about partial improvements we can make in the delivery and targeting of social interventions – quite an achievement.

PART 3
Towards Evaluation Science

' ... methodology is too important to be left to methodologists' (Becker, 1970: 3).

Much of Part Two was lost in the thoughts of the armchair philosopher and the task of Part Three is to redress the balance by addressing the concerns of the jobbing researcher. In the previous chapter I concocted a rather elaborate set of principles for the execution of a realist evaluation science. Evaluators should lead with theory, use concepts at middle levels of abstraction, recycle conceptual platforms, build models, adjudicate between plausible rival hypotheses, trust most programme assumptions whilst challenging a few, and monitor disputatiously the work of every other researcher in the same field (a.k.a. TARMATO). Although pocket illustrations were provided, there is no substitute for a full exposition accompanied with practical examples. To this end, this part of the book contains three chapters brimful of empirical materials.

Chapter 6 provides an extended illustration of the idea of 'conceptual platforms'. The issue, recall, is that evaluation research tends to start each inquiry anew instead of researching the given programme as yet another specimen of a familiar genus. Accordingly, the question under consideration is one that troubles researchers both pimply and grey-bearded, namely – where to start? Having forsaken method-driven research for theory-driven inquiry, we still have to face a formidable choice of potential drivers, a conundrum that I always think of as Weiss's (2000) question – 'which links in which theories should we evaluate?' The chapter presents an illustration of how such a platform might be conceived, diving into particularly stormy waters in suggesting a generic, conceptual anchorage for the evaluation of 'behaviour change programmes'. There are endless psychological theories of behavioural change. Many governments have been captivated by a popular version of behavioural change, going by the name of 'nudge'. The chapter suggests a different primary orientation led by a programming perspective and led by an evaluation question – what are the components of behavioural change that an intervention must prompt in order to achieve lasting outcomes?

Chapter 7 is a reworking of the same platform. Recall that the whole idea is about reusable conceptual platforms and this chapter evokes the principle by recycling the generic structure established in the previous chapter and applying it to a different domain. Again, I use a provocative illustration in choosing the example of clinical interventions as the guinea pig. The effectiveness of clinical interventions turns on the application of the specific remedy, medicine, prophylactic, antidote, purgative, tonic, drug, balm, surgery or therapy. At the same time, however, there is always a behavioural change component in which the patient seeks out, decides upon, participates in, stays with, co-produces, exits and comes to terms with the treatment and whatever befalls as a result of the treatment. What would the evaluation of clinical interventions look like if this behavioural sequence was the conceptual platform? How would inquiry on clinical interventions be organised if they were regarded as social interventions?

Chapter 8 is the *denouement* of the entire tale. Moreover, it takes to heart Becker's old war-cry denouncing the professional 'methodologist'. It faces the sceptic's blunt challenge – so, Pawson, let us see you practice what you preach! The chapter is based on a large-scale realist synthesis of the complex and contested evidence-base of the potential effectiveness of a ban on smoking in cars carrying children. Other versions of this research are already in the public domain (Pawson et al., 2011a; Wong et al., 2011). This chapter uses the review to show how each of the seven strategies in the TARMATO typology can be incorporated in the one study. To be sure, I have emphasised that the analysis of complex policy domains is only really accomplished by deploying a sequence of studies scrutinised by a jury of diligent onlookers. Nevertheless, the green shoots of the TARMATO principles should be discernible in any good realist inquiry and this investigation is presented as a modest step in that direction.

SIX

Invisible Mechanisms I: The Long Road to Behavioural Change

It makes intuitive sense that better working conditions would improve productivity. In the same way it is clear that street lighting or closed circuit television should work by increasing surveillability. Plague reduction should work by drowning witches, and fever should be reduced by the extraction of overheated blood. We have been too ready to assume that how crime prevention *should* work is the way that crime prevention *does* work. (Smith et al., 2002)

Evaluation research bestows credit on interventions. It is often defined as the systematic determination of the merit, worth, and significance of programmes. This chapter concurs with the epigraph above in pondering whether evaluators always give credit where credit is due. Smith et al.'s suspicion, and it is one that applies well beyond crime prevention, is that the way interventions are conceptualised in evaluation research often leads investigation to assess and valorise only a small portion of the active ingredients needed for change. Indeed, sometimes, entirely the wrong agent is designated as possessing causal powers. Note that the thesis, engagingly put as it is, is not about intervention content. The remedy to the attribution problem does not lie in the enlightened escape from simplistic, medieval thoughts about the benefits of garrotting, leaches, oracles, witch-drowning and blood-letting. The argument is a methodological one, namely that social and behavioural change happens slowly and painstakingly, that a whole sequence of measures is required to bring about profound and lasting change, and that methods of evaluation research are not always up to scratch in being able to identify the crucial concatenations.

This chapter seeks to develop this thesis with a closer look at the core realist concept of the programme mechanism. Mechanisms are agents of change. They describe how the resources embedded in a programme influence the reasoning and ultimately the behaviour of programme subjects. Studying mechanisms propels the researcher right to the business end of interventions but, as we now know, that business is always complex. Accordingly, the chapter seeks to throw light on the presence of an overlooked set of programme mechanisms so deeply buried that they are almost invisible. We are not chasing shadows here. We are not dealing in exotica. The processes I have in mind are missed because they are tacit, mundane, over-familiar, and taken for granted. They stare evaluators in the face and as a result they are often overlooked. And yet, as I will attempt to show, they are often responsible for a goodly part of the impact of a goodly number of interventions.

To obtain a first glimpse of some of these subdued corners of interventions it is worth considering, in very general terms, how programmes are assembled. Policy making is energised by the hot new idea. Attention is thus drawn immediately to the unique properties and powers of the new 'measure', 'treatment', 'therapy', 'mechanism of action', or 'theory of change'. To be sure, other eyes are also on the prize, namely impact on the intended outcome. Accordingly, interventions find support and are brought to life if there are persuasive reasons to believe that a new-fangled idea might have a significant leverage on a long-standing problem.

But what happens next? The machine takes over. The intervention is assembled in a series of standard, bureaucratic procedures. The programme has to be organised and delivered – sites are mulled over and selected, resources are drawn in and allo-cated, staff roles are planned and allotted, and subjects are recruited, processed, cer-tificated and stood down. The working hypothesis here is that these routine features, the generics of programming, often have as profound an influence on the behaviour of programme subjects as do the big ideas. People enter programmes at the margins and sometimes quite tangentially. They have an existing life outside programmes. There are always other programmes. Life offers many new opportunities besides pro-grammes. And once within the ambit of a programme there are many opportunities to quit or stay. And even within those choosing to be camp followers, there is a range of behavioural commitments from passing interest to dull compunction to abiding passion. There are many such collateral pathways for so-called 'programme subjects' to consider, and the manner in which participants choose to navigate their way in and around interventions has been overlooked in evaluation research. These strategies for journeying through, rather than responding to, interventions deserve a sustained programme of research and this chapter sets out a brief agenda for such inquiries.

1   The first part of the chapter provides some examples, some sightings of these shy creatures. Quite deliberately, the search for invisible mechanisms travels across the policy waterfront and covers prisoner education, psychotherapy, body mas-sage, crime prevention, youth mentoring and disability benefits. Such a breadth of vision fulfils one of our ambitions for realist evaluation science. Working at this level of abstraction grabs a gain on complexity. Ground coverage begins with a cross-domain adumbration of the hidden ingredients of behavioural change.

2   The purpose of this Cook's tour, fulfilled in section two, is to build a generic conceptual platform for studying behavioural change within interventions. The challenge of moving from insider to outsider in any walk of life is considerable. On offer is a sequential model of the totality of choices, which take the typical par-ticipant from programme outsider to programme adherent. The model culminates in

pinpointing the parallel sequence of resources that interventions need to marshal in order to prompt and sustain positive momentum.

3   The third section of the chapter considers the ramifications of the model for policy making and evaluation. The core argument is that programme builders often fail to cater sufficiently for the invisible, tacit elements of behavioural change and should build people-processing mechanisms more carefully into interventions. Likewise evaluators, with their fixation on destinations, tend to overlook the vicissitudes of the journey.

———— 1. Latent procedures in implementation and evaluation ————

Here begins the Cook's tour (i.e. swift but wide ranging) around these preliminary, peripheral, contemplative quarters of interventions. All of the examples examine findings from initiatives put to evaluation, but often my focus is to look beneath at what programme participants have made of their experience. Where and when do latent mechanisms begin to reveal their inscrutable faces?

… Behind bars

My first illustration ponders the influence of the most mundane activity, namely waiting. There is not an intervention in the world that at some stage does not put the participant 'on hold'. Figure 6.1 provides us with some direct evidence on waiting. These are data from a pilot investigation of a 'cognitive skills' programme aimed at reducing recidivism in a group of inmates in Canadian federal prisons (Porporino and Robinson, 1995). Even within this captive population one cannot require subjects to attend programmes. Subjects are volunteers and the conventional

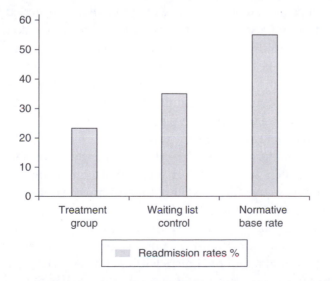

Figure 6.1   Prison readmission rates compared (*Source*: Porporino and Robinson, 1995)

way of evaluating impact whilst countering the associated 'self-selection' effect is to run a trial comparing treated subjects with those who have also volunteered but are kept, often permanently and surreptitiously, on a 'waiting list'.

What is revealed in these data? The conventional interpretation is that the intervention indeed offers benefits, as can be seen from the lower rates of return to prison of the experimentees (20%) as opposed to the waiting-list controls (32%). The fact that we are dealing with a reasonably well-disposed group is also demonstrated by the gains in the untreated volunteers as opposed to the baseline rate, where the revolving door of reincarceration revolves at over 50%. This reading only has eyes for the experimentalist's overriding concern, namely that treatment and control groups are entirely equivalent – save for the application of the programme.

But what exactly is the disposition of the control group? To be sure they are not undergoing treatment. Nor are they doing nothing – they are serving time. Nor, most significantly, are they undergoing the 'normal prison regime' – for they are also waiting. So the crucial question becomes, what are the inmates doing and thinking whilst waiting for the programme? Are they growing impatient or are they learning forbearance? Are the shelved prisoners fuming: 'I applied effing five months ago. Sameabloodygain. They pretend to be interested in your wellbeing but they couldn't organise a piss up in a brewery. What's the point of trying to change?' Or does fortitude win out? Are the jilted detainees calculating: 'Yeah, they're always playing mind games, keeping you waiting, testing you out, trying to see if you are really serious about trying to change. I'm gonna bide my time and keep my nose clean.' The answer, of course, is that we do not know. As far as I'm aware no serious research attention has ever been directed at the folks on hold. But what should at the very least be contemplated are the powerful and potentially life-changing emotions represented by our two imaginary outbursts above. And as such, ladies and gentlemen, they represent our first sighting of invisible mechanisms.

I am trying to suggest, via the inmates' notional thoughts, that the members of the 'control group' are hardly in the state of repose that is suggested by that term. Dispositions are never fixed, even in the side-wash of the intervention. This location in itself can trigger impatience or forbearance. If this data on the welcome progress of the middle group is to be believed, it would seem that fortitude rather than anger is in the ascendancy for the men held in line at this particular time. The lack of anticipated support does not turn them significantly back to the pack. At the very margins of a programme, we witness a complex calculation. A future course of action is contemplated, an opportunity along the way is spotted and then stymied, and other ways of continuing in the direction of travel are apparently discovered. Here then is a brief glimpse of the latent action of a programme – if all this reckoning and re-reckoning happens to subjects supposedly twiddling thumbs in the control condition, what other thought permutations transpire over the life-course of an intervention?

We stay within prison walls for my next illustration. The theme, however, continues – programmes are not things, not dosages but complex social situations opening up a potential menu of choices within choices. What else might entice the subject to take a seat at the intervention table? What other imperceptible offerings might be served up? Duguid (2000), a practitioner, researcher and theorist of 'prisoner education', comes up with the following counter-intuitive recipe – offer education as a rehabilitative therapy and it will fail; offer education for its own sake and it will carry over into rehabilitation.

The idea was made manifest in the Simon Fraser Prison Education Programme. This 'campus in the prison' programme ran for two decades in several Canadian penitentiaries. Its 'non-prison' features, such as the following, were heavily promoted:

- *External affiliation:* The programme is as avowedly 'mainstream' as the difficult conditions of imprisonment allowed; on offer were degrees and diplomas from Simon Fraser University; faculty crossed between university and prison; credits were transferable to outside institutions.
- *Participatory control:* The education block was separate and for the most part self-policed; provision was rolling and year-round; prisoner 'graduates' could become course tutors.
- *Open access:* The choice to enter, stay or leave the programme was that of the students and perhaps above all, talk of therapy, counselling, reform and rehabilitation was 'off-limits'.

Note that none of these features concerns programme content. The first describes a mechanism to promote entry; the second provides a reason to stay; and the third a means on which to build. It is perhaps useful to return once again to Duguid's primary proposition. He is the last to dispute the idea that other and perhaps more tangible aspects of prisoner reform, such as the improvements in employability or cognitive ability or social skills, are brought into play via such educational programmes. The contention is that these gains are facilitated because of a learning environment offering many points of contact between where the prisoners are and where they might want to be.

Before we exit the prison I call on the direct testimony of some prisoner students, for whom the workings of the non-remedial remedy is clear. I return to some interviews of my own (reported in Pawson, 1996) conducted in a UK prison, but on the same topic how education might promote change in inmates. These were hardly cosy chats. Indeed the exchanges were somewhat fiery as the men clarified who called the shots in determining their futures. A common theme was that education was not rehabilitative but that the 'hands-off' approach deepened a process of self-scrutiny that was already underway. Let me boil these sentiments down a couple of examples:

> It's not the course that's changed you as such, it's you've developed an interest inside you, you know. By and large you've got your own way of working. And you can work in a number of directions … you're sort of given advice on which way to go and that, but at the end of the day it's your own choice.

> I feel that education is a civilising process … it could well be a contributing factor in the adjustment to acceptable behaviour. Change is something that comes within you but you would be taking on board education … it's a catalyst … more than a catalyst, as I've said before, it's a civilising process.

Listen again to these words of wisdom – a 'catalyst to action' and a 'civilising process'. If I recall my O-level chemistry, catalysts are substances that increase the rate of change without taking part in the reaction. Civilising processes are a classic 'emergent process' in the sociological literature (Elias, 1969). They are a long-term outcome of collective action without necessarily being part of the volition of any individual. Here, and stemming from direct experience, are a couple more admirable ways of expressing the notion of the latent forces embedded in programmes.

… On the therapist's couch

For our next case study, we turn from the province of 'Nothing Works' to the domain of the 'Dodo's Verdict'. Alice, during her adventures in Wonderland, comes across a curious competition officiated by a dodo bird. It is a simple enough contest, a race around a lake. The twist is that no one bothers to measure times, distances, placements and so on. Instead, the dodo explains: 'Everybody has won and all must have prizes.'

This same unflattering verdict has been bestowed on psychotherapy. There are many, many different therapeutic schools. One count, made forty years ago (Parloff, 1986), estimated the number at 418. A thunderous and long-standing critique argues that the specific techniques associated with specific schools (e.g. Freudian, Jungian, Rogerian, Adlerian, behavioural, cognitive, gestalt, existential, etc. etc.) serve very limited purpose and that most of the positive effect is gained due to therapeutic relationship. This hypothesis known as 'common factor theory' associates positive change with 'non-specifics' emanating from purposeful, warm, respectful, tailor-made, one-to-one relationships between practitioner and client.

Psychotherapy has always been a hot topic for evaluation. As these inquiries grew, there evolved a comparative component in which the efficacy of rival or alternative treatments was investigated. These are known as 'active treatment comparisons'. Instead of placing patients in conventional treatment and control conditions, they are randomly assigned to one of two treatments (e.g. cognitive vs. behavioural). The two conditions are thus 'matched' as per normal trial logic. As these studies gathered pace it became possible to conduct meta-analyses of the efficacy of 'x' versus 'y'. Systematic reviews of this ilk by Luborsky and colleagues in 1975, and repeated in 2002 with a much larger sample of primary studies, came down heavily in favour of the dodo bird verdict. Very few primary studies demonstrated the superiority of one treatment over another. In the round, the meta-analysis estimates that the effect size attributable to specific therapy techniques weighs in with a Cohen's d coefficient of only 0.2 (small and insignificant in lay parlance). By this interpretation all therapies are more or less equal – and almost all should win prizes (or perhaps be amalgamated, simplified and demystified!).

Whilst debate continues to rumble about the precise arithmetical contribution of the common factors in common factor theory (Chambless, 2002), few seem to deny the significance of the 'non-specifics'. It is much more useful for present purposes to look at attempts to discern and itemise their collective content. A number of researchers have attempted to locate precisely what is common in common factor theory. Following an extensive review of the client's experience,

Tallman and Bohart (1999: 106) conclude: 'In sum, from the client's perceptive, the most important aspects of therapy are ... the personality of the therapist; having a time and place to talk; having someone to care, listen and understand; having someone provide encouragement and advice; having someone to help you understand your problems'.

Strupp (1986), from an earlier generation of research into 'non-specific factors', pinpoints a different causal mechanism, namely the guiding force of 'theory' in galvanising the psychotherapeutic process. The argument here is not about the distinctive thoughts of any of the 418 (or more) schools of thought. Rather it focuses on the very existence of 'a theory' in underpinning and guiding the intervention. The theory provides therapists with a resource capable of organising and planning the treatment. It also provides them with intensity and depth of purpose to keep them engaged over a long time. Finally, the theory may be said to certify and legitimate their particular approach. These capacities are no small matters from the point of view of the client, a point made engagingly in the following passage:

> The very fact that the therapist has a *theory* of human difficulty encourages the patient to recognise the possibility that whatever is bothering him may have happened before, to someone else. This is a powerful idea for someone suffering mightily with serious depression, or is experiencing a divorce, or the loss of a loved one, or similar emotional pain. This guy who seems to know about such things, doesn't appear to be in nearly as much agony as me ... And the guy keeps listening. Maybe the sixth or eighth time you say it, it won't hurt so much ... Not only that, even though I have been crying like a baby, he takes it seriously – he seems to think that my unhappiness *means* something. He's willing to take it seriously and interpret it with me. We work out an understanding ... which makes sense of the inchoate, the anomalous, the unapproachable. (Moerman, 2002: 95)

Whilst the enactment of programme theories may not always be played out to such a dramatic effect, once more I make the point about the potential ubiquity of the process described here. Generally speaking, people who volunteer for programmes are seeking to 'work out an understanding'. They are always on the lookout for theories – the operative issue being that it is not only therapists who trade in theories. When it comes to implementing programmes – cops have theories, teachers have theories, big brothers have theories, ward sisters have theories, and safety inspectors have theories. All of them may gather adherents.

... On the floormat

We are not yet done with the non-specific effects for there are other important conjectures claiming that they kick in before treatment even begins. Rather than garnering lessons only from academic research let us once again hear it from the horse's mouth. In this case, practitioner wisdom emanates not so much from the couch but the floormat. Latey is author of *Muscular Manifesto* (1979) and whilst specialising in so-called 'bodywork', he has clearly spent time reading the minds of his clients. In the following passage Latey (2001: 149) goes well beyond the customary recognition that patient 'self-motivation' is crucial by going on to describe how this vital spark might be encouraged and enhanced by creating certain preconditions to receiving treatment:

> I believe it helps if patients have had to surmount some difficulties in order to get to see the practitioner, as follows: i) a wait for an appointment at a time that may not be easy for them, ii) some directions to follow if practitioners are off the map of their usual movements, iii) the effort of organising their account of the problem, iv) preparing to be questioned, examined and treated in the first session. The fact that they are willing to pay for treatment, however small the fee, makes a considerable difference ... people expect to pay and do not count the cost when their health is at stake. Timeliness is also crucial. So it helps if patients have understood the problem is not going to clear up by itself, and they have reached a point where it must simply be sorted out. All the better if they have also abandoned previous attempts at treatment with enough time for it to be obvious that they have failed.

Here then is another jewellery box of invisible mechanisms that may contribute crucially to programme efficacy. To be sure, as presented, they are evidenced only in anecdote, but practitioner wisdom has a habit of being shared and is a prime source of programme theory. We have already encountered perverse effects with prisoner subjects on waiting list controls and, interestingly, Latey also recommends being positively artful with the 'keep 'em waiting' strategy. However, this is but one of a number of other pre-intervention strategies that may be transferable – intensive openings, speed off the mark, quick wins, immediate active role for client, arrival in the last chance saloon, and not forgetting that nod to the old advertising slogan, 'you've tried the rest now buy the best'.

... In Fagin's den

The roll call of invisible programme mechanisms continues as we revisit the stunning epigraph to this chapter, the first lines from a paper entitled, 'Anticipatory benefits in crime prevention' (Smith et al., 2002). This is a useful variation to our thinking about the tacit powers of interventions because the goal in this policy domain is to control and constrain potential action. Previous examples covered attempts to fire and facilitate fresh thinking and behaviour. Latent mechanisms can operate both ways. Smith et al.'s central argument is that we should never jump to conclusions about the 'self-evident' causal powers of interventions. Crime reduction, for the most part, works by persuading potential offenders that the risk of apprehension and arrest increases substantially under a newly-installed programme. Since perception is the key, the authors hypothesise that the threat of action of an intervention may be as powerful as the specifics of action.

Many programmes appear to show improvement (crime reduction) before the programme is up and running. Indeed, some seem to work without them being fully implemented. This hypothesis is forwarded on the basis of a review of the crime prevention literature. A search was undertaken locating studies containing time series data sufficiently powerful to distinguish crime fluctuations before, during and after the introduction of prevention programmes. Fifty-two such reports were uncovered, which revealed an unexpected pre-initiative drop in crime statistics. Of these, 22 had collected strong *prima facie* evidence that allowed causal attribution to 'something' occurring within the early inception of the scheme. For instance, a study of the effects of security patrols on cycle parking lots showed that announcing the scheme was followed by a reduction in crime levels before 'foot was ever laid to pedal' (Barclay et al., 1997). The unpublicised withdrawal of the patrols, moreover, did not result in an immediate increase in crime. Further 'pre-ignition effects' relating to the up-coming installation of CCTV cameras, security devices, alcohol testing, physical layout improvements and so on are discovered and corroborated in the review (Smith et al., 2002: 73–76).

So what is the 'something' that could account for these unanticipated, anticipatory effects? Smith and colleagues (pp. 78–79) list ten possible mechanisms, which I abridge thus:

- *Evaluation artefacts.* These include some time-honoured measurement headaches such as regression to the mean, difficulties with calculating moving-averages, and the perennial problem of seasonal shifts in recorded levels of crime.
- *Practitioner and subject effects.* These include improvement in knowledge and motivation of the local population and police officers on the announcement of a new scheme, which translate into increased determination, greater diligence and better performance in advance of the initiative.
- *Offender effects.* These include both the 'over-anticipation' effect, in which equipment is supposed to be operational before it actually is and the 'disinformation' effect in which publicity and hearsay carry the impression that a powerful, covert programme is already in place.

Again we see a catch-all description, in this instance 'anticipatory effects', netting a miscellany of possible mechanisms. The point for emphasis is that none of the above is part of the intended measure; all are part of the implementation and evaluation apparatus – and all are open to further and more mindful manipulation by programme planners. And, it is in this respect that the latter item in the list excites attention. If we think of crime, at least some crime, as an 'intelligence-led' operation then 'counter-intelligence' becomes an option in its curtailment.

How could such a mechanism be embodied in a formal intervention? The active ingredient in all the cases reviewed appears to centre around the circulation of information – getting the word out on the street. The optimal working example is probably the action of 'decoy vehicles' in reducing car theft. Cars and vans, similar to those favoured by thieves, are parked in high vehicle crime locations. They are fitted with technical devices making it possible to track or, sometimes, trap the intruder. Whilst this immediate and tangible mechanism is what does the job in apprehending offenders (successful patrol car chase permitting), there is good evidence that hearsay buttressed by media campaigns is the latent mechanism that really brings down overall rates in a locality (Sallybanks, 2001). The scheme makes would-be offenders ponder precisely at the point when they normally sense an easy-picking. And that rumination is deepened if they have in mind television pictures of the spectacular and embarrassing failure associated with being so outwitted. Whichever impulse wins the day, it seems that rumour and counter-rumour, intelligence and counter-intelligence about programme potency join our list of their latent mechanisms.

… At the mentor's knee

More latent mechanisms reside in another characteristic chapter in the world of interventions, namely mentoring programmes aimed at disaffected young people. As ever, the tale has broader ramifications in that it follows a pattern much observed in programme evaluation, namely – the shining success of a major demonstration project followed by the failure of subsequent 'replications'. Why is this misfortune familiar?

The best known programme in this domain is the venerable *Big Brother Big Sister Programme* (BBBS). The best known study (Grossman and Tierney, 1998: 403) reports:

> Taken together, the results presented here show that having a Big Brother or a Big Sister offers tangible benefits for youth. At the conclusion of the 18 month study period, we found that Little Brothers and Little Sisters were less likely to have started using drugs or taking alcohol, felt more competent about doing school work, attended school more, got better grades, and have better relationships with their parents and peers than they would have if they had not participated in the programme.

Alas, such optimism has not survived many replications in the US and UK (Colley, 2003). There, a more familiar sequence for the mentee is progress and setback, progress and setback, with the mentor having to spend considerable time 'fire-fighting' family feuds, drug relapse, gang violence and so on (Shiner et al., 2004). The obvious explanation for this contrast between the originator and the imitators is to look for differences in implementation and context. But what are they? A close look at Grossman and Tierney's (1998 425) description of BBBS reveals some vital clues and lifts the lid on another important set of latent programme mechanisms.

The study footnotes a formidable set of eligibility requirements, and some vital clues on the participants' aspirations lie here. We commence with a familiar sighting. BBBS is indeed a venerable programme, having existed for a hundred years, and thus sufficiently cherished to require a waiting list. Oversubscription thus prompts screening, which involves: an assessment for a 'minimal level of social skills'; ensuring that youths and parents actually 'want a mentor'; gaining the 'agreement of parent and child to follow agency rules'; successful completion of 'orientation and training sessions'; and the fulfilment of 'residential and age limitations'. Once on the programme there is 'close supervision and support of each match by a case manager who makes frequent contact with the parent/guardian, volunteer, and youth and provides assistance when requested'. The voluntary status of the mentors gives authenticity to their guidance but they also receive 'training that includes communication and limit-setting skills, tips on relationship building and recommendations on the best way to interact with a young person'. In addition to these programme requirements, the research created exclusions of its own, namely for youths with 'physical and learning difficulties' and for those 'serving a contractual obligation such as Child Protection Service contract'.

This welter of self, bureaucratic and investigatory selection is, of course, significant. It is not too brave an inference to observe that by the time they reach the evaluation, the programme is dealing with a relatively compliant and particularly persevering set of mentees. BBBS, unlike many of its counterparts, is able to create a progressive filter of motivational mechanism via a finely engineered and parallel set of programme supports. Under these conditions mentoring schemes 'work'.

... In the spectre of unemployment and AIDS

For the next illustration we change policy domains and cross continents. We also move from the uncertain beginning to the final throws of a programme. Many of the examples thus far have highlighted the need for supplementary mechanisms to raise awareness, to court interest, to engender belief and to settle participants into a programme. Boosting anticipation is, however, not a requirement in highly popular schemes with rapid take-up. For a perfect example of this scenario we focus on a *Disability Grants Scheme* introduced in South Africa at the turn of the century (Natrass, 2006). As with many welfare schemes a sometimes unspoken strategy is to limit admission to the programme. In its prior legislation, these particular benefits were designed for individuals whose illness or disability rendered them incapable of entering the labour market. The fact that many South Africans were ready, willing and able to work, but quite unable to find it, was irrelevant to the letter of this law.

This stipulation was not irrelevant, however, to thousands of scheme applicants and not a few of its officials. Given South Africa's high unemployment and HIV rates, as well as this relatively generous scheme, illness itself became an important source of income. As a result the scheme buckled under the clamour of expectations. Natrass (2006) describes a whole series of unintended consequences of this state of affairs, the most significant being the 'perverse incentive to become ill and to remain ill'. A medical officer at a TB assessment clinic describes the situation at programme entry:

> The majority of patients are really coming mainly because they are unem-
> ployed ... It seems sometimes to me that developing TB is a kind of blessing
> for some of them, that they now stand a chance of getting a grant. (2006: 8)

Moreover, once this ticket to state support is won, there is a further incentive to undermine the medical treatments that were also provided within the scheme. In words from the same source: 'People won't take their tablets ... because they want to stay in the system. Poverty is in such proportion that people will do things that could kill them to get the grant' (2006: 8).

Natrass goes on to describe the several modifications under consideration to keep the programme on track – abandoning the scheme, tapering the grant, increased supervision of treatment, the addition of an employment guarantee scheme, tax breaks for firms taking on scheme leavers, and so on and so forth. The details need not detain us here because the case is used to signal a general issue. That is to say, part of the success of any programme is to create expectations at entry but also about egress. One of the most unspoken of invisible mechanisms lies in the need for an exit strategy. Interventions need ways of engendering a particularly tricky behavioural turn: 'I'll go along with this ... but now I can go along without it'.

... Behind bars (again)

For my final illustration of the significance of small things, we return to prison. The previous example has highlighted the importance of exit strategies. All interventions have to come to an end and in general terms it is clear that egress is better facilitated if the programme is able to provide the means and the motivation for behavioural adaptations to be sustained even when intervention resources are withdrawn. Nowhere is this aspiration more difficult than in programmes delivered in prison. Many years ago Martinson (1974) wrote a pessimistic paper declaiming that 'nothing works' in the field of offender rehabilitation. Whilst significant success has now been discovered around the edges (Duguid, 2000) the ultimate stumbling block remains. Whatever changes are engendered on a programme, whatever catalytic moments are encountered, and whatever self-revelations occur whilst doing time, hopes for reform are often dashed on release when the prisoner encounters what the rest of the world feels about ex-cons.

Prisoners, of course, are wise to this eventuality and those who want a shot at going straight are keen to carry as much programme collateral as they can into the outside word. My small, anecdotal example of this occurred in a prisoner higher education course run at HMP Full Sutton as delivered by my department at the University of Leeds. The first cohort of graduates learned that they would be awarded 'degree certificates' to mark their educational achievements. There were exercised by the 'look' of these diplomas. Who would be the awarding body? Which certificate might carry more capital in the outside world? I present the competing logos as Figure 6.2, alas only in black and white.

or

Figure 6.2 Certificating behavioural change?

2. Unspoken mechanisms articulated

This section extracts the methodological moral from the above tales. It pulls together an abstract model of the pathway of change describing the cumulative, progressive, iterative transformations that typify the vast majority of behavioural change interventions. The starting point should now be clear. Social programmes do not work through Pauline conversions, divine deliverance, instant redemption or miracle cures. They work by persuading subjects to change. And subjects, from the very beginning, will be relatively recalcitrant or willing. Subjects on the threshold of a programme will ponder, wait, figure, investigate, and change their minds. Subjects over the threshold will dive in, tread warily, pull out, dawdle, support, sabotage, take over, malinger, proselytise and so on. Programmes work to the extent that they can shift the tide, moving sufficient numbers of the marginal and refractory into compliance and commitment with the intervention goals.

A complex, orchestrated series of steps is required to make a significant difference to the way people think and I have tried to illustrate the behavioural change minuet in programmes offering prisoner education, psychotherapy, muscular massage, crime deterrence, youth mentoring and disability support. Chalk has been combined with cheese in order to show that much of the responsibility for bringing about the diverse goals belongs with the mundane organisational feature of interventions. Steadily and imperceptibly, successful programmes recruit with care, create expectations, demand effort, offer sounding boards and encouragement, build and test resilience, accommodate setbacks, explain themselves, share execution and control, offer onward external continuation, and so on. All of these are mechanisms – they are resources capable of infiltrating the subjects' reasoning. They operate, so to speak, aside from the core mission. Their role is to support, enable, engender or catalyse the principal policy objective.

Figure 6.3 attempts to map the pathway of subjects from first contact with a programme to exit. It assumes that a long journey is involved and that subjects will often fall by the wayside. It contains seven staging posts, reflecting changes as subjects move from marginality to membership to exit. Each stage is depicted as a decision point for the programme subject and each stage includes a tailored intervention mechanism designed to propel the subject onwards. The top row of the figure depicts the decision chain through which contemplative subjects pass. At all stages programme participants are choice-makers. Their progress through the programme may be continuous and to plan. Or, it might stall, short circuit, or backfire. Or, to coin a phrase, subjects may move two steps forward and then one step back. The bottom row is crucial. It reflects upon the opportunity for programme planners and practitioners to develop resources, which will encourage and propel each choice in the right direction.

The figure is constructed at a level of abstraction designed to cover a wide spectrum of behaviour change programmes. The successive behavioural states are represented by the cartoon figures. I had doubts about using them to express a perfectly sober idea. Whilst they might have a certain pedagogic charm, the key idea is to portray a subject's state of thinking entirely in the abstract. The model assumes there will be refraction and hesitation, failure and drop out, rather than stately progress. Behavioural change will only occur for certain subjects, in certain circumstances, in certain respects. The model assumes, to coin another phrase, the

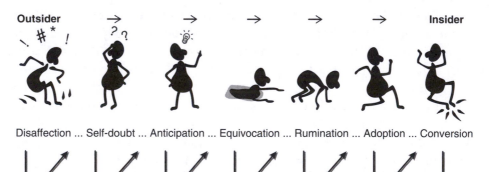

Figure 6.3 A conceptual platform for behavioural change interventions

need to draw a horse to water – purposefully, diligently and strategically – before there is the remotest possibility of making him drink. The crucial point is that there is a common pattern in the way that programmes prompt such transformation, and to emphasise the point I also present the model in narrative (Box 6.1).

Figure 6.3 and Box 6.1 represent a prototype of a 're-usable conceptual platform', described in the previous chapter as a key device in bringing learning and cumulation to evaluation research. A brief recapitulation of the basic principle may be useful at this point. The problem is the infinite capacity of evaluation to start from scratch with each newly-hatched intervention and, in so doing, discard the learning opportunity that occurs in the basic scientific instinct to compare and contrast. The first intention of the model is to provide a distillation of the many, many latent, preparatory and anticipatory processes captured in the medley of behavioural change programmes explored in the previous section. The model recognises that programme subjects, across many, many such settings are 'unsure of the next step' and notes also that this is understood in many, many successful initiatives. Comparison across cases allows one to recognise common solutions and the model expresses these in an abstract language that captures the core, underlying process. The model is thus a middle-range theory (Merton, 1967) in the classic sense of using concepts able to confederate a range of distinct empirical instances into a single schema.

Box 6.1

Behavioural change in interventions in narrative

The model begins with the outsider (1), the disaffected subject at best indifferent to or at worst antagonistic in respect of the programme's goals. For a behavioural change programme to leave the starting blocks, a close encounter is needed to accomplish the often forbidding preliminary step of persuading subjects about the risks inherent in their current activities and to seed doubt about the wisdom of their continuation. An element of self-uncertainty (2), once inculcated, leads to the possibility of presenting alternatives to current behaviour and lifestyles. These options are likely to vary in their palatability to different subjects and the intervention then needs to make a case that the particular programme pathway has some basic feasibility in the eyes of participants. An initial level of anticipation (3) is induced which may be hardened by further explanation of why the theories, ideas and resources within the specific programme are applicable to that particular subject. The subject then enters the programme with some cautious expectations (4), which are unlikely to be met unequivocally and are thus more likely to endure if immediate evidence of the promised success is presented. Regardless of such quick wins, subjects will face repeated challenges in adapting behaviour and the programme will need to assist in demonstrating how to be resilient in the face of adversity. We are now in the midst of the programme, by which stage the subject will have made numerous recalculations (5) about the wisdom of continuation. The persistence of the subjects' motivational

(Continued)

(Continued)

change can be tested and thus confirmed by ceding control of elements of the programme to the participants and assigning them responsibility for some programme
goals. Playing an active part in co-producing the intervention is a sign of arrival at
insider status (6) and of adherence to a new behavioural code. The programme is
then in a position to attest success by 'certifying' the gains. Graduates (7) leave the
programme without further need for its support and may even go on to act as ambas-
sadors to other potential subjects.

The platform also embodies another feature of model building in its deliberate
accentuation of key stages in the process of change – a strategy also incorporated
in Weber's (1949) 'ideal type' models. Any real subject passing through a real programme would likely make twenty pragmatic decisions per day on what to do
next. The model condenses and emphasises elements of the choice architecture
in order to isolate the commonly applicable processes. Once we have begun to
see the wood for the trees, the model then provides an explanatory ensemble for
understanding, predicting and planning other implementation pathways in other
programmes.

More concretely, one can say that the model already embodies the actions of
a prisoner wondering how to go straight, an osteopath seeking to drum up more
business, a cop spreading intelligence about a new crime reduction gizmo, a teara-
way sorting out his relationship with a mentor, a disabled person wondering how
to prolong support, and so on. All of these activities and more are captured by
the abstract formulation of the model. And when the continuity of constituent,
underlying processes is fully appreciated, the expectation is that the model will be
transferable. It may be able to teach us something about the choices of programme
stakeholders thus far unconsidered such as: a family pondering whether to bother
with green bin recycling, an obese teenager wondering whether to attend 'fat
camp', a car commuter dubious about the local bus services, a smoker wondering
if she will be able to quit, and so on.

In the next section, and the next chapter, I want to speak to the benefits of
reusing such platforms. Before commencing, it is sensible to deal with potential misapprehensions. The most obvious is that the model is not meant to be
applied mechanically. I make no claim that the seven phases, no more and no
less, are the exact number and sequence of steps that must occur for behaviour
change to coalesce. Recruitment, selection and preparation may be automatic
in some programmes and exhaustive in others. Subject contact with a scheme
may be momentary or long-lived. Behavioural outcomes sought may be singular
or multiple. They may be hard to reach or near to hand. Accordingly, whilst all
interventions within the family will encounter each of its phases, the model,
being an ideal type, may seem to elongate or to compress the activities in any
particular one.

Note also that the model, whilst wide ranging, is not designed to portray all possible types of behavioural change interventions in all possible policy domains. The building blocks of Figure 6.3 and Box 6.1 are drawn mostly from programmes providing new opportunities for individual subjects entering on a voluntary basis. These features mark its boundary. The platforms would have to be reconfigured had we tried to model, for instance, mandatory programmes aimed at behavioural control or, for example, community programmes aimed at collective behaviour.

Note finally that it is not a psychological model. The idea of 'stages of change' in individual choice is already embodied in many psychological constructs such as the 'transtheoretical model' and 'reasoned action theories' (Prochaska and DiClemente, 2005). These theories attempt to model people's motivational states in respect of their readiness and willingness to undergo change. Whilst the model developed here also trades on the idea that the participant's dispositions will propel or limit progress, it should be stressed that the model operates in the 'programme theory' tradition. Visually, this can be seen in the zig-zag structure of Figure 6.3. That is to say, the model describes: i) readiness for behavioural change, but also ii) the intervention's capacity to shift dispositions onto the next stage. As in all realist models, mechanisms are paramount. Mechanisms possess causal powers. Mechanisms offer resources which the subject may select or spurn. Programmes are more than mirrors of set motivational sequences; well-aimed interventions also drive dispositional change.

3. Reusing the platform – applying the model

Having established a basic model and clarified its function, the chapter goes on to examine that role in more detail, namely to support the construction and the evaluation of the next behavioural change intervention. I begin with a couple of brief remarks for policy architects on the construction of behavioural change programmes before moving to some thoughts about how evaluation might be refocused to capture its lessons.

The key implication of the model is there to behold in Figure 6.3. If policy seeks significant behavioural transformation then the coordination of whole series of ideas and agents is required to create durable change. Programmes need to construct runways rather than springboards for change. The practical problem raised here is that the tempo of construction of modern programmes often rides roughshod over the realisation of the vital preparatory and anticipatory inter-linkages in the model. Perhaps the key change in policy architecture in the UK in recent years is the dislocation of services and interventions. Once upon a time it was the task of the big public agencies (schools, hospitals, local authorities, police, etc.) to tackle generic and long-standing issues. This often left them weak at responding to new challenges but with a strong organisational capacity. Nowadays, the tendency is to design made-to-order programmes aimed at specific and pressing problems.

The upshot, already dubbed 'interventionitis' (http://news.bbc.co.uk/1/hi/education/562369.stm), is that reform is led by a constant stream of pilot programmes, demonstration projects, new deals, modernisation initiatives and so on. With so many interventions created from the egg, it is little wonder that many end up broken. In the haste to assemble new interventions, the policy maker's pen and the practitioner's eye may hasten over the latent requisites for change. This is a brave, not to say grandiose thesis. There is only room to begin testing it with two examples, one drawn from my own evaluation experiences and one from the contemporary explosion of interest in 'nudge theories' of behavioural change. The working hypothesis in both cases is that the persistence and continuity demanded in our model of the latent mechanisms of durable change is often put at risk in newly-designed and assembled programmes.

As a first illustration, consider the curious case of 'invisible programmes'. I have had some involvement in the evaluation of the endless run of UK initiatives struggling to deal with young people who are NEET (Not in Employment, Education or Training). The basic idea in most of them ('Connexions', 'Educational Maintenance Allowances', 'Learning Agreements', 'Activity Agreements) is to supply some combination of a modest financial incentive plus the services of a personal advisor to guide the young person back into some form of EET. An unexpected feature cropped up during the pilot interviews. It transpired that several of the participants on these programmes had no perception that they were 'on the programme'. In answer to gentle probes about their experience of programme X, service Y, and so on, it was clear that they had no idea that they had encountered the said schemes. This was nothing to do with any inner state of anguish or befuddlement. What happened, as one put it, was that 'some bloke' had told them that they needed to see 'some other bloke' if they wanted to retain basic benefits and support.

The fact that they could not 'name' their programme is not in itself fatal, for the intervention label itself does not have causal powers. It does, however, indicate that referral to these programmes often does not and often cannot pay close attention to the detailed initiation and motivation building stipulated in the early stages of the behavioural change model. The interventions in question involved assembling a mighty nationwide delivery apparatus hastily and, in some instances, from scratch. In the first of the above mentioned programmes, the worthy desire to better integrate aspects of youth work and career advice led to the wholesale reorganisation of these agencies – re-branded on the High Street as the Connexions service. The roles of the advisors responsible for delivering one-to-one support were often indecipherable amidst the institutional turmoil. Clients arrived in the middle of the intervention simply by dint of referral from one part of the educational and welfare system to another. If they experienced a bond of trust and were prompted into self-reflection that was largely due to the happenstance of encountering a particularly skilled mentor. In short, a significant proportion of participants found themselves on the scheme without any buy-in to the scheme. Whilst I have raised no more than anecdotal evidence in support of it, this scenario haunts several of the most ambitious behavioural change programmes, the implication being that latent preliminaries are as vital as big ticket apparatus.

For my second exhibit I turn to the upper reaches of policy making. At the time of writing there is considerable interest in so-called 'intelligent programming'. As ever, there is an ideological dimension to the proposal, the idea being well suited to the current UK government's political instinct that it is better to encourage people to change their own behaviour rather than to rely on legislation, performance management and enforcement. I make no attempt to referee such high level banner-waving, for the point of interest is about how behavioural change is conceived in the current wave of intelligent interventions. The widely acknowledged source of inspiration is the work of Thaler and Sunstein in their book *Nudge* (2008). Well placed members of the Cabinet Office have pressed these ideas into service in a range of practical interventions (Dolan et al., 2010). Well placed observers have had the opportunity to comment critically on the grand design in a House of Lords, Science and Technology Select Committee Report (2011).

Nudges are provided when policies are put in place so altering the 'choice architecture' within which people make their everyday decisions. For instance, it is claimed that: fitness benefits will accrue if buildings are constructed with fewer lifts requiring occupants to haul that excess poundage up the staircases; organ donation will improve if people are required to opt out rather than to opt in to donor registration; energy consumption will decrease if householders are provided with meters clocking up instantaneous charges; healthier eating in children will follow if school meals provide salad as a default option and sweets are removed from eye-level shelves and checkouts in supermarkets.

I want to add to the critical attention given over to nudging via a comparison with the behaviour change model developed in Figure 6.3. I begin with points of accord. Realist evaluation has an old slogan. Programmes do not 'work' in and of themselves; rather it is their subjects' choice that makes for success (or failure). In this respect, I am a committed Thalerist and a devoted Sunsteiner. Indeed the notion of 'adjusting the choice architecture' is a brilliant way of expressing the idea of programme mechanisms. Programme mechanisms describe how the resources available in a programme influence the participants' reasoning and subsequent behaviour. Mechanisms add, subtract or refine options in order to influence choices. Mechanisms nudge.

This fundamental precept of behavioural change is no basis, however, for the ideological preference for low key 'intelligent programming.' So, for instance, it is a complete mistake to imagine that legislation involves a heavy handed compulsion that is somehow the converse of the quiet awakening of individual choice. Legislative programmes, too, work via adjustments to the choice architecture. To anticipate an example covered in detail in Chapter 8, consider what is required for the successful implementation of a ban on smoking in cars carrying children. Legislators need to be persuaded of the extent of risks to car-confined children. Public opinion needs to be sweetened on the same grounds. Tobacco companies need be persuaded not to dare mess with children's lives by opposing the legislation. The police need to be convinced that it is their job to enforce public health legislation. The public need to believe that the law will be enforced. Orchestrated mind-bending, rather than gentle hints, seems the order of the day. Conversely, as noted in the Lords inquiry, some of Thaler and Sunstein's suggestions on the power of the subtle nudge actually require muscular support mechanisms to achieve the purported effect. Pester power might be reduced in the supermarket by removing check-out sweets and eye-level goodies, but persuading shopkeepers to do so requires a hefty political shoulder charge.

The real problem with nudge thesis, then, is that it isolates the complex business of behaviour change into tiny isolated compartments. *Nudge* is a truffle box of compelling examples but they are compelling precisely because they deal in miniature kerfuffles. The problem of inattentive targeting in men's urinals might indeed be reduced by a well placed etching of a housefly upon which to take aim. The leaping, hideaway alarm-clock going by the name of *Clocky*™ might well irritate the habitual snoozer into rising in order to turn the damn thing off, but these are hardly telling issues for social policy. But as soon as one confronts complex, wicked problems, the behavioural change requirements become tough and manifold. Figure 6.3 represents a simplified, ideal-type model of the long road to behavioural change. Each of the requisite mechanisms might perfectly well be conceived as a nudge but the point is that they have to be orchestrated by many hands in many places over a considerable time.

I make these two examples do rather a lot of work here, but they do begin to signal broader lessons for the conception and construction of interventions. That is to say, programme building for behavioural change should follow the dynamics of Figure 6.3. We should stop thinking of programmes as embodying some dominant propellant for change. A series of sturdy and time-honoured mechanisms is also required to pull in and pull along subjects in different states of preparedness for change. To reuse a metaphor, programme planners need to design runways rather than springboards.

Our basic model of gradualist change also has profound implications for the conduct of evaluation. The basic thesis is to push the study of tacit programme mechanisms higher up the research agenda. Such a call does not involve the rejection of existing methods and strategies; it is an argument for reconfiguring the research portfolio. In the case of all four suggestions to follow, the proposed inquiry could be undertaken using primary research capturing the latent processes as they unfold, or with a secondary review piecing together their imprint across a variety of programmes and services:

Study the stages. More research attention should be paid to focusing on the specific stages in the above model – they and the theories involved should become objects of inquiry in and of themselves. This would automatically bring to the surface the importance of latent mechanisms. For instance, there is hardly an intervention in the world that does not create queuing points at entry and during processing. Normally, waiting lists are regarded as a sign of failure. In UK health services research, millions of pounds are spent on prompting and investigating the means to their reduction. Yet, as we have seen, there are instances when waiting can build resolve and can prompt careful self-reflection. It would be enormously interesting to investigate the pros and cons of 'waiting lists' in a variety of different interventions, revealing no doubt diverse tipping points when their function changes from proving ground to detection bloc.

Another ubiquitous challenge lies at the endpoint of the model. Many interventions work under the wistful assumptions that the behavioural gains, once prompted, will remain intact on the withdrawal of the intervention. Above, I provided a particularly telling example of the contrary outcome, when welfare support turns into calculating, long-term dependency. I should add that this problem occurs in many other interventions that deal in material provision; it is proving equally difficult to wean bankers off their bonuses. The problem is that exit strategies are often considered only as an afterthought, once the mistaken assumption about the staying power of programme gains has been uncovered. A rather obvious solution is to devote specific and significant research attention to the point where the end of intervention is nigh. What is needed is careful synthesis, policy sector by policy sector, of the various strategies in which provision has been tapered, transferred or transformed to the mutual benefit of the participant and provider.

Study delivery variation. More advantage should be taken of the natural variation in programme delivery. Programme 'adaptation' is an inevitable feature of popular, widely instigated interventions. For instance, in health care systems the same innovation will be trialled across a number of wards or units or hospitals. In regeneration programmes a number of different localities are often created to testbed the latest ideas. In drug-harm reduction schemes there is often 'rollout' across many schools and youth centres. Such comparisons are important not only for the customary purpose of charting outcome difference across cases; they could also open to scrutiny many subtleties of programme induction and throughput management. How has access been managed differently between case A, B and C? And did it involve that same subtle mix of the red carpet treatment and rug pulling? Was there a difference in opportunities for programme participants to learn from each other and influence the direction and content of the initiative? In general terms, cases should be compared along the journey rather than at the destination.

An example of such comparative implementation design can be found in Greenhalgh et al.'s (2009) study of Modernisation Initiative in a London Hospital. Various forms of reorganisation were studied across three services (stroke, kidney and sexual health). This illustration covers just one of the programme's aims, namely increasing patients' involvement in providing support for other users. The particular initiative thus had a behavioural change component aiming to shift cadres of patients from service users to peer supporters. It proved difficult to recruit and retain peer mentors and outcomes varied widely across the three schemes. One mechanism that proved vital in implementing the objective turned out to be the building of trust between volunteers and hospital staff (i.e. phase 6 of Figure 6.3 referring to 'ceding control'). To create this bond requires substantial and sustained contact between professionals and volunteers within well-defined clinical routines, a situation that applied most clearly in the Kidney services. Stroke services did not have the requisite routine contacts, nor was close physician–client interaction ever part of the sexual health service philosophy. This influence of this crucial little configuration shot to significance because of the 'comparative process' design.

Explore drop outs and dead-ends. Realist evaluation has always sought gain in a programme's misfortunes. If the purpose of evaluation is to discover for whom, in what circumstances and in what respects a programme works then uncovering subjects, situations and aspects wherein the programme fails can be most helpful in the future targeting of the intervention. If we find sub-groups of young people terminally toughened or totally terrified rather than 'scared straight' by prison visit schemes, then we have a better picture of the middle ground of subjects who might be responsive. The idea here is simply to extend this point of principle to all the latent preliminaries and processing mechanisms that guide the subject's journey. Figure 6.3 describes the long road to behavioural change. It is a highway with many junctions and slip roads. The subject may not accept that they have a problem; they might decide that the programme theory is for other suckers; they may surmise that the quick win is not worth a hill of beans, and so on. Subjects may exit at any stage and miscreants include not only those waving goodbye but those continuing without any commitment to the programme objectives.

The crucial task for evaluation then becomes: how and to what extent can such forms of routine resistance be anticipated and calmed? A perfect example of how this idea might find its way into evaluation can be found in the passage I quoted earlier from the *Muscular Manifesto*. Lacey's musings were used as a vivid illustration of practitioner wisdom on the little things that made a difference to programme outcomes. But they can also be conceived as formal hypotheses capable of being put to empirical test. For instance, he posits that his physical therapy works better if the subject is required to put together a detailed history of their problem, if they have tried and failed with previous treatments, if they have to wait for a sought after appointment, and so on. These are powerful and largely untested hypotheses. For example, it would be fascinating to know, and perfectly possible to research, just how influential to programme success is the previous 'personal history' of failure.

Study programme history. Rather than always chasing after the newly-minted programmes, more long-term evaluation of existing interventions should be conducted. What happens upstream clearly conditions what occurs downstream. Most obviously, a poorly recruiting programme or one that recruits the 'wrong' type of subject is already on the highroad to failure. But one suspects that flows and blockages occur throughout the life of a programme, with equal significance for its fortunes. There are always refractory phases in the intervention pathway and long-standing programmes stand longest because they are likely to have deciphered the optimal routes. They will have tinkered; they will have cracked the recruitment problem; they will have learned how to promote reliance and stubbornness in mid-phase; they will have recruited help from their graduates, and so on. Learning about the ways and means is crucial to understanding ends. The evaluation of programme history is maddeningly absent in programme planning (Pollitt, 2008).

It is important to temper this recommendation. In the experimental paradigm it has always been suggested that 'programme integrity' be tested before it is put to trial. Campbell tried, perhaps in vain, to recommend long-term follow up in the evaluation of compensatory education and deviance prevention interventions (1988: 308). Many, many scholars have recommended that mature interventions rather than demonstration programmes should be the staple of evaluation (Hawe et al., 2009a). All of these suggestions are perfectly sensible but all of them terminate in a standard outcome evaluation. The suggestion here is literally about procuring histories. Why and how did the programme develop from year to year? The inevitable escape of a programme from its original plans will have been met in effective programmes by many unheralded adaptations to its management and delivery. These are the stories that need to be told and the lessons that need to be assimilated.

A basic thesis of the book is that evaluation research would be much improved if programmes, especially new programmes, ceased to be its unit of analysis. The four examples above provide a glimpse of some alternative starting points. They all involve thinking 'outside the box'. It is expedient, however, to close by asking a tough question, namely – who funds research outside the box? None of these strategies sits within a particular policy jurisdiction; none of them mirrors conventional 'departmental' responsibilities. Who is going to support this research?

SEVEN

Invisible Mechanisms II: Clinical
Interventions as Social Interventions

Our exploration of the significance of latent mechanisms continues with a modest look at the mammoth field of clinical interventions. Recall that the broad thesis here is evaluation can only grow as a science if it learns lessons from investigation to investigation rather than each inquiry emerging freshly out of the egg. I have suggested that this objective can be furthered by the creation of 'reusable conceptual platforms'. The chapter tests the reusability hypothesis in time-honoured fashion by extending the model developed in the previous chapter to a further case, indeed by confronting it with a critical case, namely clinical interventions. In orthodox medical science, the causal powers of such treatments reside at the physiological level, allowing medication to attack viruses, kill cancerous cells, relax blood vessels, heal bacterial infections, boost the immune system and so on and so forth. The crucial mechanisms of action identified here are organic and not social. What counts is the capacity of physical actions and pharmacological ingredients to act on biological systems. Yet even here, in these unlikely waters, there is a decisive opportunity to make profitable use of the conceptual platform established in the previous chapter.

There is no denying this absolute difference between clinical interventions and social programmes. Much of what we know to be true about medical treatments is won in basic science. Because of research in the laboratory and under the microscope there is a significant sense in which we know how treatments work before we put them to the test in the field. That test is, so to speak, confirmatory – to discover to what extent and how safely the treatment works in the general population of sufferers. And there's the rub. Any field test of a drug's efficacy has to cope with the real contingencies of treating real people. To deal with these modalities, to try to calm the potential contribution of human volition to the treatment process, clinical science has evolved the methodological wonder known as the placebo controlled trial. It is thus appropriate to complete our tour of invisible mechanisms with a look at the most famous of all, namely the 'placebo effect' in medical trials. Despite Moerman's artful quip (2002: xiii) about how easy it would be to write a book on placebos – 'because it would have nothing in it' – it turns out that there is a massive literature on the said topic.

The powerful and plural placebo ———

There are many variants of randomised, placebo-controlled trials but the one that offers the greatest promise in trying to differentiate treatment effects from placebo effects operates with three groups of participants, namely 'experimental', 'control' and 'untreated'. Subjects are randomly assigned to the three conditions. The first two receive a 'treatment' without knowing whether it is real or placebo. The third is simply 'untreated'. The idea is that this strategy will perform the hat-trick – differentiating real effects from placebo effects from the null condition.

It turns out that the logic of the 'three arm trial' is not as watertight as it first appears. One significant problem is all too familiar from our previous exploration of social programmes, most especially in relation to the protracted overture to the Big Brother Big Sister mentoring schemes, namely – at what point should one consider that an intervention has begun? In the case of clinical trials, Moerman ponders the same issues – at what point does treatment commence? And on this basis he goes on to make a powerful claim: 'It is logically and conceptually impossible to have a "no-treatment group" in which disease runs its natural course'.

He asks us to consider more closely the experience of subjects in the non-treatment group:

> In order to do a trial, people have to be recruited and diagnosed for the condition under study: they receive some sort of examination, maybe an intensive and dramatic one. They give informed consent, perhaps after reading a long and complex document describing the study, the various treatments under review, and so on. They are then randomly assigned to three conditions: drug treatment, placebo treatment, and no treatment. It's not clear what one will tell the group getting 'no treatment'. Certainly their participation can't be blind to them: they know they aren't getting any drugs or placebos; a reasonable inference might be they are healthy enough not to need any. And there has to be a follow up, an assessment of the condition of the subjects after some period of time, or a diary of symptoms has to be kept. While these people have not had pills, they have had a great deal more than nothing. (Moerman, 2002: 26)

The same argument has been made earlier about subjects on 'waiting list' controls in social interventions. They are not in a state of repose. Waiting in the wings of a trial can provoke a range of responses, which have never been properly examined. Moerman in the quotation above makes a 'reasonable inference' about how non-treatment may be interpreted. However, the notion that such patients reckon that they must be able to get by without treatment is only one of a number of plausible conjectures. At the opposite end of the scale, it is possible that the dearth of treatment in the null condition could promote despair about absence of hope rather than optimism about marginality of need. Alternatively, disappointed members of this group might feel compelled to seek out additional therapies completely beyond the ambit of the trial. Many, many other conjectures might intervene according to condition and circumstance. The crucial point is that it is impossible to design out human volition by experimental manipulation.

Note that this same stricture applies to the contrast at the heart of the much more familiar, two armed RCT, namely to those getting the drug and those receiving the placebo. These groups are responding to 'whatever it is' without knowing 'what it is'. However well the assignment is concealed, indeed if it is concealed perfectly, this leaves the subject swallowing the pill in a quite different state of mind, and a curiously apprehensive state of mind, from a subsequent patient taking the medication in the safe knowledge that it is an approved treatment. Moreover, Moerman's point about the conditioning force of the entire experimental paraphernalia applies to these groups as well. That is to say, the difference between the experimental and control group is not simply that one receives real treatment and one receives inert treatment. The latter group is also diagnosed and recruited to the trial. They learn something about their condition and possible remedies. They are put though a battery of tests which are followed up. To paraphrase, they receive 'a great deal more than nothing'. A whole string of such treatment modalities squirrels into the trial, rather than being designed out of it.

The sensible inference to be drawn from the above is that clinical treatment is a long and complex journey capable of attracting diverse inferences in the minds of inference-making subjects, that it is impossible to prevent them cogitating on their role in the trial, whatever it is, and that it is impossible to assign arithmetically some part of the treatment effect to the drug and some part to the placebo (see Box 7.1). Moreover and perhaps more significantly, these attempts to corral such anticipatory effects in the 'controlled experiment' bear little relation to how these latent mechanisms escape into all aspects of real, 'uncontrolled' treatments. Here, patients arrive in the clinic in quite different states of readiness and anticipation – for which they receive pills and potions and consultation and care. A rather different strategy is called for to understand these complex pathways.

Box 7.1

How large is the placebo effect?

In the first and still the most famous review of the placebo effect, Beecher (1955) made the claim that in 15 trials he examined there was a general pattern whereby both experimental and control groups tended to show improvement, with one third of the membership of the control group typically responding to placebos. Kienle and Kienle (1997) reject these findings, arguing that Beecher had cherry-picked the studies, had used heterogeneous outcome measures and had confused two arm and three arm trials. A later major review of three arm trials by Hróbjartsson and Götzsche (2001) claimed that 'compared to no-treatment, placebo had no significant effect on objective and subjective outcomes'. Glorious dispute followed in the same journal, including a rejoinder by Einarson and Hemmels (2001) pointing out that many of the 'no-treatment' groups in the studies reviewed did in fact maintain some form of treatment. A further complication is based in the point that placebos do not work as strongly in clinical trials because subjects do not know whether they might be getting the real or the sham treatment. Studies made in which patients think they are receiving the actual treatment rather than its possibility are claimed to show a significantly stronger placebo effect (Vase, 2002). Finally, note that there is scattered literature indicating that the placebo effect varies considerably by condition (coughs versus cancer) leading to the claim that the large-scale, meta-analytic reviews fail to differentiate treatment modalities. Kirsch et al. (2002), for instance, maintain that the placebo effect is particularly large in antidepressant treatment.

The moral of this tale is that it is unwise, indeed impossible, to pin an overall number on the placebo effect without a more thorough dissection of its many forms.

The final proposition of Box 7.1 provides the theme for the remainder of this chapter, for the history of placebo research is the story of how the core idea of 'placebo' has, by dint of close empirical research, been broken down into a number of component social and psychological processes. Rather than being defined by default as the improvement attributable to inert pills, sham procedures, snake-oil salesmanship and so on, a whole range of 'active' placebo mechanisms have been unearthed, located in the reasoning process of patients in responding to the total apparatus of medicine. What we learn about these 'meaning effects', operating in clinical conditions where they were once considered marginal and a nuisance to boot, may be informed appreciably by the previous lessons from social programmes where they are much closer to centre stage. Our conceptual platform may well be reapplied with advantage.

Accordingly, the purpose of the remainder of this section is to build a model of clinical treatment (Figure 7.1) by drawing parallels with the model of social programmes as in Figure 6.3. The argument is the same – change happens slowly and painstakingly, that a series of measures is required to bring about profound and lasting change, and that the orthodox methods of (clinical) evaluation are not always up to scratch in being able to identify the crucial concatenations. The new model portrays treatment as a sequence, a patient pathway with the equivalent stages from anxious arrival at the threshold of an intervention to graduation and exit. It also makes use of the same scaffolding, zigzagging between the subjects' decision points and the practitioners' facilitation opportunities located over the course of the treatment. It is presented at the same high level of abstraction, embodying ideal-type processes that characterise all treatment pathways. Throughout, the model tries to capture an unfolding drama described by

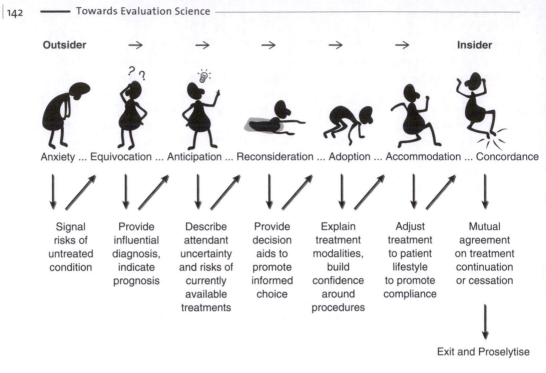

Figure 7.1 A behavioural change model for clinical interventions

Skrabanek and McCormick (1998) as the 'mutually reinforcing effect [of] the physician's belief in the treatment and the patient's faith in the physician'.

In order to stress the family resemblance between the models, Figure 7.1 is presented using the same structures and symbols. Quick eyed readers will observe that one stick figure is replaced by a new recruit and all march to a slightly different rhythm. The labelling of the ensuing actions and reactions is, of course, more specific than in Figure 6.3. Whilst this remains a generic model, it operates at one level of abstraction down from the 'universal' model of behavioural change programmes. Despite these local differences the overall argument remains the same, namely that the success of clinical interventions requires close attention to the unfolding of all stages in the behavioural change sequence. The model has seven stages; the full implications of the model will be put to consideration once all components have been spelt out. We commence at stage one, one that will be familiar to all – feeling unwell and with a degree of anxiety, and uncertainty about the meaning and significance of symptoms.

1. Interpreting symptoms – resistance and delay in seeking treatment

Our model of social interventions began with 'outsiders', subjects in a perturbed state not yet ready to participate in the mainstream and with severe doubts about the wisdom of doing so. Successful social programmes, it was argued, respond by publicising the message that the subject is not alone in their predicament and by seeding doubt and signalling the risks about remaining in this state of detachment. The parallel process whereby patients take their first step into medical treatment can be equally fraught, even though services provision for health problems is comparatively vast, as is folk wisdom about appropriate remedies. Whilst the specific risks posed by a social problem and an undiagnosed condition are quite different, both are dealt with by providing some kind of challenge to prevailing conceptions.

In the case of acute and life-threatening conditions the stakes may be particularly high should there be a delay in coming forward for treatment. The effectiveness of some therapies (angiosplasty, thrombolytic agents etc.) for coronary heart disease diminishes by the hour following a severe attack. Delays of diagnosis in breast cancer of three months or more are reported to lead to a 12–19% drop in 5-year survival rates (Richards et al., 1999). In general, clinical efficacy is highly susceptible to pre-intervention procrastination in seeking treatment as it is distributed across a trial population. The average success rate for a treatment can hide significant individual differences associated with the longevity of the disease (Kravitz et al., 2004).

Against this background, a body of research is gathering with the aim of understanding resistance and hesitation in seeking treatment, both in terms of the causes and potential solutions. People stand back from diagnosis on the basis of complex deliberations about themselves and the clinical institutions. The picture emerging from evaluations of campaigns encouraging people to seek early treatment is of the need for 'tailor-made invitations', closely fitting the patient's condition, circumstances and prior expectations. Gone are the days where pure ignorance was seen as the problem and one-size-fits-all, 'educational' campaigns were deemed the solution. Procrastination runs deep and requires a more subtle awakening.

For instance, the REACT (Rapid Early Action for Coronary Treatment) campaign (Raczynski et al., 1999) was shaped by the existing evidence on 'risk factors' known to limit effective response to acute myocardial infarction (AMI). The manner and timing of the response to such attacks is rough and ragged because: i) AMI symptoms are diffuse, ii) AMIs, unlike other conditions, offer no opportunities for behavioural rehearsals, iii) the presence of bystanders and family members is vital in avoiding delay, iv) clinician advice for those displaying earlier symptoms is crucial but difficult to organise equitably and systematically. The REACT programme sought to address each constraint in a multi-factor campaign, including actions aimed at at-risk individuals, their families, their communities and their professional providers. Each component was 'theory-based', perceiving symptom recognition as a communication problem rather than a clinical issue. Luepker et al. (2000) can be usefully consulted on the evaluation of efforts to mount the initiative flexibly to mirror the experience of different communities and individuals. The programme is noted here not because it cracks the problem but rather for its careful articulation of the problem. It demonstrates the complex social dynamics at the very inception of treatment and their significance for long-term outcomes.

The reasons that women give for seeking or delaying treatment for breast cancer are much studied (Ramirez, 1999) and also demonstrate vividly the variability of choice making at the threshold of clinical interventions. Facione and Facione's (2006) inquiry examined the 'cognitive structure' of this decision in minute detail. They compared the thinking of 13 women seeking 'immediate' diagnosis with a group of 15 'delayers' who had had symptoms for at least three months (with eight displaying symptoms for more than a year). The authors describe the inhibited progress along the decision tree as follows: 'People form early preferences on how they would like to respond to a high stakes dilemma. They structure their arguments for the value of one chosen alternative while mimimizing the values of the other alternative not to be chosen. They may seek selectively for facts that support that choice' (2006: 3138).

Coming to details, the authors note that the reasoning of both groups was permeated by fear. However, 'Women who sought diagnosis used the fear to motivate seeking a diagnostic visit and described the visit as relieving uncertainty and anxiety. Women who delayed described experiencing anxiety, sadness and depression ... associated with concerns about biopsy and breast loss ... concluding that these negative emotions were best avoided by delaying' (2006: 3144). Borrowing on the experience of others led to a similar bifurcation. The recalcitrant claimed that friends' or relatives' experiences with biopsies were relevant to their own decision to delay: 'My lump is just like hers, benign'. In women who sought diagnosis, 'positive stories of well treated cancer and benign biopsies were used to explain the advantages of seeking diagnosis' (2006: 3144).

As with social interventions, these examples confirm the need to commence interventions by meeting the subtleties of subject choice by interrogating those choices. They demonstrate the need to abandon the notion that resolution lies in information campaigns for the uninformed. Facione and Facione (2006: 3147) go so far as arguing that the providers' responsibilities extend to 'challenging, correcting and reframing' many of the commonly used justifications for treatment delay. Our model thus commences with the dynamics of symptom interpretation as its first element. It is impossible to rid subject choice from the decision to enter programmes or seek treatments, the point is to make it better informed but also more reflexive and self-critical.

2. Diagnosis is treatment (and a teachable moment)

The sub-title here follows a famous paper by Brody and Waters (1980) who claim that providing a diagnosis is itself a miniature treatment carrying its own effect and one that can shape the progression of an illness. The authors argue that the simple act of giving an authoritative name to the symptoms and identifying a time-honoured, clinically-approved treatment can itself have a therapeutic effect. Doing so gives meaning to symptoms, which otherwise the patient feels are hard to pin down and describe. Clarification on the 'true meaning' of the 'warning signs' may begin to develop reassurance. The process described here runs in close parallel with our social programme mechanism of opening up a sense of anticipation that life need not necessarily run along limiting, predetermined channels. Social programmes are successful by dint of being able to catch the moment when this reconsideration is in play.

In the context of research on diagnosis of 'non-specific abdominal complaints', van Dulman and Bensig (2002: 295) describe the process more closely:

> Physicians perform cognitive interventions by explaining to the patients the connection between the meaning and the perception of their complaints, encouraging physical and psychological relaxation, identifying negative ideas and replacing them with patient-specific positive ideas. After a visit to their physician, patients frequently modify their ideas about the cause of their complaints and often already feel less concerned once they have been reassured that they have not contracted a life threatening disease. This reassurance can manifest itself in a reduction both in physical complaints and in the accompanying use of health services.

Diagnosis, of course, may not always act beneficently. A diagnosis is a label and labelling theory tells us that ascribed meanings can also be condemnatory and stubborn. Rodger et al.'s (1999) retrospective cohort study of carriers of the hepatitis C virus (HCV) demonstrates this effect over a remarkably lengthy period. Serum had been stored and frozen from patients visiting the infectious disease clinic in Melbourne between 1971 and 1975. It was tested in 1988 and an attempt was made to locate carriers of the virus. Of the 34 chronically infected subjects 15 knew of their status before this follow up; the remainder being unaware. A battery of quality of life (QOL) measures was then administered with the following results:

> those aware of their positive HCV serostatus had a significant reduction in QOL scores in 7 of the 8 scales compared with the population norm. These individuals had a subjective perception of extremely poor physical and mental health leading to limitation of daily activities, bodily pain, poor social functioning and emotional problems. In contrast, the group that was unaware of their HCV status had significantly lower QOL scores in only 3 scales (general health, vitality and mental health). (Rodger et al., 1999: 1300)

Since Brody and Water's pioneering paper, the idea of making use of special opportunities within the diagnostic period to influence the future direction of treatment has been broadened via the concept of the 'teachable moment' (McBride et al., 2003: 156):

> The label 'teachable moment' (TM) has been used to describe naturally occurring life transitions or health events thought to motivate individuals to spontaneously adopt risk-reducing health behaviours. The occurrence of TMs is supported by accepted conceptual models that emphasise the importance of cues in prompting motivation for behavioural change ... The concept is appealing because timing formal interventions to take advantage of these

naturally occurring events might increase the effectiveness of self-directed and low-intensity interventions that are also low in cost and amenable to widespread dissemination.

McBride and colleagues (2003) illustrate the influence of teachable moments on smoking cessation. The same advice on quitting was offered in the course of the following events: i) office visits (to GPs); ii) notification of abnormal test results; iii) pregnancy; iv) hospitalisation and disease diagnosis. As with many social interventions, the shaping influence of context is profound. Studies of cessation rates after these encounters showed significant differences: i) 2–10%, ii) 7–21%, iii) 10–60%, iv) 15–78%. The authors go on to develop hypotheses about how formal interventions might be shaped and timed, the better to promote positive choices. This TM 'programme theory' stresses that advice gets across more readily if it: a) personalises risk, b) chimes with ongoing emotional changes, and c) stresses the patients' wider obligations to kin and to peers.

For obvious reasons, the first formal diagnosis of a health complaint is a significant turning point, the handling of which may prompt distress or confidence building, which reactions themselves may go on to impede or facilitate further progress in the treatment pathway. The model now turns to the next point in that chain.

3. Treatment (pure but not so simple)

Thus far our model of clinical interventions has been played out in the community, home, waiting room and doctor's surgery and, unsurprisingly, it carries many of the same dynamics as social interventions. As such, it yields comfortably to explanations from psychology and sociology. But at this point our reworking of the generic conceptual platform plunges under the skin, arriving at what many would regard as 'treatment proper', namely the application of therapies, remedies, surgical interventions, pills, unguents and potions. The mechanisms of action here, clearly and unequivocally, belong in the realms of pharmacology, chemistry, genetics, biology, physiology etc. Investigation of why and whether such treatments work thus depends significantly on basic science, laboratory investigations, animal experimentation and clinical trials. In this case, the treatment is applied and the body responds.

The crucial issue to be confronted concerns the extent to which this phase can be treated in isolation from other stages in the pathway model. Do the social constraints disappear? Evidence-based medicine has in the past tended to be fiercely protective of this arena, arguing that there is a hierarchy of evidence on treatment efficacy, namely that the aforesaid apparatus (of basic science, laboratory investigations, animal experimentation and, above all, clinical trials) is sufficient to answer the crucial question about effectiveness. Whilst the splendours of this science are there for all to see, they do not forbid a role for human agency.

The elbow room for human choice and uncertainty rests on something we all know – namely, that the same treatment produces different results in different people. Kent and Hayward (2007a), express the ensuing dilemma as follows: 'Because many factors other than treatment affect a patient's outcomes, determining the best treatment for a particular patient is fundamentally different from determining which treatment is best on average'. Formally, this problem is recognised in the trials literature as the heterogeneity of treatment effects (HTE): 'When HTE is present, the modest benefit ascribed to many treatments can be misleading because modest average effects may reflect a mixture of substantial benefits for some, little benefit for many and harm for a few' (Kravitz et al., 2004: 661).

Such a proposition is horribly familiar in social programmes, where there are always winners and losers (with a horrible tendency for them to balance out). Likewise, there are many different personal and contextual circumstances which leave patients with different levels of responsiveness to treatment (Umberson and Montez, 2010). In terms of the individual – diet, age, lifestyle and general state of fitness can make a significant difference. Their medical history, the degree of the progress of the disease and the extent of co-morbidities are also highly significant. Social contexts, like work environment can increase susceptibility to disease and limit opportunities for the implementation and action of treatments. Even geography can make a difference with, for instance, the prevalence of penicillin-resilient bacteria varying considerably by region and country. Alongside all of these contexts stand differences in human genetics. The ability of the body to absorb and metabolise a drug varies considerably. The new discipline of 'pharmacogenetics' studies how our individual genetic inheritance endows us with a range of different drug transporters and receptors, which in turn are key in controlling the body's response to treatment (The Royal Society, 2005).

Kent and Hayward (2007b) have found a striking way of highlighting the significance of this mass of contingencies, boiling them down into stark vignettes. The following tells the tale of the contrasting benefits of endarterectomy (a straightforward but not risk-free surgical procedure to remove blockages of carotid arteries to reduce the risk of stroke). The original European Carotid Surgery Trial (ECST) trial resulted in the recommendation that everyone with a blockage of over 70% should be so treated. However ...

> Consider, for example, Cesario and Viola. Four days ago, Cesario – who is 76 years old – suddenly, though temporarily, lost control of his right hand and the ability to talk. A cerebral angiogram (an X-ray of the arteries that supply the brain) showed that his carotid artery was 90% blocked and the plaque has an irregular border. Based on the trial, according to the ECST model, his risk of stroke over the next 5 years is over 40%. Viola, on the other hand, is 59 years old. More than three months ago, she experienced transient loss of vision in one eye (suggesting a clot in the vessels supplying her eye rather than her brain). She has had no symptoms since. Her carotid

blockage was 70%, and the plaque was smooth. Based on Viola's characteristics, her risk of stroke in the next five years is less that 5%. Moreover,
because Viola is female and has very high blood pressure, her risk from
surgery is higher than Cesario's. For Cesario the benefits are clear; for Viola,
the risks of stroke from the surgery itself would outweigh the benefits.
(Kent and Hayward, 2007b: 68)

In the space of a paragraph we can see the analytic logic in construction. Factors conditioning the effectiveness of treatment are varied and multiple, and it is their muliti-
plicative action that determines the ultimate efficacy of treatment. A paradigm shift
beckons in clinical research. Rather than the traditional blockbuster trial, the move
to a detailed risk-based, sub-group analysis is underway. The key is to explore systematic differences within as well as between experimental and control conditions. This
move is rather reassuring to the realist evaluator with its echo of a familiar mantra
that the crucial task is to explain 'what works for whom in what circumstances and
in what respects'. One should add that, even for enthusiasts, personalised medicine's
goal of 'the right medicine for the right patient' is decades away. Risk stratification is
used presently in only a tiny minority of trials (Kent et al., 2010).

These developments are not awaited here, since the aim is to incorporate the
ensuing complexity and ever-present uncertainty into the behavioural change
model. The typical situation remains that bodies arrive for treatment in quite different states of repair because they are controlled by capricious, wilful human
agents. Not only does each patient represent a different medley of risk factors,
the system for identifying and itemising them precisely and coherently is only
partially in place. Note, that in addition to all of this input heterogeneity, the risk
agenda also brings fuzziness to clinical outcomes, for we also now have to reconsider what counts as 'success'. Classically, within the RCT, the result that counts is
whether 'treatment provides the cure'. But the notion of a curative outcome has
been massively stretched in modern medicine, which also concerns itself with
prolonging life, improving its quality, reducing pain, providing succour, preventing secondary infections and side effects, and so on. Success on all of these fronts
is also conditioned by patient choice and medical history as well as culture, demo-
graphics, genetics etc.

The crucial point then is that the onward treatment pathway is never established or predictable. There is always judgement to be exercised by the physician
and the patient. Cesario and Viola represent the doctor's dilemma but so do Bill
and Ben in decisions on balancing benefits and risk (incontinence/impotence) in
treating slowly developing prostate cancer, as do Sharon and Tracy in their decision about whether to go ahead with breast implants against the unknown risks
about the safety of their manufacture. And so it is to a greater or lesser extent in
every treatment decision. Our model of behavioural change continues to zigzag
onwards. Precepts are challenged to reframe our understanding of symptoms,
diagnosis is offered raising hopes of remedy, only for HTE to reawaken the spectre
of uncertainty.

4. Informed choice of treatment and decision aids

As we have just seen, it is a rare condition these days that does not generate at least a modest dilemma over which clinical pathway should be chosen. This situation is sometimes described as 'professional equipoise' – the predicament in which clinical science provides no definitive indication about which of two or more treatments may provide the optimal remedy. Accordingly, it is now a common cry that greater patient involvement in choosing their own treatment may lead to improved outcomes. One consequence of this trend is the promotion of 'decision aids', tools for patients' consumption that explain treatments and their potential risks and benefits. According to one authority (O'Connor et al., 2007) decision aids were accessed more than 8 million times in 2006, mostly through the Internet – this datum itself being a stunning sign that treatment is played out in the public sphere as well as in the clinic. Decisions made at this juncture and on this basis may turn out to be wise or unwise. Any comprehensive model of the treatment process needs to incorporate the effectiveness of attempts to inform patient choice.

On closer inspection, the introduction of informed choice or shared decision making turns out to be difficult to manage. Stewart's (1995: 1422) pioneering review of experiments on patient choice reveals some subtle examples of dynamics that can help to clarify the latent mechanisms involved:

> In one study ... the fact that a woman was able to choose the kind of breast surgery to have [mastectomy or lumpectomy] was not found to be related to emotional health outcomes. In another ... going to a surgeon who permitted, but did not force the choice, *was* found to be related to positive outcomes. I would suggest, therefore, that it was not simply the decision making power of the patient that was effective but, rather, the provision of a caring, respectful and empowering context in which a woman was enabled to make an important decision with both support and comfort.

The dilemma portrayed here, whilst horribly specific, harbours a striking resemblance with the lot of many recipients of social programmes described in the previous chapter. Subjects always choose but rarely choose the choices open to them, or know that much about them. Conversely, the deeper the contemplation of the choice, the more informed the choice, the more determined is the subsequent pursuit of the choice.

Many patients, of course, still prefer to delegate treatment decisions to their physician. Ford et al.'s (2003) synthesis shows that the desire for involvement varies by type, severity and longevity of a patient's condition. Against this background, studies of the efficacy of shared decision making tend to generate distinctly patchy outcomes. Choices on whether to start, stop or continue with hormone replacement therapy (HRT) represents a good example of clinical equipoise. Murray et al.'s (2001) inquiry compared a group of women making the choice using an 'interactive, multimedia decision aid' versus those receiving 'normal clinical care'. After three months decisional conflict was significantly lower for the experimental group, GPs felt that significantly more patients had taken the lead in decision making, and significantly more of them had decided against HRT. These differences, however, turned out to be short lived and shrank to non-significance at nine months. Such studies require careful excavation to decipher the delicate balance of outcomes. No such attempt is made here, the point being that we find ourselves back in the classic social programme territory. Decision aids are no panacea. These schemes only work for certain groups in certain situations over certain durations and in certain respects. Without understanding these contingencies the onward fate of the chosen treatment remains uncertain.

Studies focusing on the physicians' handling of shared decision-making (Elwyn et al., 2000) reveal the subtleties required it its implementation and also help explain its variable effectiveness. The first and considerable hurdle is to test the patient's appetite for participation rather than to assume its presence, a dilemma demonstrated vividly in one doctor's remarks on how not to introduce parity: '"Hey this is shared decision-making time … let's do it" … I think patients would think I have gone barmy if I did that'. Elwyn and colleagues go on to propose a sequential model of the stages through which informed choice may come to effective fruition, and which can be summarised thus:

- Opening up the possibility of, and opportunity for, shared decisions;
- Exploring the patient's ideas and fears with their problem and possible treatments;
- Portraying clinical equipoise, rather than indecision, during initial explanation of treatment options;
- Identifying the preferred format for the patient to understand information on the various treatments;
- Pausing the processes to check understanding and reactions to the data;
- Rechecking the patient's acceptance of their role as joint decision-maker as choices harden;
- Offering a cooling-off period and follow-up before arriving at the final decision.

Whilst this miniature 'model within a model' requires further testing before it can be endorsed as 'evidence-based practice', it provides an elegant practical exemplification of the social dynamics in this fourth stage of the pathways model. It adds significantly to the general thesis wherein the singular notion of treatment is seen to dissolve into an array of social processes.

5. Interpreting the treatment modalities (and the doctor's theories)

Our model arrives at the commencement of treatment and we turn to the social side of its initial delivery. Pills are swallowed, shots are injected, instruments are inserted, salves are applied … and the reasons for these procedures are also explained. We are told what to expect. We are forewarned and forearmed about how it will feel. The potential power of this explanation has long been acknowledged – a function captured in the lionising title of a landmark paper by Houston, 'The Doctor Himself as a Therapeutic Instrument' (1938). Nowadays, we would be more likely to cede that power to institutional arrangements, long internalised by a public availing itself of comprehensive health service provision. Not only are we informed that the treatment is designed to treat A, and it works through B, and that it has possible side effects C, and that it should not be applied if one is already taking D, all of that advice, in the UK at least, comes wrapped officially in the box carrying the NHS prescription.

As documented earlier, social programmes work more adroitly if there is immediate evidence to participants of 'quick wins' and, just as significantly, the presence of some authority who is able to attribute the gain to the intervention. The early stages of medical treatment are prone to the same influences, but can be even more powerful in their reinforcing effects by dint of institutional authority. A doctor's counsel is automatically more compelling than the youth worker's advice.

Moerman (2002: 35) provides an anecdotal example of the doctor as an active ingredient, which provides a glimpse into the underlying mechanism. It comes in the form of testimony from one of ten men in a placebo trial of knee surgery. The patient was a member of the control group and therefore unaware that he had undergone sham surgery in the form of three stab wounds in the knee to mimic the visible results of arthroscopic surgery. The outcome (and the surgeon) is described as follows:

> I was very impressed with him, especially when I heard that he was the team doctor with the [Houston] Rockets … So, sure, I went ahead and signed up for this new thing he was doing … The surgery was two years ago and the knee has never bothered me since. It's just like my other knee now. I give a lot of credit to Dr Mosley. Whenever I see him on TV during a basketball game, I call to the wife and say, 'Hey, there's the doctor that fixed my knee'.

The significance of this transfer of conviction in the application of a treatment has been a constant source of dispute. It is the epicentre of the placebo debate. I will not repeat the earlier arguments about the power and the limitations of double-blinded randomised controlled trials. The problem with the blinding remedy from the perspective of this chapter is the basic logic – the attempt to purge a mechanism from the treatment process when the real point is to understand its functions, positive and negative. The bottom line is that one cannot cancel out the doctor's influence in real diagnosis and treatment. Real doctors are not anonymous. Real doctors don't write teasing, suspenseful prescriptions for 'X' or maybe 'not X'. No one can 'conceal' from them that which they have prescribed. As long as there are medics, their convictions will play an active role that cannot but influence medical outcomes.

The conventional placebo controlled trial turns out to be a blunt instrument, hugely important in arriving at a ball park figure of the efficacy of a somewhat artificial application of a treatment but of little use in understanding how to maximise that efficacy. I must not throw baby out with the bathwater here, however, for it is quite possible to convert the RCT into an instrument for investigating the dynamics of the doctor's advice. Several ingenious and well conducted trials help us understand the mechanism involved when treatment is first applied.

One of the cleverest is a trial by Pollo and colleagues (2001) involving recovering patients following cancer surgery. It is significant because it investigates the most fundamental and routine act of implementation, namely telling the patient what the medication is and does. The patients in the trial, following normal practice, were given standard doses of analgesics (painkillers) shortly after surgery and then at intervals over three days. In addition they were put on an intravenous drip (IV) containing only a saline solution. This IV acted as the placebo and the experiment turns on the different explanation given for its function. Group 1 were told nothing about the contents or purpose of the IV. Group 2 faced the classic blinding routine of being told that the IV was either a further real analgesic or a placebo. Group 3 was told that the IV contained a further painkiller.

The outcomes of these different regimes were measured by charting requests for additional painkillers. These were real patients in real recovery and it was normal practice for them to be able to 'top-up' the standard dosages, if they wished to do so. Group 3 requested 34% less analgesics than group 1 and 16% less than group 2. This, of course, is one experiment on one portion of a treatment in a highly specific locality for a highly specific condition. But it does begin to show the authority of 'mere' verbal instructions.

Thanks to further studies of this ilk the ground is solidifying under the claim that the explanatory accompaniments to medical treatment can moderate its immediate clinical influence. The lesson here, however, is not just the need for further research on the tricks of the trade of physician–patient communication. It is important, from the point of view of theory building, to specify the mechanisms in operation at this point in Figure 7.1. Once again, I charge Moerman (2002: 45) with helping us to locate the lasting lesson: 'Doctors know lots of things. Many of the things they know they are unaware of knowing (as is true for many of us in this life). But it is the depth of their conviction which conveys to patients the power of their treatments.'

What this suggests is that professional confidence in the knowledge that a treatment works provides considerable assurance to patients, allowing them to interpret the immediate action of that treatment. Such powers of conviction, however, are not only in the gift of the self-assured physician. Much of the endorsement is tacit and institutional. The doctor provides a prescription and an explanation. But before that, we already know that the drug has been licensed, quality-assured and safety-checked. And after that, when the drug is dispensed, there is a huge organisational scaffolding in which our identities are checked, we pay for the privilege of receiving the treatment (or are absolved from it) and we receive further detailed advice in explanatory leaflets. We are provided with gold-plated advice on what to expect. Social programmes often have to provide such authoritative scenario-building from scratch and can never match such levels of reassurance.

6. Compliance with treatments (and more teachable moments)

Healthcare choices cease only on death. Decisions made well after diagnosis is completed and a course of treatment is underway may still influence its efficacy. Just as the subjects of social programmes ruminate persistently on their continuing utility, patients have ultimate liberty to choose whether or not to follow medication and care regimes. Here, in the penultimate step of our behavioural model we confront another large body of research on 'compliance with treatment'.

Lack of adherence to the experimental condition is another methodological bugbear of the clinical RCT. Dracup and Meleis (1982) conducted a pioneering inquiry attempting to fathom the reasons for an initially successful and subsequently unsuccessful trial of the same drug for reducing blood pressure. It turned out the hypertension regimen was followed by 80% of patients in the former trial compared to only 50% in the latter. Since these early studies, research has turned to the reasons for non-compliance and that rationale, once again, lies in the ubiquitous choices and beliefs of the patient (McGavock, 1996). As seen throughout the earlier stages of our model, people confronted with an illness try to deal with it through their own experience, resources and folk wisdom. Later, when they arrive at a consultation, diagnosis and choice of treatment, patients still bring with them a set of ideas and expectations about health and illness. There is no fixed moment in which lay knowledge capitulates to professional expertise, with the result that adherence to treatment can wobble throughout the entire intervention.

Donovan (1995), for instance, reports on patients' self-experimentation in modifying the prescribed drug intake to diminish the risk of side effects and in order to discover the lowest drug dosage that seems effective for them. Even more subtle is the discovery of 'drug holidays' and 'white-coat adherence', in which compliance is timed to meet medical check-ups and consultations (Raynor, 1992). Highly complicated treatments result in some of the most informative evidence on the compliance problem. In a study of adherence with physiotherapy regimes for osteoarthritis, Campbell et al. (2001: 133) note:

> Initially, all informants complied with the physiotherapy regimen to some extent, usually citing loyalty to the therapist ... The reasoning underlying compliance in the longer term was more complex. While most understood and acknowledged that they should undertake the exercises and taping often and regularly, many only managed a restricted programme, usually those easiest to accommodate into daily routines or which seemed to convey the most benefit.

Turning to how practitioners might respond positively to these subtleties of compliance, we encounter once more the potential of 'teachable moments'. The dynamics and difficulties here are much the same as described in previous discussions. A trial by Grunfeld et al. (1999), on patient satisfaction with follow-up arrangements for breast cancer check-ups provides a simple example of the opportunities and of the drawbacks. Patients were randomised into two groups – i) continuing routine follow-up in outpatient clinics, or ii) routine follow-up with their own GP. Tellingly, the response rates to follow-up in the hospital group fell 10% more than in the GP group. The study concentrates, however, on patient satisfaction with specific arrangements. In this respect the GP group outscored the outpatients on almost all of the 15 items in a satisfaction survey as they related to the quality of service, consultation and continuity of care. The authors are keen to stress that these results go well beyond simple messages about optimal settings for follow-up. Patients value the importance of 'seeing a doctor you know' and perceive a clear and unsurprising advantage with respect to GP follow-up. However, 'receiving a thorough examination' is also deemed vital for staying on the programme and in this respect both situations (95% positive) cater equally well. Teachable moments, being social arrangements, only work for certain subjects in certain circumstances.

7. Concordance and exit

We arrive at treatment's end and the patient's exit. But because we have concentrated on the invisible, routine, social contributions to clinical interventions, the denouement is not a tale of the now fully-recovered patient, nor indeed the fairy tale of them going on to live happily ever after. As with social programmes we need to complete the model by considering what it means to 'graduate' and by charting how exit is best conceived and managed. Much thought has been given to these matters, perhaps most notably in the Royal Pharmaceutical Society (1997) report: *From Compliance to Concordance*. Their considerations are captured admirably in these anecdotal remarks from a member of the working-party:

> When we first met, one of our group (which included doctors, pharmacists, nursing and social science researchers) innocently inquired which of us habitually took medicine as prescribed. There was an embarrassed silence. Most confessed to such recidivist misdemeanours as abandoning courses of antibiotics after the first day or two. Once we began to examine the literature, we found ourselves questioning whether it was non-compliance or compliance that constituted deviant behaviour. (Marinker, 1997)

The Society's deliberations culminated in the production of the much vaunted 'concordance agenda'. The rationale is to rethink the problem from one of failure to enforce and reinforce treatment instructions to one in which patients' and health professionals' viewpoints should be merged on mutually agreed goals. In the words of the (1997: 11) report:

> Concordance is based on the notion that the work of the prescriber and patient in the consultation is a negotiation between equals and that the aim in the consultation is therefore a therapeutic alliance between them. This alliance in the

end may agree to differ. Its strength lies in a new assumption of respect for the agenda and the creation of openness in the relationship, so that both doctor and patient can proceed on the basis of reality and not of misunderstanding, distrust and concealment.

The journey through the whole of the clinical pathways presented in Figure 7.1 is premised on need for concordance. Potential clashes of opinion lurk at every turn and progress through the model depends on whether patient and physician agree, differ, or agree to differ. This set of options remains until the very end and they can be just as sharp in the decision to discontinue treatment. Two treatments in particular have raised concerns over the management of the exit strategy, the use of opioid therapy for the relief of chronic pain and the group of drugs used to relieve the symptoms of depression. Fine and Portenoy's (2009) paper on the former begins with a reminder of the several reasons why any treatment might be withdrawn – absence of actual or perceived effect, poor tolerability, the presence of a comorbid condition that might worsen under further application of the main treatment, and persistent problems with adherence to dosage. Similarly, the discontinuation of the antidepressant treatment may lead to problems with dependence and withdrawal distress (Rosenbaum, 2005).

And with these issues the need for a measured exit strategy becomes paramount. For the evaluator, the interesting feature of such managed withdrawal is that the strategies involved are the perfect mirror image of the attempts to wean recipients off long-term welfare benefits (recall the discussion of South Africa's disability grants in the previous chapter). Clinical exit strategies include the slow tapering of the dosage as well as the addition of or switch to alternative treatments or counselling. Failing these, the option remains of reverting to the original or equivalent drug treatment.

As with everything else in the model, exit proves complex and open to success or failure. Accordingly, the NICE guidelines on depression recommend detailed consultation on the withdrawal of treatment with respect to: 'previous treatment history, ... the consequences of a relapse, residual symptoms, response to previous treatment and any discontinuation symptoms'. Significantly, one other consideration is added to this list: 'the person's preference' (2009: 36). To their very conclusion, treatments only work with dual commitment from physician and patient.

Implications for healthcare evaluation ——

Whilst clinical treatment is vastly different from most forms of social interventions, there is commonality across the dozens of investigations discussed in the above section. What these inquiries tell us is that the path from illness to wellness, should it materialise, is a transition rather than a deliverance. A whole range of collateral, one might indeed say complementary, mechanisms facilitate the journey. Best practice in medicine rests on unleashing biological and physiological change but it also involves interweaving an array of psychological and social processes – some of them rather more opaque than others. Evidence-based medicine and evidence-based policy are cousins that should be encouraged to embrace rather than squabble.

With this harmonious thought we reach the final objective of the chapter, which is to provide some speculative comments on the ramifications of the treatment pathway model. It is pertinent to begin with a forceful reminder that, like its social programme counterpart, Figure 7.1 is a middle range, ideal-type model. It trades on a level of abstraction that cannot capture every decision and every prompt offered in the programme pathway but which is able to illuminate a common diagnosis–treatment dynamic from which all interventions can learn. The point of trying to manufacture such a conceptual platform, recall, is that it is reusable. Rather than having a million studies on a million treatment contingencies, such a platform can act as a gathering point for what we know and a launching point for new inquiries, which accordingly do not 'start from scratch'. Figure 7.1 is thus forwarded, as a rough prototype, as a potential starting point for such an endeavour. Its potential as a gathering and galvanising point for inquiry is much the same as noted for its counterpart in the previous chapter. Five more specific ramifications are spelt out in a little more detail.

1   Understanding the processual nature of treatment should persuade us, and hardly for the first time, that the evidence base to support clinical practice needs to harness a multi-method, multi-case and multi-objective approach. There is a need for basic trials, close monitoring and rigorous summative evaluation to chart progress through many significant outputs and outcomes. Qualitative research is needed to understand the interpretative processes that lead people in and out and in and out of different phases of treatment. Comparative research is required to understand the powerful influence of institutional context in shaping which treatment decisions are followed in which circumstances. Basic science, microscopic observations in the laboratory, animal studies, and preliminary pathophysiological studies in human volunteers are required to develop the treatment. Tribal loyalties and hierarchies of evidence have stood between these perspectives. Hopefully, enough has been said about the iterative and cumulative nature of all the stages in the treatment process to show that none of their respective tasks can be understood in splendid isolation.

2   The phases in the model should become major sites for investigation and review in their own right. There should be more treatment-contemplation studies, more diagnosis-reaction studies, more teachable-moment studies, more decision-aid studies, more concordance studies, and so on. To a modest extent, this shift is already underway. Indeed some aspects, such as shared decision-making, have been regarded as 'paradigm shifts', attracting their own journals and professional audiences (Moumjid et al., 2007). There are problems, however, with the current state of the art. Being 'medical science', studies of the behavioural accommodation to treatment are usually conducted in RCT style, comparing outcomes, for

instance, of groups choosing treatment with and without a decision-aid (Murray et al., 2001. These often fetch up with disappointing outcome differences because they do not venture into the black box. The same point applies to the growth in meta-analytic reviews of 'behavioural medicine' that confine evidence to that obtained in RCTs (Gravel et al., 2006). Once again, the danger lurks that such reviews only inspect for net effects. Enhancing each stage in the decision pathway requires a different impulse for different patients in different conditions. For instance, finding ways to improve compliance with treatment will differ significantly according to treatment modality: a lifetime's hypertension medication, a complex physiotherapy regime, a cancer survival plan, following a contraceptive regime, adapting to lifestyle changes, etc. And when this is understood individual and cultural differences will need to be tackled.

3   Particular treatments for particular conditions should be studied with more emphasis on the linkage of the different stages of the model. To what extent does practice upstream condition what happens downstream? This idea that empirical research should inspect the integrity of the implementation chain is common in the evaluation of social programmes. The most interesting mode of such investigations takes the form of a 'weak links in the chain' analysis and discovering these may help redirect effort to points where programme theory and programme practice are at odds (Pawson and Sridharan, 2010). Whilst the number of stakeholders and institutions involved in the clinical treatment chain can be very large, the constituent healthcare processes do possess a 'theory of change' that can be investigated in the equivalent manner. One example is a call from Demark-Wahnefried et al. (2005) for a systematic assessment of the contribution of teachable moments across the three phases of cancer care: primary advice about better exercise and diet; secondary guidance about continuing screening for associated problems and neoplasms; tertiary recommendations measures on the management of long-term and palliative care.

4   Because of the complexity of the treatment process, service delivery innovations designed to create improvement often spring leaks, fire unintended consequence and sometimes end in broad failure. An important part of evidence-based-everything is to learn from failure. As with the evaluation of social interventions, it follows that more effort should be expended on researching anomalies, outliers and unexpected outcomes in healthcare programmes. A good example of this is the study mentioned above explaining the paradoxical outcomes of subsequent trials of the same drug (Donovon, 1995). 'Lack of adherence' to treatment was discovered here and this led to a pocket of investigations explaining the phenomenon – self-experimentation to diminish side-effects, fitting treatment to daily routines, faking good in consultations etc. If we begin here, with the notion that subjects always undertake interventions in ways that 'seem right for them', a permanent line of inquiry is opened. Inflexibility of provision in the patient's eyes may well be a general problem in what is predominantly a top-down game. The

much-vaunted move from a 'compliance' to a 'concordance' agenda has methodological as well as philosophical implications. Exploring outliers, not as failures but as critical cases, is an efficient way to test and refine theory. Publication bias towards 'positive' findings could disappear eventually – if the empirical agenda turned to explaining rather than measuring outcomes.

5   More evaluation effort should be targeted at those interventions where latent forces loom largest and most controversially. Because their physiological, microbiological mechanisms of action are apparently inert, absent or unknown, much complementary and alternative medicine (CAM) has been subject to charges of quackery. If, however, we take as the starting point that all interventions work by capturing hearts and minds as well as healing bodies, then a calmer approach to CAM evaluation can be contemplated. Bellavite and colleagues (2006) have produced a sequential, multiplicative and, thus what looks to my eyes, sound template for such evaluations:

> One can assume that in a homeopathic cure a complex interaction of these mechanisms occurs: (i) a small physical action of extremely low-dose remedy, (ii) the activation of centres responding to 'placebo effect' due to beliefs, expectations of the patient and (iii) the endogenous healing mechanisms. If this is the case, the therapeutic effect is due not to the sum of these factors but their product and any procedure decreasing or shutting down one of them (as blinding undoubtedly does) may markedly affect homeopathic cure, much more than allopathic drug effect.
>
> Issues such as interpersonal, physical, non-verbal rapport and empathy (in whatever treatment) could be studied as change mechanisms in their own right. There would be ample room here for the golden rule of studying the 'same' programme delivered in different ways. Homeopathy delivered from the UK high street (by *Holland and Barrett*) will have totally different dynamics than when developed in prolonged relationship with the registered practitioner.

This chapter has sought to demonstrate that, viewed from the perspective of the totality of mechanisms that prompt behavioural change, social programmes and healthcare interventions have much in common. Many clinical evaluators have been and remain dubious about this proposition fearing, perhaps, a loss of rigour emanating from the arrival of the soft science. Equally, many social scientists prevaricate – wary of the danger of comparing complex social interventions to the swallowing of a pill. Somewhat uneasily, a complementary perspective is dawning with appreciation that much that is efficacious about treatment lies well before and considerably after the point of treatment.

EIGHT

Synthesis as Science: The Bumpy Road to Legislative Change

There are known knowns. These are things we know that we know. There are known unknowns. That is to say, there are things that we now know we don't know. But there are also unknown unknowns. These are things we do not know we don't know. [Donald Rumsfeld, Former United States Secretary of Defence, 2002.]

This book has contemplated a grand challenge – to consider the scientific roots of evaluation research and to rethink them from a realist perspective. I have left the most ambitious chapter to the end. In Chapter 5, I sketched an overall strategy to combat the perils of programme complexity. Evaluation researchers should proceed by seeking to gain the widest possible understanding of the array of potential influences that shape the fortunes of the policy or intervention under study. They should construct, collectively and cumulatively, evidence on as many of these contingencies as possible, whilst knowing full well that they cannot cover all of that infinite, indefinite ground. Any particular inquiry should, therefore, stand foursquare on the shoulders of what has gone before. But what it also must do is operate within a balance sheet of problems solved and problems that remain unanswered and then prioritise and target investigation on those unresolved issues. Finally and crucially, it must seek to defend the utility of the partial knowledge that accrues in the continuing process.

Whenever I utter this mini-manifesto, I am always reminded of an unflattering resemblance to the notorious statement used as the epigraph to this chapter. Rumsfeld's circuitous and circumspect proposition on the fallible basis for forward planning won the 2003 *'Foot in Mouth'* award from the Plain English Campaign. Given his confident and certain pronouncements on weapons of mass destruction, many commentators might have preferred conferral under a *'Please Practice What You Preach'* award. This chapter, however, comes in praise of Rumsfeld's Dictum. It is a profound distillation of the predicament of evidence-based policy. Evaluation research can be thought of as a never-ending journey.

We seek to justify policy decisions on the basis of 'known knowns' and indeed after a hundred or so years of formal policy inquiry there is solid evidence on some aspects of some interventions. Equally, no inquiry can cover every aspect of an intervention and by definition will have concomitants that, for practical purposes, we choose to leave aside (aka 'known unknowns'). Equally, all interventions have uncharted histories, emergent processes and paradoxical outcomes that we have yet to encounter or imagine (aka 'unknown unknowns'). The whole point is the steady conversion from one state to the other, from incomprehension to unfamiliarity to understanding.

Against this background, the purpose of the chapter is to demonstrate how to apply, within a single investigation, the entire repertoire of strategies that I have promoted as the 'realist response to complexity' (recall the TARMATO typology in Box 5.1). I want to show how to build an inquiry by using: i) programme theory as the unit of analysis; ii) conceptual abstraction to maximise sources of available evidence; iii) recycled conceptual platforms to provide a stock-in-trade framework for each analysis; iv) model building to extend the range of questions asked and answers provided; v) adjudication as the main means of assessing and building evidence; vi) the trust–doubt ratio as the means of filtering questions to pursue and questions set aside; and vii) organised scepticism as the jury on all discretionary judgments made in the inquiry.

For my illustration, I draw on a review recently carried out with colleagues on the potential effectiveness of a law banning smoking in cars carrying children (Pawson et al., 2011a). The work was carried out with collaboration from the UK National Institute for Health and Clinical Excellence (NICE). Its public health team had a particular interest in legislative interventions (e.g. compulsory car seat belts and motorcycle helmets; banning hand-held phones in vehicles; smoke-free bars, workplaces and public places; prohibiting under-age tobacco/alcohol purchase; limiting sales of non-prescription medications; compulsory nutrition labelling; and so on) given their potential muscularity as compared to the normal run of health promotion and information campaigns.

The review was funded by the UK Economic and Social Research Council (ESRC), funding being provided for further development of systematic review methodology. There was indeed a considerable methodological challenge here, law-making being very much outside the regular reach of systematic review topics. Legislative interventions carry all the complexity catalogued in Box 3.1. Effective laws have to be justified, designed, drafted, publicised, rendered unambiguous and made enforceable. They have long implementation chains requiring that new statutes navigate the competing expectations of law-makers, pressure groups, enforcement agencies and the public. And, in this instance, they also have to accommodate the diverse sensibilities of smokers and non-smokers, parents and children. For these reasons the case study provides us at the outset with a reasonably typical and abundant subset of knowns and unknowns.

The method used, perforce, is realist synthesis and the following exposition can be regarded as a further piece of 'show and tell' for those coming to grips with the method. Other published papers present and scrutinise the primary evidence in much greater detail (Wong et al., 2011). Here, I reconstruct the 'logic of inquiry', providing a two-part account of the discretionary judgements made in: a) building and b) testing the programme theories. The inquiry is chronicled from conception to execution to aftermath, signalling the usage of the above seven strategies as they come into play.

Building the programme theories

Realist synthesis reconstructs the programme theories that have given rise to an intervention before going on to test those theories using available, primary research. My previous advice on the elicitation of these initial theories has stressed the use of multiple gathering points – grey literature, policy documentation, interviews with key programme architects, and formal social science theory (Pawson, 2006a: 79–82). When it comes to complex interventions, reviewers face a potential overabundance of theories from which to choose, a state of affairs that has become known as 'the swamp'. Unless research priorities are established at this point a review will sink under its own weight. Further guidance is thus needed to answer one of the foremost challenges of the strategy, namely – how does one derive the programme theories that will be put to review?

There is no exact formula to be followed in exiting the swamp. It is, however, possible to describe four broad strategies for arriving at a manageable and optimal set of initial hypotheses:

- Situate the review on an existing conceptual platform.
- Engage in a continuous process of hypothesis selection and hypothesis shedding.
- Focus the selection of theories on points of policy discord.
- Develop lines of inquiry, breaking each theory down into themes and sub-themes

Conceptual platform

Figure 8.1 illustrates the preliminary framework published as a precursor to the review (Pawson et al., 2010a). Temperamentally, realist synthesis can be considered world weary. It starts with the assumption that there is nothing entirely new in the world of public policy and that any specific intervention should be investigated in the light of the findings of previous inquiries on the same 'family' of programmes. Although our focus was to be on the specific merits of a ban on smoking in cars with children we anticipated that this would be informed significantly by an understanding of the fortunes of public health legislation in general. We pulled together material on the existing prescriptions and proscriptions mentioned above, seeking to distil a common programme theory that could be tested in detailed research on any one of them. Law making, we discovered, proceeds slowly, inching its way through three stages depicted on the left hand side of the

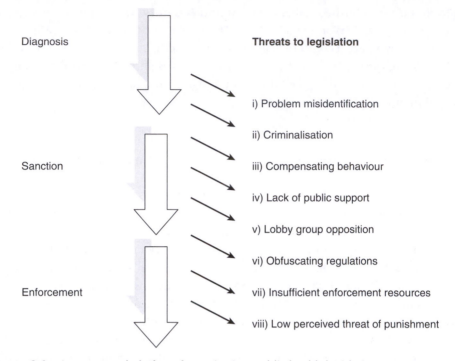

Figure 8.1 A conceptual platform for reviewing public health legislation

figure. Firstly there is detailed risk analysis demonstrating why some feature of existing behaviour and conduct can be considered deleterious to public health. Secondly, the dynamics of compulsion are mulled over, designing the sanctions regime and the penalties considered capable of modifying these high risk practices. Thirdly, an enforcement regime is designed and implemented to apply the sanctions. These three elements provide the backbone of legislation.

The real theory-building behind public health law, however, lies in the ability to anticipate and bring under control various 'threats' to effective legislation. Unwilling subjects face up to restrictions or requirements by adapting, manipulating, circumventing or ignoring them. Accordingly, intelligent law making also anticipates the ways in which legislation might prevail in the face of such opposition. Figure 8.1 thus lists in its right-hand column a typical set of 'threats to legislation', which should be anticipated and overcome in the making of sound public health statutes. The figure is accompanied by pocket illustrations providing brief examples of the typical dilemmas encountered at each stage. Possessing such a generic framework sensitises the reviewer to the long-standing issues within the policy domain and acts as first base for deriving the programme theories to be reviewed.

   i *Problem misidentification.* This refers to ambiguity and uncertainty in the basic diagnosis of risk. To be effective legislation needs credible, authoritative evidence that the behaviour to be targeted really is a major contributor to a public health problem. A particularly troublesome example of risk assessment is the three-fold classification of 'controlled substances' introduced in the UK Misuse of Drugs Act 1971. The categorisation is based on the potential 'harms caused', with penalties and enforcement effort increasing as one moves from class C to class A. Throughout its history, ministerial and advisory heads have rolled as the science behind the classifications has come into question (Monaghan, 2010).

ii   *Criminalisation and blame.* This is the classic unintended consequence facing laws dealing with 'minor infractions'. Some subjects pursued and prosecuted under new legislation may become toughened in their attempts to pursue the now illegal behaviour. For example, Wolfson and Hourogan (1997) forward an 'amplification of deviance' hypothesis in the case of some young adults prosecuted under the US liquor drinking ban and the tobacco purchase legislation. They point to evidence that arrest and repeat violations continued to increase after legislation.

iii   *Compensating and displaced behaviour.* This refers to the problem that legislation may target a risky behaviour, only for the influence to be countermanded by the subject finding further outlets for their misdemeanours. For example, reckless driving may continue even under the sanction of the law – a goodly proportion of drivers continue to drive whilst disqualified, very many over-hasten when clear of enforcement cameras and road humps, and some, now securely harnessed, drive faster and more carelessly than they would otherwise do (Huang and Cynecki, 2001).

iv   *Lobby group opposition.* Vested interests do not lie down and die in the face of new legislation. Public health law has had a tendency to tread on the toes of the industrial giants in the food, alcohol and tobacco industries (Nestle, 2007). Accordingly, their lobby groups have often responded by seeking to obstruct, delay or repeal pending legislation under the old common law doctrine about restraint of trade: 'it is the privilege of a trader in a free country, in all matters not contrary to law, to regulate his own mode of carrying it on according to his own discretion and choice'.

v   *State of public support/opinion.* American suffragette Carrie Chapman Catt reminds us of the next battle ground in effective legislation. 'No written law has ever been more binding than unwritten custom supported by popular opinion'. An unpopular law will become embroiled in implementation discord. At the other extreme, a law that simply imitates popular opinion will make little difference. Alcohol restriction is generally unpopular and generates all manner of means to circumvent it (World Health Organization, 2005). By contrast, a case is argued that the declining support for corporal punishment allowed Swedish legislators to ban it – rather than the law promoting attitudinal changes (Roberts, 2000).

vi   *Obfuscating new regulations.* Public health law often has to maintain a fine dividing line between acceptable and unacceptable responses to new regulations. Especially in the face of complex legislation, opponents often attempt to pick and choose *how* they concur with the law. 'Fake compliance' may be a problem in these circumstances. Wansink and Chandon (2006) discover that products required to carry fat *and* calorie *and* carbohydrate *and* sodium information are often promoted as 'healthy' in respect of their best performing characteristic (despite it often being the odd one out).

vii   *Low perceived threat of enforcement.* Laws may be ineffectual if miscreants believe they are unlikely to be caught or prosecuted, especially if the offence is brief and, in the subject's mind, unlikely to be witnessed. There is a significant pattern, to which I return later in the chapter, wherein drivers' use of handheld phones declines in the first months after a ban but rebounds during the subsequent year (McCart et al., 2006). Turner and Gordon's (2004) study of pupils' perception of school smoking bans indicates that many youths regard enforcement regimes as tokenistic.

viii *Insufficient enforcement resources.* Laws may be ineffectual if they are hard to police and lie at the boundaries of conventional interpretations of criminal behaviour. Police routinely report that enforcement of seat belt and handheld phone laws are wasteful of limited resources (McCart et al., 2006). Jacobson and Wasserman (1999) compare differential rates of enforcement across tobacco control laws, with clean indoor air regulations being rarely policed, whilst teen access laws received a significant amount of vendor compliance checks.

Note again that this model was constructed and thus informed our research design before we embarked on the specific review on the effectiveness of banning smoking in cars carrying children. It is a further example of the idea of rooting realist synthesis in the infrastructure provided by reusable, middle-range conceptual platforms. Figure 8.1 operates at a level of abstraction that applies to any piece of public health legislation, its recurring themes providing a common vernacular to shape any potential investigation with that family. Our reconstruction arrives at the specific piece of legislation to be reviewed. The topic was chosen because a potential ban on smoking in cars carrying children had captured a significant wave of interest in senior policy circles at the time. Later, I will describe how that tide ebbed but let me stick to the script in noting that this scenario captures the very rationale of research synthesis – knowledge accumulates within a research community about a family of interventions and this leaves it at the ready to interrogate any upcoming manifestation.

Hypothesis selection and hypothesis shedding

The iron law of complexity says that one cannot review everything but having the platform of Figure 8.1 meant that we were in a position to commence the second of the above strategies for exiting the swamp, namely the continuous process of hypothesis sifting. Some research questions now beckoned urgently whilst others could be reasonably parked. The conceptual platform anticipated certain themes that were indeed uppermost as we explored the literature on the specific ban on smoking in cars carrying children. Readers can probably reconstruct our reasoning in supposing that the effectiveness of this particular ban will turn strongly on crucial items within themes on risk, public support, pressure group opposition and enforcement described in Figure 8.1. This led to a (reduced and renumbered) set of core questions chosen to guide our review, listed in Box 8.1.

Just as significantly, this refined framework consigned some potential aspects of the proposed ban to the discard pile. We thus made several early decisions eliminating from our inquiry processes that feature in the generic platform. Here is a brief list of some of the casualties, identified under the numerals in Figure 8.1: i) the key risk involved is not one of 'driver distraction' and the core objective is not to further reduce the opportunities for smoking and the harm done to smokers; ii) deviance amplification, 'revenge' smoking in front of the kids, would not be triggered following the prosecution of a parent; iii) 'displacement' smoking may well occur but not necessarily in environments in which children would be put at risk; vi) whilst efforts might well be made to disguise smoking to avoid prosecution, these would be piecemeal and not result in any collective, systematic obfuscation of the law; and viii) although ambiguities might arise in the drafting of the law (e.g. what is the cutoff age for an exposed 'child'?) these definitional quandaries would not be the most difficult burden facing enforcement.

Box 8.1

Core questions on the efficacy of a ban on smoking in cars carrying children

1 **Is the risk sufficient to justify a law?** Reviewing the evidence on the precise health risk involved when children are subjected to second-hand smoke in a vehicle cabin.
2 **Is there likely to be public support for such a law?** Reviewing the evidence on whether and why a public consisting of smokers and non-smokers might support the ban.
3 **Is there likely to be effective pressure group opposition to the ban?** Reviewing the evidence on whether the traditional and truculent opposition of the tobacco industry would apply in this case.
4 **Is the law enforceable?** Reviewing the evidence on the smoking public's perception of the likelihood of enforcement and whether the police will give it priority.

To be sure, we found material on all of these issues in the literature and, indubitably, all of them could be subject to reviews of their own. The practical point is that many, many questions have to be set aside in the review process and having a prior, generic template gives some order and reason and openness to the foreclosure of hypothesis. One of my solutions to the problem of researching complex programmes was to call upon the assistance of Campbell's trust–doubt ratio. He estimated, recall, that over 90% of potential questions have to be put aside in evaluating a particular intervention. Here we see that proportion building.

Policy discord

The next strategy in hypothesis selection is to focus on policy debate. Recall that the realist approach always gives precedence to explanatory ambitions. In terms of the questions in Box 8.1 the objective is to deliver explanations on why or why not the toxicological risk is significant, why or why not the public will lend support, why or why not the tobacco lobby will put up a fight, why or why not enforcement will work. In order to maximise explanatory import it is useful to see how the impeding policy looks from both sides of these fences. Accordingly, theory development should always seek out plausible rival hypotheses with the aim of putting them to empirical adjudication. It should begin with both the 'whys' and the 'why nots'.

Whilst high Popperian in its origins, this desideratum is a mundane feature of policy discourse, a point made in another paper published as an *amuse-bouche* to the main review: 'The Today Programme's Contribution to Evidence-based Policy' (Pawson et al., 2010b). Amongst the UK chattering classes this BBC radio programme is regarded as the premier news outlet. Imminent and potentially vexatious policy ideas allow for a stock *Today* format in which a policy protagonist is cross-examined by the presenter, acting as antagonist. The body of the interview is then given over to a well-briefed probing for potential weak links and blind spots in the said policy reform. The well-prepared guest will have anticipated the onslaught and come armed with counter evidence to support their proposals.

Here I come to the point. This process of extracting the rival interpretations underlying prospective interventions and the close cross-examination of the supporting evidence for each is realist synthesis in miniature. It follows a key realist principle enunciated in Figure 5.5, namely that it is impossible to find iron-clad evidence to prove a proposition but that it is quite possible to find evidence that adjudicates between rival propositions. An apt illustration is provided in a *Today* interview with Professor Terence Stephenson, head of the UK Royal College of Paediatrics and Child Health (17 July 2009). He makes the case for banning smoking in cars carrying children.

The first question, on the level of risk involved, calls for some foundational evidence and Professor Stephenson is ready: 'If you light up a single cigarette in a car the levels of toxins or poisons are a hundred times the safe limit or twenty-five times the levels you'd find in a smoky bar'. The interviewer, Sarah Montague, is not easily brushed off and counters by calling on some commonsense wisdom about how smokers and their passengers often come to an accommodation on ventilation. Stephenson is ready, rejoining that 'Even if you open up the windows and turn on the air-conditioning, toxin levels will be twenty-three times the safe limit'.

Challenge and retort continue across a range of practical and ethical issues, ending in more brittle ground for our expert. Under questioning about who is going to enforce such a ban, given the police's limited resources, Stephenson replies implying that the threat of enforcement may be significant in itself, citing the menace involved in Ontario's $250 on the spot fines. He continues with some more impressionistic data, 'we have had legislation to stop mobile phone usage in cars and that's enforced and it has a huge deterrent effect. My experience is the number of people using mobile phones in their cars has gone down hugely even though the number of prosecutions in quite small.'

My point here is not about winners or losers in this particular scrimmage or indeed about the dreadful quality of the evidence presented that morning but about the format. By concentrating on policy discord we know that items like 'ventilation', 'precedents created by previous bans', 'self enforcement' and 'comparison with mobile-phone bans' might all usefully find their way into a review. Stephenson and Montague continued to ding and dong, all of their debating points triggering items for our review. Not only does the cross-examination draw out key research issues, it also demonstrates the function of evidence. Good policy formation, programme building and law making is a matter of anticipating practical challenges to interventions and pre-installing further counter-measures to circumvent them. Good evidence-production is a matter of seeking data to judge the success or otherwise of ploy and counter-ploy, hypothesis and counter-hypothesis. Evidence adjudicates between the rival propositions.

Lines of inquiry

My fourth strategy for hypothesis-building is to progressively break each programme theory down into appropriate themes and sub-themes. What one finds in investigating any particular issue raised in a review is that the evidence will often provide part of the answer but in doing so will normally raise a set of further, unanswered questions. This inevitability simply reflects the never ending nature of scientific inquiry. Realist synthesis tries to understand what it is about an intervention that works for whom, in what circumstance, in what respects, over which duration and so on. This is an infinite task and in the course of inquiry in a complex policy environment different permutations of these explanatory elements grow ceaselessly. Inquiry thus has a delta structure depicted in Figure 8.2. Certain lines of inquiry may be pursued with explanatory gain but others have to be foreclosed and such a decision has to be made at every stage in the review process.

Topic	Themes	Theories	Sub-theories	Sub-sub-theories

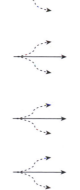

Figure 8.2 Tributaries of evidence

To illustrate with the present inquiry, the research team started with a topic (larger, bold arrow), the effectiveness of a potential ban on smoking in cars carrying children. We made the judgement that the four broad themes, namely risk, public opinion, tobacco lobby activity and enforcement would carry the most crucial evidence. Thus commenced the main lines of inquiry (straight arrows) with other potential themes (curved dashed arrows) being dispatched as explained above.

Investigating onwards, let us say with the risk theme, we encountered the basic theories of toxicology, the foundational one being to identify the precise substance likely to damage health. It turned out that tobacco smoke is comprised of a thousand different elements. Being secondary research, and as Campbell advises, we thus took on trust the toxicological sub-theory that respirable smoke particulates of less than 2.5 microns in diameter carry the major burden of risk (further straight arrows). As a result, other available evidence on, for instance, nicotine concentrations in vehicle cabins, was discarded from the review (further curved arrows).

Later in the same line of inquiry we discover another sub-theory that risk was also partly determined by the ability of the body to metabolise dangerous substances. This ability varies genetically – a further sub-sub-theory we chose not to follow. It also varies with age and whilst there is good evidence to suppose that children's bodies are in general terms more susceptible to toxins (Bearer, 1995), there is no specific evidence in this in relation to secondhand smoke, any appropriate test of the theory being unacceptable for ethical reasons. Another sub-sub-theory thus curves away from our review.

Put metaphorically, we can say that good systematic reviews have a structure rather like a river delta. One cannot follow every tributary and decisions have to be made throughout the syntheses on which are the most profitable streams and rivulets to follow and which can be left untravelled. The result, of course, is the steady accumulation of the magnitude of the trust–doubt ratio.

Testing the programme theories

Armed with this considerable immersion in generics (key issues in public health legislation) and specifics (key debating points on the potential ban) and disarmed of the need to travel every brook and burn, the research team considered itself finally ready to confront the evidence. In this second section of the chapter I seek to show how we used data from primary research to answer the four questions set out in Box 8.1. As noted, I will not offer a comprehensive account of how we located, extracted and assessed all of the accumulated evidence, but concentrate instead on explaining two research strategies that are unique to the realist approach: i) synthesis as a form of explanation building, and ii) seeking defensible partial knowledge as the goal of inquiry and the source of decision support.

Before I commence, it is worth noting another little 'gift' bestowed by rooting research synthesis in programme theory – namely, that it automatically generates multi-method, multi-mode inquiry. Of the items in Box 8.1, question one points us in the direction of toxicological data, question two has an evidence base rooted in survey research, question three takes us to political science, and question four calls upon crime prevention evaluation. Despite the fact that the review deals in these very different forms of data, their usage is the same – explanation building.

1. Is the severity of risk sufficient to justify the law?

The most obvious way to answer this question is to seek out evidence on whether children subjected to secondhand smoke in vehicles suffer more health damage than those who are not so exposed. We discovered five papers that attempted to supply evidence in this form. Evans and Chen's (2005: 244) research provides a typical example utilising a Canadian community health survey to chart the association between home and vehicle environmental tobacco smoke (ETS) and chronic bronchitis. Results are reported as follows:

> The proportion of respondents who reported ETS exposure in the home and vehicle was 9.0% and 8.4% respectively. The prevalence of self-reported doctor diagnosed bronchitis was 1.5%. When considered separately, home and vehicle ETS were both statistically associated with chronic bronchitis in children and adolescents aged 12–19 years ... When home and vehicle exposure were considered together and sex, age, allergies, marital status and race were controlled for, home ETS exposure was not a significant predictor of chronic bronchitis while vehicle ETS was.

In short, the study lays claim to an intricate little web of associations, which are presented as a sufficient basis for a ban. But can the data be regarded as conclusive? The evidence here is, of course, associational and derives from self-reported survey data and so comes with the standard caveat that correlation does not imply causation. The findings are highly susceptible to the vagaries of memory, subjects having to recall events many years in the past. Results are also subject to bias through arbitrary question wording, the key associations being calculated based on self-reports on 'regular exposure to ETS', a phrasing that may well carry a different meaning from respondent to respondent. Another well known technical difficulty with such questions, which may well be present here, is 'systematic exposure misclassification bias'. Survey participants with active respiratory symptoms and a formal diagnosis have much more cause to recall exposure to ETS (Hu, 1999).

These technical problems aside, this study also suffers the ever-present methodological headache – complexity itself. The research task here is to assess the contribution of one micro-environment, itself consisting of a spasmodic history of hundreds of car journeys taken over many years and under many conditions, and then comparing them to a lifetime of irregular exposure to many equally complex air quality environments, and then attempting to discover the onward influence of the former but not the latter upon the individual's health profile, a complex dynamic which itself responds to many, many influences other than air quality. Even the most powerful longitudinal research system could not track all of these pathways and this one-shot survey provides only rough estimates in respect of a few byways of the process. Such research is indeed tantamount to discerning the influence of the needle in the haystack. What is produced are some indicative traces of evidence on risk rather than any conclusive findings.

As ever in evaluative inquiry, direct evidence on cause and effect is hard to come by and, as ever, it is often better to construct the evidence via a theoretical model. What is needed here, to coin a phrase, is a reusable conceptual platform with which to assess the toxic risks. Not being toxicologists, it was some way into this inquiry before we discovered the standard framework for assessing the toxicological risk, known as the dose–response chain (Figure 8.3). Once discovered it proved an indispensible tool for ordering and interpreting data from the available research.

First is the matter of the pollutants under study. Secondhand smoke is a complex mixture of thousands of chemicals emitted from burning tobacco, all with potential health effects, 50 of them considered to be potentially carcinogenic by the US Surgeon General (US Department of Health and Human Services, 2007). At step two there is prevalence, the extent of within-vehicle smoking and smokers, also difficult to monitor closely in the private space of a moving vehicle. Thirdly, we move to the rear seat of the car and the equally taxing matter of estimating the extent to which children experience secondhand smoke in this location. Step four is susceptibility. Science is only beginning to understand how sensitivity to a potential toxin varies from one individual to another, with genetic makeup, metabolic variation, body mass, rate of breathing all bringing variability to the response. Children's bodies are suspected of showing greater sensitivity to most toxins, another factor that should be inserted into the risk equation. Finally we come to health impact, once again difficult to chart because of the potential pathways of so many toxins to so many organs and thus to myriad disease pathologies – short-term, long-term and terminal.

Such a framework provides for a more powerful assessment of the risk underpinning a potential ban on smoking in cars carrying children even though the evidence on each stage is far from complete. I proceed by assessing some typical data from each stage. Several studies have attempted measurement, under different driving conditions, of pollutant levels in cars when smoking occurs in the vehicle. In most cases, a volunteer smoker is asked to light up and an air quality monitor, substituting for the child, is set to record the fluctuations in toxicity levels. The pioneering inquiry (Edwards et al., 2006a) provides some representative

Figure 8.3 The causal chain of toxicity: from dose to response

findings. The principal investigator drove the car (in which no smoking had previously occurred for 10 months) while another investigator smoked cigarettes under specified conditions. Data was collected using a *TSI SidePak* AM510, a portable real time air quality monitor measuring average levels of dangerous, respirable particulates (known as 'PM$_{2.5}$') over 1-minute periods. The *SidePak* was located on a child's booster seat in the rear of the car at approximately the height of the nose of a small child sitting in the back of the car. Ambient air quality was monitored before the experiment began. Three cigarettes were smoked: with window open and cigarette held outside; with window half open and cigarette in car; and with all windows closed.

Mean PM$_{2.5}$ levels during smoking of the first cigarette were 199 µg/m^3, (peak 217 µg/m^3), during the second cigarette 162 µg/m^3 (peak 181 µg/m^3), and during the third 2926 µg/m^3 (peak 3645 µg/m^3). Fifteen minutes after the third cigarette was extinguished, PM$_{2.5}$ levels were 631 µg/m^3, and did not return to the baseline level until almost 40 minutes after the cigarette had been put out. PM$_{2.5}$ levels observed during smoking were many times higher than in ambient air (3–4 µg/m^3) which was measured 'next to a busy traffic roundabout'. In summary and in terms of orders of risk magnitude, one can say that this study uncovers considerable variation of toxicity across the smoking conditions but these are insignificant alongside the almost thousand-fold difference between the closed and ambient conditions. Such data might understandably be termed 'hard evidence' and indeed they come closest to the elusive 'known knowns' in this review. A more accurate description of their status might read 'conditional knowns'. In specific and specified circumstances – small cabin space, low speeds, windows closed, passengers in close proximity, several cigarettes smoked etc. – vast levels of toxins are observed.

A full risk assessment, however, requires that we pursue the remainder of the dose response chain. Particulate levels at the peak of 3645 µg/m^3 may be considered potentially deadly but whether that potential is realised depends on prevalence and exposure. Although smoking behaviour is hard to discern in the close confines of private vehicles, several studies have ventured here and I report briefly on some typical findings. On the matter of prevalence, we know that the percentage of adults who smoke is declining but checked in at around 20–25% in the UK and the US in 2008 (UK ONS and US Centers for Disease Control data). Martin et al. (2006) made the first estimation of how much of this was imported into the car using roadside observations of the number of vehicles carrying a smoker at a particular point. The prevalence rate was 4.1%, seemingly low until one takes account of that fact that smoking will not occur at every moment of a journey and that 4.1% of just a few thousand journeys per day will leave many hundreds of passengers per day at risk.

On the matter of exposure, results of a survey reported by Leatherdale et al. (2008) contain some indicative estimates: 'In 2006, 28.1% of children (810,000) of Canadian youth in grades 5–12 were exposed to smoking whilst riding in a car at least once in the previous week and 4.6% (131,300) were exposed to smoke while riding a car on a daily basis'. Commonsense wisdom would say that not all drivers smoke and that not all smokers partake perpetually whilst driving and that not all parents who are smokers will do so whilst transporting the kids. Nevertheless, evidence of the type reported here shows that this is still a hard core of exposure. Again, whilst this is relatively small in percentage terms, we can say that on a national basis hundreds of thousands of children will be affected, a figure perfectly capable of triggering legislation.

As we have seen in the Edwards et al. (2006a) data, the specifics of the smoking encounter can also make a considerable difference to exposure. One of these conditions, especially, has aroused much research interest. What happens when the driver opens windows or operates the air conditioning? This 'ventilation solution' has long been a major contention of the tobacco lobby and evidence is needed to settle the debate. I turn to the most rigorous inquiry on this proposition. Ott et al.'s (2008) study involved more than a hundred air change measures in a variety of vehicles under many different ventilation and driving conditions.

The first aim of the inquiry is to provide some metrics on air change – just how much air is shifted under different conditions? The basic measure used in this regard is air changes per hour (ACH) and opening a single window by 3" turns out to 'increase ACH by 8 to 10 times'. Ventilation, it seems, brings about significant air change (hardly surprising for that is what it means) but what of the effect on dangerous toxins? Ott and colleagues provide the most comprehensive body of data on particulate mass concentrations, which I summarise brutally as follows: peak exposure level during smoking with windows closed is 3184 g/m³; with windows open by 3" this drops to 608 g/m³, and with windows fully open peak exposure reduces further to 371 g/m³.

Ott et al.'s study confirms that ventilation does reduce the presence of toxins. We have further evidence here of the extraordinarily high levels of contaminants under adverse conditions. We also have new evidence with the above data of the fall in exposure rates under more benign circumstances. But as noted earlier, evidence that settles one issue has a habit of opening others. In relation to the ventilation data we still have the vexing problem of knowing whether these reduced but not inconsiderable rates can still be considered harmful. Even more perplexing and frankly unlikely is whether they could be accommodated in legislation. One of the core lessons from a public health legislation conceptual platform is to avoid ambiguity in drafting laws and it is hard to imagine anything other than rank confusion arising in a law offering exemptions for ventilation.

Our journey through the risk equation remains incomplete for we still have to establish whether the exposure rates (under any of the above conditions) should be considered dangerous. One way of approaching this question is to examine precedents and relativities – comparisons of the vehicle toxicity data uncovered above with measurements of air quality made in other domains already subject to smoking restrictions. The rationale for doing so is obvious – 'if intervention was needful *there*, then surely the same applies *here*'. This sentiment is uttered in virtually all lobbying for banning smoking in cars carrying children. The 'smoky bar', the bête noir of public health advocates, is the favoured precedent and I turn to an inquiry that throws some light into that smog.

Edwards et al. (2006b) have carried out the most substantial study of air quality in pubs and bars in the UK. It was conducted in 2005, before the introduction of smoking bans in these establishments. Sixty-four pubs came under scrutiny, chosen to span different communities. The mean fine particle level ($PM_{2.5}$) across all sites was 285.5, though as with in-car measures, large variations in air quality were uncovered according to pub location, usage, time of week, time of day etc. In the worse category (pubs in deprived areas) mean levels were 400 $\mu g/m^3$, with a range of 54–1395 $\mu g/m^3$, figures that the authors and indeed policy makers considered as strong support for this particular ban.

Unfortunately, drawing parallels on air quality levels across the two situations is not straightforward. Recalling the in-car studies, peak levels under closed conditions are over 3000 $\mu g/m^3$, seemingly much more dangerous. Then again, if a comparison is drawn with mean levels in a fully-ventilated car, Ott et al. provide a reading at 97 $\mu g/m^3$, which is at the lower end of the establishments above. The upshot, perhaps laboured by these simple comparisons, is that as toxic environments go, both cars and pubs present risky locations but this varies widely according to context and usage. The crucial difficulty is the matter of the duration of exposure. Many of the vital reported measures are of 'mean prevalence'. These means refer to quite different time intervals and circumstances. In-car, the mean typically refers to air quality during the smoking of a single cigarette and not the entire journey. In-pub, the mean refers to the contributions of many smokers over an extended period of time. Much of the argument for banning smoking in such venues centred on the high levels of air contaminants that persisted over the entire shift of the bar worker. In a world of complex, conditional outcomes, there is no such thing as a clear precedent.

Another option for gauging the risk associated with in-vehicle smoking is to compare it with publicly-sanctioned benchmarks – the formal air quality standards recognised by official agencies such as the US Environmental Protection Agency (EPA). I will not dwell on the detailed data here for they present exactly the same difficulty in terms of comparability. Two exposure figures are presented in the EPA's (2009) report limiting the acceptable mean standards of ambient air to 15 $\mu g/m^3$ annually and 35 $\mu g/m^3$ in a 24 hour period. It is perfectly clear that even brief in-car exposures at over 3000 $\mu g/m^3$ will contribute enormously to exceeding the daily recommended limit. Inevitably, there are provisos. The EPA is required to produce standards for the widest range of potential toxins in the widest range of environments and, accordingly, guidelines are all embracing. The crucial difference is that $PM_{2.5}$ levels reported in the car studies focus on instantaneous and short-term exposure; the EPA concentrates on the cumulative harm of long-term exposure. As with the smoky bar studies, there is no precise basis for comparing like with like.

Reviews always face inconsistent evidence and I close this brief examination of air quality standards with the pronouncement of the Office of the US Surgeon

General (2007): 'The scientific evidence indicates that there is no risk-free level of exposure to second hand smoke ... The US Surgeon General has concluded that breathing even a little second hand smoke is bad for your health'. If true, this benchmark renders redundant all of the previous attempts to measure precise $PM_{2.5}$ concentrations and we move to unequivocal support for the in-car ban. How is this zero magnitude to be explained and should it be regarded as an authoritative, scientific standard for the in-car smoking ban?

It transpires that it is underpinned by a fundamental change in the interpretation of 'risk'. In classic academic toxicology an ancient principle governs the measurement of risk: 'All substances are poisons; there is none which is not a poison. The right dose differentiates a poison from a remedy'. Known as the Paracelsus Principle, it is often rendered 'the dose makes the poison', under the idea that a substance only becomes poisonous when ingested at above some safe or acceptable level (Pagel, 1982). Caffeine is often forwarded as an exemplar – commonplace in a range of foodstuffs without leading to illness but capable of causing death at 50-times standard exposure levels. Historically, The Paracelsus maxim is the basis for the dose–response curve (as in Figure 8.3) and historically, it has been considered the cornerstone of public health standards, used to define the acceptable concentrations of contaminants in food, public drinking water, and the environment.

More recently an alternative credo has come to the fore, known as the precautionary principle, and it transpires that the Surgeon General's newly-established baseline is squarely based on this premise:

> The precautionary principle states that, in cases of serious or irreversible threats to the health of humans or ecosystems, acknowledged scientific uncertainty should not be used as a reason to postpone preventive measures. The principle originated as a tool to bridge uncertain scientific information and a political responsibility to act to prevent damage to human health and to ecosystems. (Martuzzi and Tickner, 2004: 7)

Two principles collide. Should our review side with Paracelsus or Precaution? Given that this is a manifesto for scientific evaluation, it should come as no surprise that the realist perspective sides squarely with Paracelsus. The precautionary principle lumps together the dangers of a lifetime's exposure to a non-smoking spouse from a smoking partner with the infinitesimally small exposure to a passer-by, when passing a marooned smoker expelled to the street corner. The precautionary principle betokens a move from evidence to advocacy. It forecloses debate and stifles the search for further evidence. By definition the zero emission, zero concentration, zero tolerance standards are not empirically derived – they concede that the evidence is not yet in.

Precautionary standards are based on the idea that 'scientific uncertainty' prevails. Scientific uncertainty, however, is not the same as scientific ignorance. The dozens and dozens of studies reviewed in our study reveal conditional truths about the dangers of exposing children to secondhand smoke in cars. They provide a serviceable basis for building an explanation of risk levels and here lies the main conclusion to the first section of the review. Science cannot say that there is some absolute risk level 'X $\mu g/m^3$' associated with secondhand smoke and that the risk level 'Y $\mu g/m^3$' discovered in the rear seats of vehicles exceeds it by 'Z%'. However, it *can* provide evidence on the myriad conditions that contribute to risk and this provisory, qualificatory knowledge is the proper base for decision support in policy making.

Thus in summary, it can be said that: i) because of the highly confined cabin space, and ii) under the worse ventilation conditions, and iii) in terms of peak contamination levels, the evidence permits us to say that fine particulate concentrations are of a level, iv) very rarely experienced in the realm of air quality studies, and this will constitute a significant health risk because v) exposure to smoking in cars is still commonplace, and vi) children are generally more susceptible to toxic risks, and vii) that they will be open to further contamination if their parents are smokers.

2. Is there likely to be public support for such a law?

Wise legislators consider not only the grounds for a law but also its acceptability to the recipient community. Gathering evidence on the public support is a routine task of social science and this section considers the certainties and uncertainties in the evidence provided by the methods of opinion polling. The analytic structure is the same. We sampled survey data on a potential ban from both smokers and non-smokers and discovered highly instructive evidence, suggesting broad support for a law. Before we leapt on this conclusion we examined supplementary propositions on why this evidence might or might not be trusted, our final understanding resting on the balance of evidence adjudicating between the various hypotheses.

Our review uncovered dozens of attempts to gauge levels of support for in-car smoking bans, much of the evidence being drawn from questionnaire items in national public health surveys. Here, I make do with one illustrative fragment. Bauman et al. (1995) undertook the first major attempt to gauge opinion in a random household survey in New South Wales, Australia, charting responses to the question, 'do you think it should be illegal to smoke in cars when travelling with children?' as follows: 'of the 1461 adult responders, 72% agreed, 27% disagreed and 1% were undecided'. Results of this approximate order of magnitude have been subsequently reported in several other countries, most especially New Zealand and Canada.

Since the crucial task here is to gauge headwinds to the passage of the law through the climate of public opinion, the most pertinent data relates to the attitudes of the most palpable foes, namely smokers. Unsurprisingly, the ban finds less favour with smokers than it does with non-smokers. Far less obvious is the main tendency uncovered, an overall level of positive support for a law amongst those who smoke. For example, Dunn et al.'s (2008) Australian study reports 'Most respondents believed that laws prohibiting smoking should be implemented as soon as possible in cars (74.2%) and homes (71.9%). Smokers were less likely to support laws prohibiting smoking in cars being introduced now or as soon as possible (61.7%) than were non-smokers (74.2%).' Looking across the research, we detected potential signs that support for the ban might be growing over time, accumulating in Thomson et al.'s (2008) New Zealand *Adult Smokers' Survey* reporting that only 3.0% of this potentially antagonistic population agreed with item 'Do you think smoking should be allowed in cars with preschool children in them?'.

No method of systematic review treats its primary data at face value. Quality appraisal criteria must be applied. There are two problems with the evidence highlighted above – attitudinal responses can be unreliable and these data, perforce, provide only a snapshot of opinions at a particular time and place. Survey responses can never be taken entirely at face value. Well known technical problems exist due to the slipperiness of question wording. Public compassion might well differ for 'children', 'children under ten' and 'pre-school' children, not to mention the 'elderly', 'pregnant women' and so on. All of these reference points were used across the surveys reviewed in order to specify those who might be protected under the ban. An alternative explanation lurks for the peak patterns of support recorded, namely that it is exaggerated by subtleties and sympathies embedded in the question wording. Even more of a threat in the present case is the 'social desirability effect'. Survey respondents, naturally enough, prefer to be on the side of the angels and thus often 'fake good' (Choi and Pak, 2005) when confronted by a stranger asking questions about sensitive topics. Put in a nutshell, the problem is that smoking addicts, who suffer routine stigma on top of slow poisoning, may well choose to dissemble. The other major quality appraisal drawback is the 'snapshot' nature of survey research. The tendencies and patterns indicated above might not carry much sway for all policy makers. Trends that apply in the open swards of New Zealand or in smoke-averse Australia might not apply to their bailiwick. In general it is true to say that the studies reviewed in this section were all made in jurisdictions which were at least in the initial stages of contemplating such a ban. The poll that policy makers yearn for is the sample of 'their patch, right now'.

In summary, the review finds itself in the customary fix that direct evidence fails to provide the all-clarifying datum. There are some highly positive indications here on the levels of public support, even amongst smokers, but is there any way of hardening this inference further? In a theory-driven analysis, the way forward is to explore theories indicating *why* there might be such levels of support and then go in search of further evidence to test these auxiliary hypotheses. This work took the review away from the automobile and beyond the particular ban under consideration. In examining the wider research on smokers' attitudes to smoking, three potential explanatory theses in particular struck us as worthy of investigation: i) smokers' protective instincts towards children, ii) smokers' regret about the smoking habit, and iii) smokers' experience of denormalisation.

There are many studies, both quantitative and qualitative, indicating that smoking is modified routinely in the presence of children. Here I illustrate just two typical nuggets of information from studies that spell out the rationale. Gillespie et al.'s (2005) New Zealand survey reports that smokers already care about protecting children from the harm of secondhand smoke (SHS) and nearly half will not smoke in the presence of children:

> Of the respondents who reported that they did not smoke at all when they were around children, nearly half (46.5%) said that this was because they did not want to expose children to SHS. Setting a good example for children was also reported as an important reason for not smoking in the presence of children (25.6%).

The fifty Scottish smokers in Phillip et al.'s qualitative study (2006) on 'smoking ethics' also made their concerns about the effects of secondhand smoke quite clear, the most important consideration being not to harm children. 'Many thought that children were particularly at risk because they were still developing', with this consideration being more important than aesthetic concerns (e.g. the smell of the smoke). Smokers reported complex modifications in their tobacco usage. All manner of partial restrictions operated, which 'would become stricter in the presence of children and grandchildren, or relaxed if adult visitors were smokers'. There is evidence here that many smokers want to share some part of the instinctive responsibility to protect powerless, vulnerable children and this becomes a potentially important stanchion in explaining the paradoxical survey data.

A different body of evidence teaches us that smokers, as a collective, are most unusual in the ranks of peer groups inasmuch as they are ambivalent about membership of their own group. Many studies, over the years, have demonstrated that significant proportion of them want to quit. Several different estimates exist in the literature, a recent paper by Lee and Kahende (2007) suggesting that in the US in any given year nearly 2 in 5 cigarette smokers try to quit, but fewer than 1 in 10 succeed. Many subsequent studies have tried to understand the dissonance that follows as smokers come to terms with cessation failure in the face of addiction.

I highlight the largest study attempting to gain a measure of the degree of contrition. Fong et al. (2004) conducted a random-digit-telephone survey of 8000 smokers across four countries (US, UK, Canada, and Australia). Subjects responded to the statement: 'If you had to do it over again, you would not have started smoking'. The proportion who agreed or strongly agreed was 90% and was nearly identical in each country. On the basis of this evidence the authors declare that: 'Regret is a near-universal experience among smokers'. Methodological caution about potentially leading question wording, superficial telephone interviews, and, in this instance, the possibility of 'faking sorrow' must always be expressed. Nevertheless, these orders of magnitude are rarely seen in opinion polling and, together with the persistent data on the numbers seeking to quit, there is evidence of a powerful tendency here.

But with what consequence? Fong and colleagues argue that near-universal regret is a powerful constraint on a smoker's future choices and, accordingly, that knowledge of this should feed into tobacco control policy. A straightforward inference is that remorse about their own habit means that even hardened smokers will have little interest in conscripting a new generation of smokers. In short, smokers do not and will not tend to proselytise. 'Regret' may be a significant part of the explanation for the muted levels of opposition to the ban on smoking in cars carrying children and thus becomes another serviceable fragment of evidence explaining the survey findings.

What of the third problem – that the vast majority of the positive survey findings emanate from countries in which tobacco control has already gained purchase? Whilst this may reduce its domain of application it also introduces a potential explanatory tool. An obvious corollary is that support for a particular ban is elevated, the more extensive the previous legislation in that policy domain. If smoking bans have been enacted on public transport, followed by office and indoor workplace restrictions, followed by smoke-free restaurants and finally bars, pubs, and gambling venues, then a useful auxiliary hypothesis is that public opinion is progressively softened up for the next location, namely private cars. Known colloquially as 'domino theory' and in tobacco control circles as the 'denormalisation theory', this thesis has also come under considerable research scrutiny.

Hammond et al. (2006) analyse further results from the four nation study reported on earlier that pertain directly to the smokers' perceptions of denormalisation. Most smokers (81%) agreed with the statement that 'there are fewer and fewer places I feel comfortable smoking'. An identical percentage agreed that: 'society disapproves of smoking'. Further research from Fong et al. (2006) probed more directly the smoker's experience of legislation. Adult smokers were surveyed by telephone before and after the implementation of the Irish workplace smoke-free law in March 2004. The relevant and paradoxical finding was that: 'Increase in support was most dramatic in venues where pre-policy support was lowest (for example, bars/pubs and restaurants), suggesting that policy makers that stay the course in implementing comprehensive smoke-free policies are likely to experience increased support among smokers after implementation'. Coping with bans, it would seem, is part of the everyday lot of the smoker.

The labour of review ends, once again, with conditional and corrigible truths. A sizeable number of studies has shown significant levels of support for a ban on smoking in cars carrying children. The vast majority of this evidence comes from surveys and opinion polls. These methods trade in tendencies and probabilities rather than uniformities and certainties. There is always an imponderable gap between what people say and what they do. Moreover, this evidence is narrow in its population base, emanating from localised studies in specific time periods. However, these indeterminacies do not negate the contribution of the evidence reviewed. A more compelling source of certainty lies in the process of explanation building. The importance of public opinion is not just a matter of a percentage of affirmation here or a percentage there. Attitudes are rooted in reasoning and those roots are open to investigation. In this case, the solidity of smokers' support for a ban is attested in three further bodies of evidence on the grounds for that support, namely their shouldering of the widespread belief about the vulnerability of children, their sentiments of regret about taking up smoking, and their acknowledgement that sympathy for the smoking habit is already on the decline.

As with all hypotheses, these conjectures are provisional, falsifiable and open to further testing. It is quite possible, for instance, that the denormalisation thesis requires further refinement. The working hypothesis, put crudely, is that smokers become used to being pushed around. But does this apply in their personal private spaces and is the car regarded as such a space? These are known unknowns. But they should also be considered sub-sub-theories capable of being put to the systematic test. I shall not do so here, noting in passing another wee observation from Phillips et al.'s (2007) Scottish study: 'Smoking restrictions in the car seemed to be more robust than in the home, suggesting that the car occupies an intermediary position between public and private space; its confined nature also seemed to encourage stronger rules'.

3. Is there likely to be effective pressure group opposition to the ban?

Cigarettes occupy a distinctive but not unique place in modern commerce. In liability law they face the perpetual challenge of being condemned as a 'tangible good that may cause harm'. And yet their sale, save for restrictions on youth purchasers, is perfectly legal. Legislation restricting smoking behaviour has thus tiptoed its way through the judiciary – attempting to restrict a potentially dangerous activity whilst recognising the legality of its market. Against this background, it is well documented that the tobacco lobby has mounted a sustained campaign attempting to thwart the steady encroachment of legislation. Truculent opposition has been mounted against smoking bans in public places, against health warnings, against advertising restrictions and, until 1998, against the very idea that smoking was a health risk (Glantz and Balbach, 2000).

Under review here is the narrower question about whether the tobacco industry will mount opposition to the banning of smoking in cars carrying children. It turns out that there is precious little published evidence on this issue – given that it covers a very recent twist in legislation. Only a very few jurisdictions in Australia, Canada and Malta have enacted the ban. What is more, lobbying is a covert business, much of it out of the public eye and absent from research reportage. Our search on this issue began by seeking materials on existing tobacco company resistance to legislation banning smoking in cars carrying children. Basically, there was only one sighting in an academic journal and a fragmentary one at that in a passage from Freeman et al.'s (2008: 64) analysis of Australian newspaper coverage of the ban:

> Invoking the protection of vulnerable children in the debate about smoking in cars called up an almost invincible sub-text for advocates. Unlike all other advocacy for smoke-free areas, this debate was not contested by the tobacco industry or other commercial interest groups ... Indeed, one tobacco company was publicly supportive of legislation.

It turns out that British American Tobacco (Australia), (BATA) was the supportive party in this instance. I contacted their press office who provided me with their submission to the Preventative Health Task Force:

> *Smoking in cars carrying children: BATA Position Summary.* BATA supports the sensible regulation of tobacco products, while ensuring that adult smokers can make informed choices about the use of such products. We accept that environmental tobacco smoke is an issue of public importance and believe that smokers should be mindful of others' comfort and should not smoke around young children. We do not support attempts to ban or regulate against smoking in private dwellings or private vehicles that are not containing children. We believe that people should not smoke around young children. However, we think this is more effectively achieved through education and encouraging greater personal responsibility amongst smokers.

Here then we have a tiny fragment of evidence obtained by a little detective work rather than any formal method of systematic review. Does it allow for prognosis? Will tobacco companies always react to this particular piece of legislation in a similar, conciliatory manner? The answer, of course, is an emphatic 'no'. Realist synthesis, however, remains undaunted by partial knowledge and the inexorable line of advance is to make sense of a pocket datum by enwrapping it in explanation. How does the episode fit within the wider struggles for ascendency between the tobacco companies and the tobacco control lobby? This was the question we set ourselves in this segment of the review and it provided the spur to further innovation in our search and analytic methods. This certainly did not feel like meta-analysis but neither did it involve further adventures of the amateur sleuth. The method was more like that of the military historian, understanding how battle lines had been drawn in the past in order to make sense of how a current conflict might be handled.

I can only offer a potted history of our military history here. Carefully worded sentiments such as those in the BATA submission above can be found on the websites of every single tobacco company. It has not always been so. The phase 'tobacco wars' is often used to describe the 50-year battle of lawsuits between the opposing lobbies (Glantz and Balbach, 2000). These authors describe a long string of tobacco company tactics such as hiking up legal costs for opposing plaintiffs, attacking the 'junk science' behind claims that smoking and secondhand smoke causes disease, seeking delay in legislation by calling for further evidence on ventilation solutions, raising economic arguments about loss of business, publishing research on the stress caused by smoking cessation, buying influence through the funding of university business institutes, and so on.

Such ploys continue save for one crucial element. The scientific arguments on health risk have been lost. For instance, the R. J. Reynolds's website concedes bluntly that 'Cigarette smoking is a leading cause of preventable deaths in the United States' (http://www.rjrt.com/). As can be seen in the BATA statement quoted previously, the dangers of secondhand smoke are also acknowledged. The major upshot of the medical establishment's hard won victory on these matters was the 1998 US Master Settlement Agreement (MSA). This is an accord struck between US tobacco companies and the State Attorneys General, which released the companies from some vituperative lawsuits and long-term tobacco related health care costs – in exchange for immediate compensation payments and the curtailment of certain cigarette marketing practices. This linkage between the MSA and company policy on children and young people can be observed directly on the R.J. Reynolds website:

> After many years of intense national debate, the major issues regarding cigarette marketing and underage smoking have been comprehensively addressed through a Master Settlement Agreement signed Nov. 23, 1998, by the major U.S. tobacco companies and 46 states and a number of U.S. territories ... The MSA prohibits taking '... any action, directly or indirectly, to target Youth ... in the advertising, promotion or marketing of Tobacco Products, or ... any action the primary purpose of which is to initiate, maintain or increase the incidence of Youth smoking ... ' (http://www.rjrt.com/)

Here then is the legal leg-iron preventing the companies from directly promoting cigarettes to young people and the source of the website cry that 'we believe that people should not smoke around young children'. Evidence thus gathers suggesting an unmolested path for the particular legislation under study. The tobacco lobby is unlikely to mount a sustained, formal and overt campaign of opposition to any proposed ban on smoking in cars carrying children. Clear and very public testimony places a direct and legally binding onus on the tobacco companies to 'practice yourself what you preach'. Whether covert operations remain is, of course, an open question. For present purposes it is considered another uncharted review tributary (Figure 8.2). For those with an inclination to follow it, it might be instructive to note papers by Healton et al. (2006) which reposts that 80% of US adult smokers report beginning smoking before age 18 and estimates annual revenue from youth consumption at $1.2 billion, and by Connolly et al. (2010) on the poisoning in some children following the introduction of Camel 'Orbs', 'Sticks' and 'Strips' (flavoured 'candy-like' products that release nicotine and tobacco upon chewing).

The substantive conclusion is thus clear. In terms of overt actions, such as counter litigation opposing a ban on cars carrying children, the tobacco companies have scant room to manoeuvre – being trapped in a pincer movement of their own conciliatory, legally-underwritten pronouncements and the invincibly powerful sub-text on the 'protection of children' that is applied by the smoke-free lobby. The methodological conclusion is also clear and repeats itself. Direct evidence on the likelihood of lobby group opposition is scant and likely to remain so due to its hidden and politicised nature. It is, however, possible to build on the meagre available evidence by explanation building. The evidence is used to construct an account of the manoeuvrings through which the warring parties have sought to gain advantage. Good evidence has already accumulated showing the pattern of lobby group advance and resistance. An analysis of these *rules of engagement* demonstrates, in the specific instance of the legislation about children, how the machinations fall conclusively against the tobacco industry.

4. Is the law enforceable?

This section of the review takes us much further down the implementation chain. It assumes that all the grizzly obstacles in the form of risk measurement, regulation drafting, public support, lobby group opposition and so forth have been settled. Appropriate legalisation is on the statute books. It is illegal to smoke in cars carrying children. If you continue to do so – you will be fined. But will you? Jacobson and Wasserman (1999: 567) remind us of one of Figure 8.1's key threats to public health legislation, in that these laws sit on the margins of the criminal justice system and thus often lack clarity in this vital enforcement stage:

> When deciding what their legislative goals should include public health advocates need to incorporate ... the locus of enforcement and implementation responsibility and the sanctions available to the enforcement agency. Failure to specify enforcement mechanisms in the legislation will lead to delays in implementing and enforcing the laws as well as compliance problems.

In respect of a law banning smoking in cars carrying children the potential impediments are clear. It is quite possible that the legislation will be stymied at street level in an unholy alliance between smokers' scepticism about whether a fleeting infraction will be detected and police ambivalence about the lack of a mandate and the absence of resources to act in this arena. This fourth phase of the review followed the normal theory-driven regime of: i) uncovering the expectations of key stakeholders on the enforcement of such a law, and ii) assembling the evidence on how and with what success the subsequent enforcement strategies have worked.

   Both tasks, especially the latter, posed severe methodological problems. Because these laws have only recently arrived on the statute books in very limited jurisdictions, little is published on the planning of enforcement and virtually nothing on its actuality. Such a scenario threatens the very idea of evidence-based policy – novel interventions do not and, seemingly, cannot have an empirical base on which to foot policy recommendations. The previous section on lobby group activity involved a hard struggle to draw inferences from an information base that was hidden. Here, it is almost non-existent. Is retreat inevitable? Should reviewers seek sanctuary in the common cry – 'more research is needed'? Readers might anticipate my answer by recalling the realist motto that there is nothing new under the sun in the world of policy making. Realist synthesis interrogates ubiquitous programme theories rather than unique programmes. Accordingly, this section shows how these theories can be modelled (Box 5.1) to reach out to consanguineous bodies of evidence.

As noted, the review began with the discovery that the theories behind enforcement of this smoking ban were many and inconsistent. Our search of a programme theory took us through grey literature such as 'The New South Wales Tobacco Action Plan: A Vision for the Future' (www.health.nsw.gov.au/pubs/2005/tobacco_ap_vision.html) and 'A Smokefree Future: A Comprehensive Tobacco Control Strategy for England' (Department of Health, 2010). Modern policy documents of this ilk operate glossily at high levels of abstraction, covering 'visions', 'rationales', 'targets and target groups', 'strategies for preventing uptake', 'strategies for aiding quitting', and then 'delivery'. Alas, on this vital latter matter the prose goes purple and often travels barely beyond identifying responsible bodies and partnership. We were able to find little practical detail in the formal literature on how the legislative arm of tobacco control was to be policed.

More specific ideas on enforcement tend to be voiced by the practitioners who will ultimately bear responsibility and these entered the review radar in a bricolage of news reports and web commentary. Longer versions of the review quote these programme theories, chapter and verse. It is sufficient here to say that Jacobson and Wasserman's words proved prophetic – different jurisdictions opt for quite different enforcement regimes. There is considerable agreement that the putative offence, being difficult to discern, would be difficult to police. Consensus then disappears on who should take responsibility for enforcement and how they should do so: the police using periodic crackdowns; the police using opportunistic monitoring; the police using secondary enforcement; enforcement by agents of the public health authorities; community surveillance and public disapproval; self-regulation under the symbolic authority of the law. In short, every strategy from tough enforcement to no enforcement is mooted. The expectations of the public are, of course, part and parcel of the enforcement equation and here too scrutiny of the appropriate blogs and websites revealed widespread scorn from these stakeholders about the likelihood of being caught, arrested and punished.

The review thus moved forward with a core theory about offender scepticism and what are best described as rival theories about optimal enforcement regimes. This is not an unfamiliar situation in policy analysis nor a particular impediment to realist synthesis as one of its key motifs is to 'adjudicate' between contending theories (Figure 5.5). I turn, however, to the real stumbling block – the sheer lack of published evidence with which to provide a resolution to the squabble about enforcement. Whilst it is perfectly true that there is scant formal evidence on the enforcement of bans on smoking in cars carrying children, dozens of other laws, bans and edicts operate in similar scenarios and this resource provided the basis for a simple model (Figure 8.4) that we used to tease out the enforcement riddle.

Offence characteristics

- in-car
- private space
- difficult to spot and intercept
- low perceived risk of enforcement
- limited police resources

Banning hand held phones

Compulsory child restraints

Smoking ban with children

Model of conditions for effective enforcement

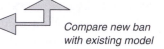

Compare new ban with existing model

Figure 8.4 Enforcing the ban: a similarities and differences model

In this instance we are interested in a hypothesis on whether enforcement works in a configuration defined by three primary elements: 'cars', 'smoking' and 'children'. Prohibitions already operate on other smoking activities, on other in-car activities and on other behaviours infringing on the welfare of children. Many of these share the same core difficulties – the offence is hard to spot and difficult to intercept; offenders are sceptical about being caught; police have other priorities and limited resources; a 'private space' is under surveillance; and so on. Often such legislation has many more years under its belt and, more to the point, has amassed a body of evaluation tracking the efficacy of enforcement. Accordingly, in this section of the review, empirical work begins with two near neighbours. In this summary, I undertake a rapid assessment of the research on the mode, extent and success of the enforcement of: i) bans on using mobile phone in cars, and ii) obligatory use of safety restraints when carrying children in cars. After coming to an understanding of how enforcement works in these two domains, following the design in Figure 8.4, I consider their contextual similarities and differences with the law under study.

Banning hand held phones in cars. Johal et al.'s UK study (2005) is one of many showing a significant immediate reduction in usage following the law. Roadside observations recorded a reduction in prevalence from 1.85% to 0.97% over a period of ten weeks before and ten weeks after the introduction of legislation. However, longer term follow-up studies (e.g. McCart and Geary, 2004; Hussain et al., 2006) show a clear 'U' shaped effect of the legislation. Usage rates fall steeply after the law comes into effect but, with time, climb again. The only exception to this rule was seen in Washington DC (McCart et al., 2007) where immediate post legislation usage rates were maintained.

Many other studies shed light on why there may be a 'rebound' in usage and thus offer potential advice on how it may be avoided. The underlying reason for a lack of compliance is plain and reported in several studies. Fosse et al. (2009) carried out a pre- and post-law survey in North Carolina, discovering that the pre-law 'hunch' that there would be relatively little enforcement was actually reinforced by their post-law experience of enforcement activities, or lack thereof.

Studies by McEvoy et al. (2006) in New South Wales and Rajalin et al. (2005) in Norway also indicate that cell-phone using drivers feel that it is unlikely that they would be caught. Drivers were aware of the law, its consequences (criminalisation) and safety risks (liability for crashes) – but, in the absence of expectations about enforcement, significant levels of recalcitrance remain.

So how can risk perceptions be raised? Unsurprisingly, research reveals that substantial and sustained enforcement is the basic requirement. McCart et al.'s (2006) study in Washington DC (the case without the substantial 'rebound') found that in 12 months following the enactment of the law 9718 citations were issued for drivers talking on hand held phones (8% of total vehicle citations) as well as a further 4500 warnings. Taylors et al.'s (2007) studies in Melbourne found similar levels of activity. Significantly, they also noted the use of supplementary tactics to maintain the law in the mind's eye. These include the targeting of drivers at particular risk (for young drivers the ban includes hands-free phones), the use of plain-clothed 'spotters' passing on 'sightings' to arresting officers, and the instigation of periodic, high-visibility 'days of action' to refresh the initiative. Study after study shows that this particular ban is not discharged by legislation alone. Sustained enforcement activities, high-visibility, prescribed penalties, further targeting and periodic blitzes seem the order of the day.

Compulsory child safety restraints. Evaluations of laws mandating child safety restraints in cars have been underway since the 1980s and tend to show highly significant positive results. Wagenaar and Webster's (1986) pioneering study of the impact of such a law in Michigan provides us with some typical results. Data on the usage of seat restraints was based on accident records and thus on direct observation rather than on malleable self-report. Use of restraints increased from 12% to 51% after the introduction of the law (a 25% decrease in injury also followed). The authors apply appropriate caution on the matter of attribution, noting that the new law was accompanied by a high profile information campaign. Significantly, as with many other such studies (Zaza et al., 2001), no specific data was collected on the extent of police efforts to enforce the legislation.

A later Japanese study by Desapriya et al. (2004) used official traffic accident data to measure the effectiveness, benefits and usage of safety seats for child passengers. Their data covered the period before and after the introduction of legislation in 2000 requiring all 0–5-year-old children to be restrained. Usage increased from 8% (1998) to 60% in the first year, dropping back to 51.7% by 2003. The researchers provide a number of explanations for the increase and partial drop in compliance. The Japanese legal system at the time was overburdened with existing prosecution requirements and enforcement was seen as more time-consuming than warranted by the offence. Most significantly, penalties were low (with demerit points on licences rather than monetary charges). Furthermore, the authors report that there was an absence of media and educational campaigns on the safety benefits of child restraints. This is a significant result – the law impacted (if with some fade) in inauspicious circumstances in which enforcement effort is minimal.

A recent Italian study by Collarile and colleagues (2008) begins to explain why. The study charts an increase in usage from 74.7% to 92.5% following the introduction of a law mandating the use of child safety restraints. It also uncovers telling information on the motivations behind the change. Nearly all (95.5%) parents were aware of the consequences of disobeying the law on child restraints whilst driving. However, it was not the fear of the penalty but the protection of children that drove compliance: 'The most frequent reasons for using child restraint systems were ensuring child safety (reported by 99.2% of responders), avoiding monetary fines (16.7%) and avoiding losing licence points (13.6%)'. Many, many other studies replicate the findings, arriving at the same conclusion as Aspler et al. (2003): 'parents did not need to be persuaded to use child restraints'.

The evidence provides a clear indication that enforcement regimes and compliance levels differ in these two 'neighbouring' public health laws. The safety seat legislation seems to have more self-momentum. The majority of child restraint legislation is followed by a sustained increase in compliance and even in those cases in which police action is negligible, compliance rates do not return to pre-legislation levels. Cell phone compliance, by contrast, dissipates more rapidly and more markedly without a systematic programme of crackdowns.

This brings us to the tricky business of making inference across to the ban on smoking in cars carrying children. Put simply – is it closer to the laws on cell-phones or safety-seats? All three misdemeanours are similar in that they occur in the private spaces of family cars. All three are hard to detect in busy traffic without the intensive use of police time, a resource for which there is much competition. All three involve pulling over and arresting the drivers on the grounds of 'reasonable suspicion' and thus have to overcome a range of legal technicalities. There are, nevertheless, crucial differences between them, which gives grounds for supposing that one of them provides a superior precedent:

I   A classic premise in evaluating the effectiveness of criminal law is to investigate the possibility of 'displacement'. In this instance, stubborn cell-phone addict may (at some expense) continue to parlay by going hands-free. However, complying with the safety restraint legislation requires safety seat installation and the cigarette addict's only recourse from the law is a smoke-free car.

II   The respective misdemeanours involve a potential difference in policing responsibilities. Driver inattention is a traffic offence and is the raison d'être behind the mobile phone ban, whilst improvement in public health is the prime mover in the safety seat and smoking legislation.

III The potential victim of failure to comply with the laws is different. In the cell phone example the law is there to protect other drivers, pedestrians and indeed cell-phone users from accident and injury. In the cases of the seat belt and smoke-free laws, the welfare of children is paramount.

On all three dimensions, the smoking and child seat legislation share more in common with each other than they do with the cell phone ban and on these grounds an inference might be drawn that enforcement patterns might also be more similar. The third comparison is especially compelling. The evidence indicates that the steady increase in usage of child restraints in cars is rooted in motivations about safeguarding children rather than a strategy of avoiding fines. Whilst there is no evidence to report on how families have adapted to the ban on smoking in cars carrying children, the research discussed earlier (core question 2) suggests that there are striking levels of *pre-intervention* public support for the ban on the same grounds.

Drawing parallels with the enforcement regimes in these two kindred 'in-car' laws allows us to arrive at a policy conclusion. The smoking ban in the presence of children bears close similarities with the legislation on child safety restraints and may be expected to be self-enforcing to a considerable extent. Whilst the urge to safeguard children may be expected to be the mainstay of compliance there is no evidence to suggest that it is the entire solution. A modest supporting programme combining safety promotion and education, alongside periodic but well publicised sanctions may also provide initial impetus.

Let me reprise the methodological warrant for the above proposition. Evidence-based policy normally requires that interventions have a history and undergo many replications. The laws banning smoking in cars carrying children have not rolled out sufficiently to gather a significant evidence base on their enforceability. Instead, I have proposed that a theory-driven approach may be drafted in to do the job. As before, this works by explanation building – the explanations in this instance having a further layer of complexity. Different laws require different enforcement regimes – ranging from those based on self-compliance to those requiring rigorous surveillance and punishment. The evidence on safety restraint compliance and hand-held phone abstinence allows us to build an explanation showing that the former has been enforced more successfully thanks to a tide of public support. The theory also specifies the range of conditions about police priorities, victim identities and displacement opportunities, which have fostered this support. This theory about the supportive contexts for optimal compliance is then fed back to the law under consideration and conclusions are drawn about its likely efficacy.

To be sure, this is a long, long inference chain. Inevitably, some of the links must be considered provisional and, over time, will benefit from further refinement. Nevertheless, the evidence is there, providing a further stanchion to help support the policy decision.

Conclusion ———

> The empirical basis of objective science thus has nothing 'absolute' about it. Science does not rest upon rock-bottom. It is like a building erected on piles. The piles are driven down from above into the swamp, but not down to any natural or 'given' base; and when we cease our attempts to drive our piles into a deeper layer, it is not because we have reached firm ground. We simply stop when we are satisfied that they are firm enough to carry the structure, at least for the time being. (Karl Popper: *The Logic of Scientific Discovery*, 1992: 94)

This chapter has dealt with a fleeting episode in a specialised corner of policy making, dealing with one type of intervention, aimed at a very specific form of behaviour. And on this basis I want to draw some huge conclusions. I begin by noting that there is no such thing as a typical policy intervention or a quintessential programme. Legislative instruments of the type considered here are worlds away from interventions based on, say, financial incentives or peer learning or community building. But what they all have in common is a sprawl of ambitions, stakeholders, localities and histories. What they all have in common is complexity. In this respect, evidence-based policy has to deal with a standard predicament. Research synthesis can only provide partial information on the mêlée of issues facing the decision maker. That information, as reported here, is likely to draw upon inquiry conducted in diverse research traditions, formal and informal. Moreover, that information is also likely to be partial in research quality and in political leanings.

Accordingly, the ultimate function of this chapter is to celebrate the warrant of partial evidence. That celebration begins with a recapitulation of Popper's words from Chapter 1 on the same theme. Science, he says, never furnishes us with irrefutable 'facts'. Rather it produces conditional truths. X follows Y only in certain conditions and the job of science is to provide a closer and closer specification of those conditions. That labour never reaches a conclusion. We build explanations in the process of empirical work and investigation stops – at least for the time being – when we have enough data to carry the developing explanation. This is the logic of scientific discovery and it should be the guiding principle for evidence-based policy. What is good enough for Popper is certainly good enough for Pawson.

The chapter is entitled 'Synthesis as Science' and the aim was to drive a large number of piles into the available swamp of evidence on a particular policy proposal. And upon those piles it is possible to create a few modest, durable buildings. What rises from the swamp of descriptions, snapshots, measures and correlates is a 'bold structure of theories'. Throughout, I have shown that it is possible to enwrap and harden the available data into explanations. One fragment of evidence makes sense of another and these together help to account for a third, and so on. It is these explanatory configurations that are the product of evidence-based policy. Recall, for example, how porous survey evidence on support for this smoking ban solidifies thanks to attitudinal data on the near-inviolable beliefs on child welfare, which coheres with further testimony on the near-universal regret about starting smoking, which is further cemented in smokers' accounts of consent to ever-tightening restrictions. The whole exercise has this structure and through it decision making becomes more rational. To paraphrase – we simply stop when we are satisfied that explanations are firm enough to carry the policy decision.

The review process as a whole commits realist synthesis to a repeated and perpetual process of theory-testing. Scores of hypothesis are raised, questioned and refined with the aim of proving reasonable coverage of the swampy ground of public health legislation. In attempting to traverse all corners, the research called upon the seven strategies recommended in Chapter 5 as the 'realist response to complexity'. It used 'programme theories' as the itinerant unit of analysis, 'conceptual abstraction' to maximise sources of available evidence, a stock-in-trade 'conceptual platform' to provide a widely reusable framework for the syntheses, 'model building' to reach further into proxy sources of evidence, 'adjudication' between many rival pro-gramme theories as the main means of building evidence, and the 'trust–doubt' ratio as the means of filtering questions to be pursued and questions to set aside.

The seventh stratagem, recall, is to rely on 'organised scepticism' as the jury on all the discretionary judgements made during the inquiry. This feature describes a questioning, collective research culture rather more that a research method. Clearly this is something that is hard to press into service in a research team of three, though it might be said there were moments when we argued between ourselves. Rather more in evidence was a process that Elster describes as devil's advocacy. 'One has consistently to think against oneself – to make matters as dif-ficult as one can. We should select the strongest and most plausible rival expla-nations, rather than accounts that can be easily refuted' (Elster, 2007). This was where the investigation commenced, locating it in the charged political ques-tioning that surrounded the policy. To be sure, what might be described as 'col-lectively organised scepticism' requires a second and a third and a fourth party to adjudicate on our adjudications and I will say a little more about this requirement in the final chapter.

Thus we completed our realist synthesis, all six and a half strategies worth. And what was the result of these wide-ranging but incomplete labours? We began to gain a march on the complexity of policy decisions. Just as science proceeds in the absence of the killer fact, there is no all-conquering influence that goes into the construction of policy. All of the literature on policy making tells us that it is 'a recursive, discon-tinuous process involving many different steps and a host of dynamic factors over a considerable length of time' (Mintzberg et al., 1976). Realist synthesis thus makes at least a small start on investigating the multifarious steps and factors by casting the review net widely – in this instance by interrogating four quite different issues – 'toxicity', 'public opinion', 'lobbying' and 'compliance'. Note, in passing and via the example of lobbying, that there is nothing to prevent the inclusion of the political dimension in policy decisions as a topic for realist synthesis. The inquiry thus has a broad footing but what happens next? Each one of these core themes subdivides rapidly into four or five different sub-streams and the tributaries continue to develop. One question receives an answer … but it is usually a partial answer that will beget further questions … and the process carries on *ad infinitum*.

There is no reason to regret this. What the research community should be insist-ing upon is the remarkable value of the process. Each of the broad domains reviewed reveals its truths but in ways that are highly conditional and multiply contingent. Thus, smoke pollution in cars is dangerously toxic – if exposure is frequent and ventilation absent. Public opinion is likely to be supportive – especially if other smoke-free laws have been passed. Lobby group opposition may well be muted – in the word if not the deed. Compliance tends to wax and then wane – unless a deeper public sentiment can be nurtured. Such contingencies apply all the way down the implementation chain and into the smallest operational detail. If Police Commissioner O'Callaghan of Berrysweet County is convinced that public health is not a police function and she has significant institutional sway, there will be no local arrests and the law will have to rely on self-enforcement. That is the way it is with public policy. We can anticipate very many contingencies but not all of them.

Carrying that proposition forward as a golden rule of policy planning reveals the true function of evidence and the precise role of realist synthesis. Evidence does not deliver decisions; its function is to deliver decision support. When evidence is called into play in policy formation, it is never a case of simply 'following the evidence' but rather one of 'interpreting the evidence' and then 'adapting the evidence' to local circumstances. No method of synthesis can tell the policy maker what to do. Realist synthesis, being rid of such a conceit, aims to support a decision by revealing the most important contingencies that lie in its wake. If the policy is designed to do X, better implement it though A, B, C ... better to target it at D, E, F ... and better beware of the pitfalls of G, H, I ....

If, for example, we imagine policy makers and their advisors contemplating the imposition of a ban on smoking in cars carrying children and pondering the specific issue of whether there is public support, the advice above tells them not to rely solely upon survey data and some arbitrary threshold of positive opinion to carry the day. Rather, it asks them to think through a series of questions on the crucial contingencies. Is there any reason to suppose that a significant proportion of your population is not aware of the health risks of secondhand smoke? Has the car any special cultural resonance as a private space? Is there any reason to suppose that a significant proportion of your population will not support a ban promoted on the basis of children's wellbeing? Is there any reason to suppose that a significant proportion of your smokers does not regret taking up the habit? Is there any reason to suppose that a significant proportion of your population will be sanguine about their children taking up smoking? Has there already been a reasonably successful tightening of smoking restrictions in other public places? Is there any reason to suppose that a significant proportion of your smokers has not felt the press of denormalisation? The profile of answers to these questions will vary significantly from jurisdiction to jurisdiction. And whether answering them requires further empirical scrutiny or ends in top of the head calculation, the point is that the decision process becomes one of coming up with answers to these vital questions. A better framework for decision making has been provided.

Evidence does not come in finite chunks offering certainty and security to policy decisions. Programmes and interventions spring into life as ideas about how to change the world for the better. Evaluation research allows us to refine those explanations and systematic review allows a refinement of those refinements. The review process should be understood as a means of building, adjudicating and extrapolating programme theories. Evidence-based policy will only mature when it is understood that it is a continuous, accumulative process in which the data pursue but never quite draw level with unfolding policy issues. The whole point, recalling Rumsfeld's terminology if not his methodology, is the steady conversion of 'unknowns' to 'knowns'.

Conclusion: A Mutually Monitoring, Disputatious Community of Truth Seekers

'God save you, dear reader, from an *idée fixe*, better a speck, a mote in the eye.'

Joaquim Maria Machado de Asiss, *The Posthumous Memoirs of Bras Cubas*

My *idée fixe* has travelled through three previous books – *A Measure for Measures: A Manifesto for Empirical Sociology* (1989), *Realistic Evaluation*, with Nick Tilley (1997), and *Evidence-Based Policy: A Realist Perspective* (2006) – as well as spanning, as they say, numerous book chapters and journal articles. Quick eyes will spot the absence of the terms realist in the first title. Back in the 1980s, it made more sense to make claims for the viability of the 'new realism' on the rear cover. And now here I am in 2012, doggedly, stubbornly, unendingly, writing manifestos in the name of realist social science.

I have tried to demonstrate, time and time and time and time again, that social science has a remorseless appetite for heading to the poles. Sociology in the 1980s was still gripped by the positivism versus phenomenology debate. Since this time the opposing groups have modified and multiplied – idiographic vs nomothetic, qualitative vs quantitative, agency vs structure, micro vs macro, empiricist vs constructivist, post-empiricist vs post-modernist and so on. The applied sphere has demonstrated an equal appetite for such paradigmatic fissures. Evaluation research is fashioned into increasingly fragmented pockets – formative vs summative, process vs outcome, top-down vs bottom-up, emancipatory vs experimental, normative vs value-free, and so on. By and large I have recommended that social science, pure and applied, is better served by falling between stools. And the same advice applies in relation to the central issues raised between these covers – what is the status of the knowledge that accrues as evaluation attempts to explain the outcomes of complex programmes born of complex policy systems as implemented in complex social settings?

The responses to this question do not fall neatly into two opposing camps, certain strategies being more like a dash to the exit than a rush to the poles. Nevertheless, it is possible to discern a yawning gap between those who seek to control or overcome complexity in order to establish certitude and those inclined to settle for a social science of multiple truths, normative standpoints and politicised inquiry. I have sought to argue, from the middle, against absolute truths and against relative truths and for the idea that only partial truths emerge from evaluative inquiry. I take this to be the orthodox position, indeed the humdrum expectation, in scientific inquiry. Popper was fond of saying that science is informed guesswork. Well, so too is policy making. It is created out of educated hunches, it is familiar with creating both winners and losers, it is rooted in the art of compromise and it is thrashed out of the expectation that there will be some truth in what most stakeholders have to say and thus some truth in every programme theory. Truth is thus accretive. One can improve on a previous truth without assuming one has arrived at the truth, the whole truth and nothing but the truth. One can improve on programme theory under the same terms and conditions.

Let me end by considering the fate of the manifesto writer. Has my *idée fixe* any further mileage or should I take cover and anticipate the critics' mote in the eye? Interestingly, although this is a thesis on method, a crucial part of the argument here is that to succeed, scientific research and thus evaluation research need a specific social structure, namely Campbell's disputatious community of truth seekers. What is required is competitive cross-validation, a professional culture that finds strength and value in the constant critical scrutiny of each other's work. Applying the requirement to this work, I might point out that I offered some close constructive criticism of other realist studies in Chapter 2. Although the chapter is a pernickety piece of prose, the discipline needs to see much more of it. Chapter 8, moreover, is one long invitation to competitors. Over and again, I acknowledged that many potential lines of inquiry in the smoking study had stopped short, that critics might not concur with my reasons for doing so, and that understanding as a whole would benefit from the study of their rival theories. For instance, it would be perfectly encouraging for the critic to point out that smoking in cars is ergonomically complex and thus a major cause of driver distraction and go on to gather evidence thereupon. It would be perfectly possible for the critic to argue that my risk equation failed to include thirdhand smoke, the particles that are absorbed into surfaces and subsequently re-emitted (Matt et al., 2011). Another partial line of inquiry could start here. Always, there is a further question to answer.

But let us look at the bigger picture and consider if the world of policy making is ready for the caution and rectitude of *The Science of Evaluation*. Is the policy community patient enough for ceaseless, incremental, partial understanding? Everyone knows that evidence can always be trumped by politics and that policy makers are impatient. If this book were called *The Politics of Evaluation*, I would have told the 'smoking in cars carrying children' episode as an opportunity lost. Recall that the topic was chosen to catch a growing wave of parliamentary interest. A year later the tide had ebbed, thanks to the election of a UK government with quite, quite different ideas about public health and behaviour change. Our efforts and our evidence thus slumbered – unmolested.

As it turned out, in autumn 2011 a Private Member's Bill proposing such a ban was introduced in the Commons. This triggered the Department of Health and the All Party Parliamentary Group on Smoking and Health into action. Evidence was hastily assembled and meetings were requested to discuss the findings presented in Chapter 8. All of this hurly-burly, alas, was completely tokenistic. Such legalisation is introduced under an archaic parliamentary procedure known as Standing Order 23 or the Ten Minute Rule. Any MP, rather than those with cabinet or departmental responsibilities, is entitled to speak for 10 minutes to convince the house of the merits of a fresh proposal. Bills introduced under the procedure rarely progress much further, since governments routinely oppose Private Member's Bills at a later stage, giving priority to their own legislation. The Ten Minute Rule, I often think, is a perfect allegory for the attention paid to evidence. I feel a book coming on called *Catch 23*.

Unsurprisingly, we discover once again that the senior decision-makers, the politicians, are great simplifiers, though I can think of less kindly ways of saying it. Given that they trade in sound-bites, one can expect little receptivity to contingent, conditional, complex truths. What is more interesting from the perspective of the book is the likely reaction in the junior ranks – in communities rather closer to the evidence. What about the fortitude of those whose job it is to commission, produce, analyse and apply evidence? Are they comfortable with caveats? There are reasons to be pessimistic. Many years ago US senator, Ed Muskie, presiding over a US committee on health effects of pollutants, grew tired of the scientific witnesses and their attempts to convey balance and objectivity – 'on the one hand this but on the other hand that'. His solution came in the infamous call for 'one-armed scientists'. Sad to say, many parties *within* the evidence industry have heeded his message. They too have come to prefer sound-bites (Pawson et al., 2011b).

Recall, for instance, this pronouncement from the US Surgeon General on the risk of exposure to secondhand smoke (2007): 'The scientific evidence indicates that there is no risk-free level of exposure to second hand smoke'. This, I am sorry to say, is an abomination. It follows years of careful inquiry by the same body charting how different types and levels of exposure trigger different disease pathologies in different populations. It is, moreover, a denial of the 'Bradford Hill criteria', widely accepted as the logical structure for investigating and defining causality in modern epidemiology (Hill, 1965). Hill along with Doll produced the first authoritative study on the relation between smoking and lung cancer (Doll and Hill, 1950) and went on to establish a nine-fold model for establishing causation: i) strength of association, ii) consistency, iii) specificity, iv) temporal relationship, v) biological gradient, vi) plausibility, vii) coherence, vii) experiment, and ix) analogy. This is no place to spell out all of the details other than to point out the density of the evidential layers needed to establish causation. In particular it might be useful to point out to the Surgeon General that item (v) the 'biological gradient' refers to the dose–response curve. In short, the 'dose makes the poison'.

As a second candidate for a Muskie award, I quote Simon Chapman, a former editor of the BMA Journal *Tobacco Control:*

> Since 1976, I have published over 330 research papers, editorials, letters and commentaries in peer review journals and another 100 in throwaway journals. I have written twelve books and large reports. A few of these have been cited reasonably well. But if I had to nominate my most influential contributions, I would name my 130 newspaper opinion pieces, my letters to newspapers or some of my extended radio and TV interviews during critical periods of advocacy for change. (Chapman, 2007)

It goes without saying that lobbying is the engine of policy change and it is, of course, Chapman's prerogative to champion the cause of 'making smoking history'. Much more worrying, however, is the two-legged approach he exemplifies. Advocates know the truth; scientists pursue the truth. My concern is whether it is possible to have a foot in both camps and thus whether in his sixteen-year stewardship of *Tobacco Control,* the publication became a scientific outlet, an advocacy sheet, or a throwaway journal.

There are also reasons to be optimistic about the scientific status of evaluation. Tobacco control interventions always raise the hackles and the emotions. There are less politicised areas of policy making including those intractable, wicked ones in which it is much harder to strike out for a simple solution. In these quieter quarters evidence can and does play its quieter role. Here, it is possible to detect an increasing appetite for programme theory evaluation, a growing understanding that interventions only work for some people in certain circumstances and certain respects, a weariness about the latest chest beater bearing snake-oil remedies and thus a greater willingness to use and reconsider available evidence. What is still needed is a more powerful institutional memory to absorb and share the lessons learnt and, above all, much more belligerence in informing policy makers of the power of partial knowledge.

My first conclusion is thus to call on evaluation to begin an endless journey. It should be organised with intervention theories as the unit of analysis and it should generate a phalanx of middle-range research programmes, the first probing at the boundaries of where theory A has applicability, the second establishing where theory B holds good, the third exploring where theory C finds its domain, and so on. Such a progressive, cumulative process of inquiry is difficult to maintain. It can just as easily go around in circles. My second conclusion suggests that maintaining this ever-shifting, mutually-improving, middle ground can only be achieved collectively and through constant critical scrutiny of each other's work. What we need, to recall Moynihan in the epigraph to chapter 3, are great complexifiers, evaluators who dare not only to understand what they are about, but who will dare to share that understanding with those for whom they act.

For this finishing touch, my aim was no more than to roll together these two conclusions within a rousing call to arms. In trying to connect these streams of thought, somewhere in the back of my mind I remembered a *dernier cri* from

Donald Campbell. Having located it, I found that it contains all I want to say. Given that it was first published in 1984, I am unsure whether the need to repeat it thirty years later is a sign of maturity or a sign of stagnation in evaluation research.

> The problem is turned over to you, unfinished and inadequately formalised. But I hope that I have convinced you that we need a sociology of scientific validity, and an applied social science speciality within it, as part of the methodology we bring to our tasks. I hope that you share my conviction that this can be done in a way that still makes valid applied social science possible (or at the very least, that we can produce beliefs of enough improved validity and subtlety to make continuation in our discipline worthwhile). If you are convinced of both need and possibility, I call upon you vigorous youngsters to take up the task of creating an adequate social theory of validity-increasing social science. But if you are convinced of the impossibility, then it is your duty to publicly denounce the pseudo-science in which we inadvertently find ourselves engaged. Let us at the very least create around the problem a mutually monitoring, disputatious community of scholars who listen carefully to each other's arguments and rebuttals. (Campbell, 1988: 333)

References

Andriani, P. and McKelvey, B. (2009) 'From Gaussian to Paretian thinking: causes and implications of power laws in organizations', *Organization Science*, 20: 1053–71.

Archer, M. (1995) *Realist Social Theory*. Cambridge: Cambridge University Press.

Armstrong, G. and Norris, C. (1999) *The Maximum Surveillance Society: The Rise of CCTV*. Oxford: Berg Publishers.

Aspler, R., Formica. S., Rosenthal, A.F. and Robinson, K. (2003) 'Increases in booster seat use among children of low income families and variation with age', *Injury Prevention*. 9: 322–325.

Astbury, B. and Leeuw, F.L. (2010) 'Unpacking Black Boxes: Mechanisms and Theory Building in Evaluation', *American Journal of Evaluation*, 31(3): 363–381.

Barclay, P., Buckly, P., Brantingdon, P.J., Brantingdon, P.L. and Whinn-Yeats, T. (1997) 'Preventing auto thefts in commuter parking lots: A bike patrol in Vancouver', in R. Clarke (ed.), *Situational Crime Prevention: Successful case Studies*. Guilderland, NY: Harrow and Heston.

Barnes, B. (1974) *Scientific Knowledge and Social Theory*. London: Routledge and Keegan Paul.

Bauman, A., Chen, X.C. and Chapman, S. (1995) 'Protecting children in cars from tobacco smoke'. *British Medical Journal*, 311, 1164.

Bearer, C. (1995) How are Children Different from Adults? *Environmental Health Perspectives*, 103: (Supp 6) 7–12.

Becker, H. (1970) *Sociological Work: Method and Substance*. Chicago: Aldine.

Beecher, H. (1955) 'The powerful placebo', *Journal of the American Medical Association*, 159: 1602–1606.

Bellavite, P., Ortolani, R., Pontarollo, F., Piasere, V., Benato, G. and Conforti, A. (2006) Immunology and homeopathy. Clinical studies – part 2. *Evidence-Based Complementary and Alternative Medicine*, 3: 397–409.

Bevan, G. and Hood, C. (2006) What's measured is what matters: Targets and gaming in the English public health system. *Public Administration*, 84(3): 517–38.

Bhaskar, R. (1978) *A Realist Theory of Science*. London: Verso.

Bhaskar, R. (1979) *The Possibility of Naturalism*. Brighton: Harvester Press.

Bhaskar, R. (1986) *Scientific Realism and Human Emancipation*. London: Verso.

Bhaskar, R. (2002) *Reflections On Meta-Reality: A Philosophy for the Present*, New Delhi: Sage.

Bond, L., Patton, G., Glover, S., Carlin, J., Butler, H., Thomas, L. and Bowes, G. (2004) The Gatehouse Project: can a multilevel school intervention affect emotional wellbeing and health risk behaviours? *Journal of Epidemiology and Community Health*, 58: 997–1003.

Brody, H. and Waters, D. (1980) 'Diagnosis is Treatment', *Journal of Family Practice* (1093) pp. 445–9.

Byrne, D. (1998) *Complexity Theory and the Social Sciences*. London: Routledge.

Byrne, D. (2002) *Interpreting Quantitative Data*. London: SAGE.

Campbell, D. (1988) *Donald T Campbell: Methodology and Epistemology for Social Science: Collected Papers* (edited by E. Overman). Chicago: University of Chicago Press.

Campbell, D. and Stanley, J. (1966) *Experimental and quasi-experimental designs for research*. Chicago, IL: Rand-McNally.

Campbell, R., Evans, M., Tucker, M., Quilty, B., Dieppe, P. and Donovan, J.L. (2001) 'Why don't patients do their exercises? Understanding non-compliance with physiotherapy in patients with osteoarthritis of the knee', *Journal of Epidemiology and Community Health*, 55: 132–8.

Chambless, D. (2002) 'Beware the dodo bird: The dangers of overgeneralization', *Clinical Psychology: Science and Practice*, 9: 13–16.

Chapman, S. (2007) *Public Health Advocacy and Tobacco Control: Making Smoking History*. Oxford: Blackwell.

Charlton, G. and Barrow, C. (2002) 'Coping and self-help group membership in Parkinson's Disease: an exploratory qualitative study', *Health & Social Care in the Community*, 10: 472–478.

Chen, H.T. and Rossi, P.H. (1980) 'The multi-goal, theory-driven approach to evaluation: A model linking basic and applied social sciences', *Social Forces*, 59: 106–122.

Chen, H.T. and Rossi, P.H. (1983) 'Evaluating with sense: The theory-driven approach', *Evaluation Review*, 7: 283–302.

Choi, B. and Pak, A. (2005) 'A catalog of biases in questionnaires. Preventing Chronic Disease'. Available from: URL: http://www.cdc.gov/pcd/issues/2005/jan/ 04_0050.htm.

Clarke, M. and Stewart, J. (2003) 'Handling the wicked issues'. Chapter 23 in Reynolds, D., Henderson, J., Seden, J., Charlesworth, J. and Bullman, A., *The Managing Care Reader*. London: Open University Press.

Collarile, P., Valent, F., Di Bartolomeo, S. and Barbone, F. (2008) 'Changes in child safety restraint use and parental driving behaviours in Italy', *Acta Paediatrica*, 97: 1256–1260.

Colley, H. (2003) 'Engagement mentoring for socially excluded youth: problematising an "holistic" approach to creating employability through the transformation of habitus', *British Journal of Guidance and Counselling*, 31(1): 77–98.

Collier, A. (1994) *An Introduction to Roy Bhaskar's Philosophy*. London: Verso.

Connolly, G., Richter, P., Aleguas, A.J., Pechacek, T., Stanfill, S. and Alpert, H. (2010) 'Unintentional child poisonings through ingestion of conventional and novel tobacco products', *Pediatrics*, 125: 896–899.

Cook, T.D. and Campbell, D.T. (1979) *Quasi-experimentation: Design and analysis issues for field settings*. Boston, MA: Houghton Mifflin Company.

Corning, P. (2002) 'The re-emergence of "emergence": A venerable concept in search of a theory', *Complexity*, 7(6): 18–30.

Craig, P., Dieppe, P., Macintyre, S., Mitchie, S., Nazareth, I. and Petticrew, M. (2008) 'Developing and evaluating complex interventions: The new Medical Research Council guidance', *British Medical Journal*, 337: a1655.

Dattée, B. and Barlow, J. (2010) 'Complexity and whole-system change programmes', *Journal of Health Service Research and Policy*, 15 Supp. 2: 19–25.

Davidoff, F. (2009) Heterogeneity is Not Always Noise: Lessons from Improvement: *JAMA*, Dec 16; 302(23): 2580–6.

Demark-Wahnefried, W., Aziz, N.M., Rowland, J.H. and Pinto, B.M. (2005) 'Riding the crest of the teachable moment: Promoting long-term health after the diagnosis of cancer', *Journal of Clinical Oncology*, 23: 5814–5830.

Department of Health (2010) 'A smokefree future: A comprehensive tobacco control strategy for England', London: United Kingdom. DOH.

Desapriya, E.B., Iwase, N., Pike, I., Brussoni, M. and Papsdorf, M. (2004) 'Child motor vehicle occupant and pedestrian casualties before and after enactment of child restraint seats legislation in Japan', *Injury Control & Safety Promotion*, 11: 225–230.

Dolan, P., Hallsworth, H., Halpern, D., King, D. and Vlaev, I. (2010) *Mindspace: Influencing behaviour through public policy*. Institute for Government and the Cabinet Office.

Doll, R. and Hill, A. (1950) Smoking and Carcinoma of the Lung. *British Medical Journal*, 2(4682): 739–748.

Donovan, J. (1995) 'Patient decision making. The missing ingredient in compliance research', *International Journal of Technology Assessment in Health Care*, 11: 443–455.

Dracup, K. and Meleis, A. (1982) 'Compliance: an interactionist approach', *Nursing Research*, 31: 31–36.

Duguid, S. (2000) *Can Prisons Work?* University of Toronto Press: Toronto.

Dunn, J., Greenbank, S., McDowell, M., Mahoney, C., Mazerolle, P., Occhipinti, S. and Steginga, S. (2008) 'Community knowledge, attitudes and behaviours about environmental tobacco smoke in homes and cars', *Health Promotion Journal of Australia*, 19: 113–117.

Dusenbury, L., Brannighan, R., Hansen, W., Walsh, J. and Falco, M. (2005) 'Quality of Implementation: Developing measures crucial to the understanding of prevention interventions', *Health Education Research*, 20(3): 308–31.

Earl, S., Carden, F. and Smutylo, T. (2001) *Outcome Mapping: Building Learning and Reflection into Development Programs*. Ottawa: International Development Research Centre.

Edwards, R., Wilson, N. and Pierse, N. (2006a) 'Highly hazardous air quality associated with smoking in cars: New Zealand pilot study', *The Journal of the New Zealand Medical Association*, 119: U2294.

Edwards, R., Hasselholdt, C., Hargreaves, K., Probery, C., Holford, R., Hart, J. and Watson, A.F.R. (2006b) 'Levels of second hand smoke in pubs and bars by deprivation and food-serving status: a cross-sectional study from North West England', *BMC Public Health*, 6: 42 doi: 10.1186/1471-2458-6-42

Einarson, T. and Hemels, M. 2001 'Correspondence', *New England Journal of Medicine*, 345(17): 1277.

Elias, N. (1969) *The Civilizing Process*, Vol. I. *The History of Manners*, Oxford: Blackwell.

Ellis, F. (2008) Physics, Complexity and Causality. *Nature*, 435(9): 435.

Elster, J. (2007) *Explaining Social Behaviour*. Cambridge: Cambridge University Press.

Elwyn, G., Edwards, A., Kinnersley, P. and Grol, R. (2000) 'Shared decision-making and the concept of equipoise: the competences of involving patients in health-care choices', *British Journal of General Practice*, 50: 892–9.

Evans, J. and Chen, Y. (2005 'The association between home and vehicle environmental tobacco smoke (ETS) and chronic bronchitis in a Canadian population: The Canadian Community Health Survey', *Inhalation Toxicology*, 21: 244–249.

Facione, N. and Facione, P. (2006) 'The cognitive structuring of patient delay in breast cancer', *Social Science & Medicine*, 63(12): 3137–3149.

Felson, M. (1986) 'Linking criminal choices, routine activities, informal control and criminal outcomes', in D. Cornish and R. Clarke (eds), *The Reasoning Criminal*. New York: Springer-Verlag.

Fine, P.G. and Portenoy, R.K. (2009) 'Establishing "best practices" for opioid rotation: conclusions of an expert panel', *Journal of Pain Symptom Management*, 38(3): 418–425.

Fong, G., Hammond, D., Laux, F., Zanna, M., Cummings, K., Borland, R. and Ross, H. (2004) 'The near universal experience of regret among smokers in four countries: Findings from the International Tobacco Control Policy Evaluation Survey', *Nicotine & Tobacco Research*, 6: S341–S351.

Fong, G.T., Hyland, A., Borland, R., Hammond, D., Hastings, G., McNeill, A., Anderson, S., Cummings, K.M., Allwright, S., Mulcahy, M., Howell, F., Clancy, L., Thompson, M.E., Connolly, G. and Driezen, P. (2006) 'Reductions in tobacco smoke pollution and increases in support for smoke-free public places following the implementation of comprehensive smoke-free workplace legislation in the Republic of Ireland', *Tobacco Control*, Jun;15 Suppl 3: iii51–8.

Ford, S., Schofield, T. and Hope, T. (2003) 'What are the ingredients for a successful evidence-based patient choice consultation? A qualitative study'. *Social Science and Medicine*, 56(3): 289–602.

Fosse, R.D., Goodwin, A.H., McCart, A.T. and Hellinga, L.A. (2009) 'Short-term effects of a teenage driver cell phone restriction', *Accident Analysis & Prevention*, 41: 419–424.

Freeman, B., Chapman, S. and Storey, P. (2008) 'Banning smoking in cars carrying children: An analytical history of a public health advocacy campaign', *Australian & New Zealand Journal of Public Health*, 32: 60–65.

Funnell, S. and Rogers, P. (2011) *Purposeful Program Theory: Effective Use of Theories of Change and Logic Models*. London: Wiley.

Gamble, J. (2008) *A Developmental Evaluation Primer*. Quebec: J. W. McConnell Foundation.

Gargani, J. (2010) 'A Welcome Change from Debate to Dialogue about Causality', *American Journal of Evaluation*, 31(1): 131–132.

Geertz, C. (1973) *The Interpretation of Cultures*. New York: Basic Books.

Gillespie, J., Milne, K. and Wilson, N. (2005) 'Secondhand smoke in New Zealand homes and cars: Exposure, attitudes, and behaviours in 2004', *New Zealand Medical Journal*, 118.

Gladwell, M. (2000) *The Tipping Point: How Little Things Can Make a Big Difference*. New York: Little Brown.

Glantz, S. and Balbach, E. (2000) *Tobacco war: Inside the California battles*. Berkeley: University of California Press.

Glaser, B.G. and Strauss, A.L. (1967) *The discovery of grounded theory: strategies for qualitative research*. Chicago: Aldine.

Glouberman, S. and Zimmerman, B. (2002) *Complicated and Complex Systems: What would successful reforms of Medicare look like?* Commission on the Future of Health Care in Canada, Paper 8.

Gravel, K., Legare, F. and Graham, I. (2006) 'Barriers and Facilitators to Implementing Shared Decision-Making in Clinical Practice: A Systematic Review of Health Professionals' Perceptions', *Implementation Science No. 1*, 16. doi:10.1186/1748–5908–1–16.

Greene, G., Caracelli, V. and Graham, W. (1989) 'Toward a conceptual framework for mixed-method evaluation', *Educational Evaluation and Policy Analysis*, 11(3): 255–274.

Greenhalgh, T., Humphrey, C., Hughes, J., Macfarlane, F., Butler, C. and Pawson, R. (2009) 'How do you modernize a health service? A realist evaluation of whole-scale transformation in London, UK', *Milbank Quarterly*, 87(2): 391–416.

Greenhalgh, T., Wong, G., Westhorp, G. and Pawson, R. (2011) 'Protocol – Realist and Meta-narrative Evidence Synthesis: Evolving Standards' (RAMESES) *BMC Medical Research Methodology*, 11: 115.

Grossman, J. and Tierney, J. (1998) 'Does Mentoring work? An Impact study of Big Brothers Big Sisters Program', *Evaluation Review*, 22(3): 403–26.

Grunfeld, E., Fitzpatrick, R., Mant, D., Yudkin, P., Adewuyi-Dalton, R., Stewart, J., Cole, D. and Vessey, M. (1999) 'Comparison of breast cancer patient satisfaction with follow-up in primary care versus specialist care: results from a randomized controlled trial', *British Journal of General Practice*, 49: 705–10.

Gubrium, J., Holstein, J., Marvarsti, A. and McKinney, K. (2012) *The SAGE Handbook of Interview Research: The Complexity of the Craft*. SAGE: Thousand Oaks.

Hammond, D., Fong, G., Zanna, M., Thrasher, J. and Borland, R. (2006) 'Tobacco Denormalization and Industry Beliefs among Smokers from Four Countries', *American Journal of Preventive Medicine*, 31: 225–232.

Harré, R. (1983) *The Great Scientific Experiments*. Oxford: Oxford University Press.

Hawe, P., Bond, L. and Butler, H. (2009a) 'Knowledge theories can inform evaluation practice: What can a complexity lens add?' In J. Ottoson and P. Hawe (eds),

Knowledge Utilization, Diffusion Implementation, Transfer and Translation. New Directions for Evaluation, 124, 89–100.

Hawe, P., Shiell, A. and Riley, T. (2004) 'Complex interventions: How "out of control" can a randomised trial be?', *British Medical Journal*, 328: 1561–63.

Hawe, P., Shiell, A. and Riley, T. (2009b) 'Theorising Interventions as Events in Systems', *American Journal of Community Psychology*, 43: 267–76.

Healton, C., Farrelly, M., Weitzenkamp, D., Lindsey, D. and Haviland, M. (2006) 'Youth smoking prevention and tobacco industry revenue', *Tobacco Control*, 15: 103–106.

Henry, G., Mark, M. and Julnes, G. (1998) 'Realist Evaluation: An Emerging Theory in Support of Practice', *New Directions for Evaluation, 78*. San Francisco: Jossey-Bass.

Hill, A. (1965) 'The Environment and Disease: Association or Causation?', *Proceedings of the Royal Society of Medicine*, 58(5): 295–300.

Hope, C. and Mocan, N. (2005) 'Carrots, Sticks, and Broken Windows', *Journal of Law and Economics*, 48(1): 235–266.

House of Lords, Science and Technology Select Committee (2011) *Behaviour Change.* HL Paper 179. London: The Stationery Office.

Houston, W.R. (1938) 'The doctor himself as a therapeutic agent', *Annals of Internal Medicine*, 11: 1416–1425.

Hróbjartsson, A. and Götzsche, P. (2001) 'Is The Placebo Powerless? An Analysis of Clinical Trials Comparing Placebo with No Treatment', *New England Journal of Medicine*, 344(21): 1594–1602.

Hu, A. (1999) 'Exposure misclassification bias in studies of environmental tobacco smoke and lung cancer', *Environmental Health Perspectives*, 107: 873–77.

Huang, H. and Cynecki, M. (2001) 'Effects of traffic calming measures on pedestrian and motorist behavior', McLean, VA, Federal Highway Administration.

Hussain, K., Al Shakarchi, J., Mahmoudi, A., Al Mawlawi, A. and Marshall, T. (2006) 'Mobile phones and driving: a follow-up', *Journal of Public Health*, 28: 395–396.

Jacobson, P. and Wasserman, J. (1999) 'The implementation of tobacco control laws', *Journal of Health Politics, Policy and Law*, 24: 567–595.

Jacobson, P. and Wasserman, J. (1999) 'The implementation and enforcement of Tobacco Control Laws: Policy implications for activists and the industry', *Journal of Health Politics, Policy and Law*, 24: 567–598.

Johal, S., Napier, F., Britt-Compton, J. and Marshall, T. (2005) 'Mobile phones and driving', *Journal of Public Health*, 27: 112–113.

Kane, M. and Trochim, W. (2006) *Concept mapping for planning and evaluation.* Newbury Park: SAGE.

Kaplan, A. (1998, 1st edn 1964) *The Conduct of Inquiry: Methodology for Behavioural Science.* New Brunswick, NJ: Transaction Publishers.

Kazi, M., Pagkos, B. and Milch, H. (2011) 'Realist Evaluation in Wraparound: A New Approach in Social Work Evidence-Based Practice', *Research on Social Work Practice*, 21(1): 57–64.

Kent, D. and Hayward, R. (2007a) 'Limitations of applying summary results of clinical trials to individual patients: the need for risk stratification', *JAMA*, 298: 1209–1212.

Kent, D. and Hayward, R. (2007b) 'When averages hide individual differences in clinical trials: analyzing the results of clinical trials to expose individual patients' risks might help doctors make better treatment decisions', *American Scientist*, 95(1): 60–69.

Kent, D., Rothwell, P., Ioannidis, J., Altman, D. and Hayward, R. (2010) 'Assessing and reporting heterogeneity in treatment effects in clinical trials: a proposal', *Trials*, 11: 85.

Kienle, G. and Kienle, H. (1997) 'The powerful placebo effect: fact or fiction?', *Journal Clinical Epidemiology*, 50: 1311–18.

Kirsch, I., Moore, T., Scoboria, A. and Nicholls, S. (2002) 'The emperor's new drugs: An analysis of antidepressant medication data submitted to the U.S. Food and Drug Administration', *Prevention & Treatment*, Vol. 5(1), Jul 2002.

Kravitz, R., Duan, N. and Braslow, J. (2004) 'Evidence-Based Medicine, Heterogeneity of Treatment Effects, and the Trouble with Averages', *The Milbank Quarterly*, 82(4): 661–687.

Kuhn, T. (1962) *The Structure of Scientific Revolutions*. Chicago: University of Chicago.

Lakatos, I. (1978) *The Methodology of Scientific Research Programmes: Philosophical Papers Volume 1*. Cambridge: Cambridge University Press.

Latey, P. (1979) *Muscular Manifesto*. Osteopathic Publishing: London.

Latey, P. (2001) 'Placebo responses in bodywork', in D. Peters (ed.), *Understanding the Placebo Effect in Complementary Medicine*. Churchill Livingstone: London.

Leatherdale, S.T., Smith, P. and Ahmed, R. (2008) 'Youth exposure to smoking in the home and in cars: How often does it happen and what do youth think about it?', *Tobacco Control*, 17: 86–92.

Lee, C.-W. and Kahende, J. (2007) 'Factors associated with successful smoking cessation in the United States', *American Journal of Public Health*, 97: 1503–1509.

Lieberson, S. (1985) *Making It Count: The Improvement of Social Research and Theory*. Berkeley: University of California Press.

Long, A. (2009) 'The potential of complementary and alternative medicine in promoting well-being and critical health literacy: a prospective, observational study of shiatsu', *BMC Complementary and Alternative Medicine*, 9(19): 1–11.

Luborsky, L., Singer, B. and Luborsky, L. (1975) 'Comparative studies of psychotherapies. Is it true that "everyone has won and all must have prizes"?', *Archives of General Psychiatry*, 32(8): 153–155.

Luborsky, L., Rosenthal, R., Diguer, L., Andrusyna, T., Berman, J., Levitt, J., Seligman, D. and Krause, D. (2002) 'The dodo bird verdict is alive and well: mostly', *Clinical Psychology: Science and Practice*, 9: 2–12.

Luepker, R., Raczynski, J. et al. (2000) 'Effect of a Community Intervention on Patient Delay and Emergency Medical Service Use in Acute Coronary Heart Disease: The Rapid Early Action for Coronary Treatment (REACT) Trial', *JAMA*. 284(1): 60–67.

Mackenzie, M., O'Donnell, C., Halliday, E., Sridharan, S. and Platt, S. (2010) 'Evaluating complex interventions: one size does not fit all', *British Medical Journal*, 340: c185.

Magura, S. and Kang, S. (1996) 'Validity and Self-reported Drug Use in High Risk Populations', *Substance Use and Misuse*, 31(9): 1131–53.

Marinker, M. (1997) 'Writing prescriptions is easy', *British Medical Journal*, 314: 747.

Mark, M., Henry, G. and Julnes, G. (2000) *Evaluation*. San Francisco: Jossey-Bass.

Martin, J., George, R., Andrews, K., Barr, P., Bicknell, D., Insull, E., Knox, C., Liu, J., Naqshband, M., Romeril, K., Wong, D., Thomson, G. and Wilson, N. (2006) 'Observed smoking in cars: a method and differences by socioeconomic area', *Tobacco Control*, 15: 409–11.

Martinson, R. (1974) 'What works? Questions and answers about prison reform.' *Public Interest*, 35: 22–45.

Martuzzi, M. and Tickner, J. (eds) (2004) *The precautionary principle: Protecting public health, the environment and the future of our children*. Copenhagen, Denmark: World Health Organization, Europe.

Marx, K. (1852) 'The Eighteenth Brumaire of Louis Bonapart', *Die Revolution*. New York.

Matt, G., Quintana, P., Destaillats, H., Gundel, L., Sleiman, M. and Singer, B. (2011) 'Thirdhand Tobacco Smoke: Emerging Evidence and Arguments for a Multidisciplinary Research Agenda', *Environmental Health Perspectives*, 119(9): 1218–1226.

May, C. (2006) 'A rational model for assessing and evaluating complex interventions in health care', *BMC Health Services Research* 6: 86.

Mazzocchi, F. (2008) 'Complexity in Biology', *EMBO Reports*, 9(1): 10–14.

McBride, C., Emmons, K. and Lipkus, I. (2003) 'Understanding the potential of teachable moments; the case of smoking cessation'. *Health Education Research* 18(2) 156–170.

McCart, A.T. and Geary, L.L. (2004) 'Longer term effects of New York State's law on drivers' handheld cell phone use', *Injury Prevention*, 10, 11–15.

McCart, A., Helliga, L. and Geary, L. (2006) 'Effects of Washington, DC law on driver's hand-held cell phone use', *Traffic Injury Prevention*, 7: 1–5.

McEvoy, S.P., Stevenson, M.R. and Woodward, M. (2006) 'Phone use and crashes while driving: A representative survey of drivers in two Australian states', *Medical Journal of Australia*, 185, 630–634.

McGavock, H. (1996) 'A review of the literature on drug adherence. Partnership in medicine taking'. In *Taking Medicine to Best Effect*. London: Royal Pharmaceutical Society of Great Britain: 1–55.

McLennan, G. (2009) 'For Science in the Social Sciences. The End of the Road for Critical Realism?', in S. Moog and R. Stones (eds), *Nature, Social Relations and Human Needs*. London: Palgrave Macmillan (pp. 47–64).

Merton, R. (1967) *On Theoretical Sociology: Five essays old and new*. New York: Free Press.

Merton, R. (1968 enlarged edition) *Social Theory and Social Structure*. New York: Free Press.

Mintzberg, H., Raisinghani, D. and Theoret, A. (1976) 'The structure of "unstructured" decision processes', *Administrative Science Quarterly*, 21(3): 2246–75.

Moerman, D. (2002) *Meaning, Medicine and the 'Placebo Effect'*. Cambridge: Cambridge University Press.

Monaghan, M. (2010) *Evidence versus politics. Exploiting research in UK drug policy making?* Bristol: The Policy Press.

Morrell, J. (2010) *Evaluation in the Face of Uncertainty*. New York: Guilford Press.

Moumjid, N., Gafni, A., Bremond, A. and Carrere, M.O. (2007) 'Shared decision making in the medical encounter: are we all talking about the same thing?', *Medical Decision Making*, 27: 539–46.

MRC (2008) UK Medical Research Council (MRC) guidance on 'Developing and Evaluating Complex Intervention'. www.mrc.ac.uk/complexinterventions-guidance.

Munro, M. and Jeffrey, P. (2008) 'A critical review of the theory and application of social learning in participatory natural resource management processes', *Journal of Environmental Planning and Management*, 51(3): 325–44.

Murray, E., Davis, H., Tai, S.S., Coulter, A., Gray, A. and Haines, A. (2001) 'Randomised controlled trial of an interactive multimedia decision aid on hormone replacement therapy in primary care', *British Medical Journal*, 490–93.

Murray, E., Pollack, L., White, M. and Lo, B. (2007) 'Clinical decision-making: patients' preferences and experiences', *Patient Education and Counselling*, 65: 189–196.

Natrass, N. (2006) *Disability and Welfare in South Africa's Era of Unemployment and Aids*. CSSR Working Paper No. 147, University of Cape Town.

Nestle (2007) *Food Politics*. Berkeley: University of California Press.

NICE (2009) *Depression: The treatment and management of depression in adults*. NICE clinical guideline 90.

O'Connor, A.M. (2007) 'Using decision aids to help patients navigate the "grey zone" of medical decision-making', *Canadian Medical Association Journal*, 176: 1597–98.

Ott, W., Klepeis, N. and Switzer, P. (2008) 'Air change rate of motor vehicles and in-vehicle pollutant concentrations from second-hand smoke', *Journal of Exposure Science and Environmental Epidemiology*, 18: 312–325.

Pagel, W. (1982) *Paracelsus: An introduction in philosophical medicine in the era of the renaissance*. Basel, Switzerland: Karger.

Parloff, M. (1986) 'Frank's "Common Elements" in psychotherapy: Non-specific factors and placebos', *American Journal of Orthopsychiatry*, 56(4): 521–530.

Parvin, P. (2010) *Karl Popper*. London: Continuum.

Patton, M. (2011) *Developmental Evaluation: Applying Complexity Concepts to Enhance Innovation and Use*. New York: Guilford Press.

Pawson, R. (1989) *A Measure for Measures: A Manifesto for Empirical Sociology*. London: Routledge.

Pawson, R. (1996) 'Theorizing the interview', *British Journal of Sociology*, 47(3): 296–314.

Pawson, R. (2000) 'Middle-Range Realism', *Archive Européenes de Sociologie*, XLI: 283–325.

Pawson, R. (2006a) *Evidence-Based Policy: A Realist Perspective*. London: SAGE.

Pawson, R. (2006b) 'Simple Principles for The Evaluation of Complex Programmes', in A. Killoran and A. Kelly (eds), *Public Health Evidence*. Oxford: Oxford University Press.

Pawson, R. (2009a) 'On the shoulders of Merton: Boudon as the modern guardian of middle-range theory', in M. Cherkaoui and P. Hamilton (eds), *Raymond Boudon: A Life in Sociology*. Oxford: Bardwell Press.

Pawson, R. (2009b) 'Middle range theory and programme theory evaluation: From provenance to practice', in J. Vaessen and F. Leeuw (eds), *Mind the Gap: Perspectives on Policy Evaluation and the Social Sciences*. New Jersey: Transaction Press.

Pawson, R. (2011) 'From the Library of ...' *Evaluation*, 17(2): 193–196.

Pawson, R. and Manzano, A. (2012) 'A Realist Diagnostic Workshop', *Evaluation*, 18(2): 176–91.

Pawson, R. and Sridharan, S. (2010) 'Theory-driven evaluation of public health programmes', in A. Killoran and A. Kelly (eds), *Evidence Based Public Health*. Oxford: Oxford University Press.

Pawson, R. and Tilley, N. (1997a) 'An Introduction to Scientific Realist Evaluation', in E. Chelimsky and W. Shadish (eds), *Evaluation for the 21st Century: A Handbook*. SAGE: Thousand Oaks.

Pawson, R. and Tilley, N. (1997b) *Realistic Evaluation*. London: SAGE.

Pawson, R., Owen, L. and Wong, G. (2010b) 'The Today Programme's contribution to evidence-based policy', *Evaluation*, 16(2): 211–213.

Pawson, R., Wong, G. and Owen, L. (2010a) 'Legislating for health: locating the evidence', *Journal of Public Health Policy*, 31(2): 164–177.

Pawson, R., Wong, G. and Owen, L. (2011a) 'Known Knowns, Known Unknowns, Unknown Unknowns: The Predicament of Evidence-Based Policy', *American Journal of Evaluation*, 32(4): 518–546.

Pawson, R., Wong, G. and Owen, L. (2011b) 'Myths, facts and conditional truths: what is the evidence on the risks associated with smoking in cars carrying children?', *Canadian Medical Association Journal*, 182(8): 796–9.

Philip, K. and Spratt, J. (2007) 'A synthesis of published research on mentoring and befriending', http://www.mandbf.org.uk/resources/research/

Phillips, R., Amos, A., Ritchie, D., Cunningham-Burley, S. and Martin, C. (2007) 'Smoking in the home after the smoke-free legislation in Scotland: qualitative study', *British Medical Journal*, 2007 Sep 15;335(7619):553. Epub 2007 Sep 9.

Plamping, D. (1998) 'Change and resistance to change in the NHS', *British Medical Journal*, 4 July, 317: 69–71.

Pollitt, C. (2008) *Time, Policy, Management: Governing with the Past*. Oxford: Oxford University Press.

Pollitt, C. (2009) 'Complexity theory and evolutionary public administration: A skeptical afterword', in G.R. Teisman, A. Van Buuren and L. Gerrits (eds), *Managing Complex Governance Systems: Dynamics, Self-Organization and Coevolution in Public Investments*,

Pollo, A., Amanzio, M., Arslanian, A., Casadio, C., Maggi, G. and Benedetti, F. (2001) 'Response expectancies in placebo analgesia and their clinical relevance', *Pain*, 93: 77–84.

Pope, C. and Mays, N. (2006) *Qualitative Research in Healthcare*. Cambridge: Blackwell.

Popper, K. (1963) *Conjectures and Refutations: The Growth of Scientific Knowledge*. London: Routledge .

Popper, K. (1992, 5th edn) *The Logic of Scientific Discovery*. London: Routledge. Classics (First published in 1934 as *Logik der Forschung*).

Porporino, F. and Robinson, D. (1995) 'An evaluation of the reasoning and rehabilitation programme with Canadian federal prisoners', in R. Ross and R. Ross (eds), *Thinking Straight*. Ottawa: Air Training Productions.

Priest, N. (2006) '"Motor Magic": Evaluation of a community capacity-building approach to supporting the development of preschool children', *Australian Occupational Therapy Journal*, 53(3): 220–232.

Prochaska, J. and DiClemente, C. (2005, 2nd edn) 'The transtheoretical approach', in J.C. Norcross and M.R. Goldfried (eds), *Handbook of psychotherapy integration*. New York: Oxford University Press.

Proctor, P., Reid, P., Compton, W., Jerome, H., Grossman, J. and Fanjiang, G. (eds) (2005) *Building a Better Delivery System: A New Engineering/Health Care Partnership*, Committee on Engineering and the Health Care System, US Institute of Medicine and National Academy of Engineering.

Raczynski, J., Finnegan, J., Zapk, J., Meischke, H., Meshack, A., Stone, E., Bracht, N., Sellers, D., Daya, M., Robbins, M., McAlister, A. and Simons-Morton, D. (1999) 'REACT: Theory-based intervention to reduce treatment-seeking delay in acute myocardial infarction', *American Journal of Preventative Medicine*, 16(4): 325–334.

Rajalin, S., Summala, H., Poysti, L., Anteroinen, P. and Porter, B. (2005) 'In-Car Cell Phone Use and Hazards Following Hands Free Legislation', *Traffic Injury Prevention*, 6(3): 225–229.

Ramirez, A., Westcombe, A., Burgess, C., Sutton, S., Littlejohns, P. and Richards, M. (1999) 'Factors predicting delayed presentation of symptomatic breast cancer: a systematic review', *The Lancet*, 353 (9159): 1127–1131.

Raynor, D.K. (1992) 'Patient compliance: the pharmacist's role', *International Journal of Pharmacy Practice*: 1: 126–135.

Richards, M.A., Westcombe, A., Love, S., Littlejohns, P. and Ramirez, A. (1999) 'Influence of delay on survival in patients with breast cancer: a systematic review', *Lancet*, 53(9159): 1119–26.

Rittel, H. and Webber, M. (1974) 'Dilemmas in a General theory of planning', *Policy Sciences*, Amsterdam: Elsevier. 4: 155–69.

Roberts, J. (2000) 'Changing public attitudes towards corporal punishment: the effects of statutory reform in Sweden', *Child Abuse and Neglect*, 24: 1027–1035.

Rodger, A., Jolley, D., Thompson, S., Lanigan, A. and Crofts, N. (1999) 'The impact of diagnosis of hepatitis C virus on quality of life', *Hepatology*, 30: 1299–301.

Rogers, P. (2008) 'Using Programme Theory to Evaluate Complicated and Complex Aspects of Interventions', *Evaluation*, 14(1): 29–48.

Rosenbaum, J. (2005) 'Attitudes toward benzodiazepines over the years', *Journal of Clinical Psychiatry*, 66 (supp 2): 4–8.

Rosenhead, J. (1996) 'What's the problem? An introduction to problem structuring methods', *Interfaces*, 26(6): 117–131.

Rossi, P. (1987) 'The Iron Law of Evaluation and Other Metallic Rules', *Research in Social Problems and Public Policy*, 4(1): 3–30.

Rossi, P., Berk, R. and Lenihan, K. (1980) *Money, Work and Crime*. Academic Press: New York.

Royal College of Nurses (2007) *Our NHS: today and tomorrow*. Glossy brochure published by Royal College of Nursing. Cavendish Square, London.

Royal Pharmaceutical Society of Great Britain/Merck, Sharp and Dohme (1997) Report of Joint Working Party: From compliance to concordance. Achieving shared goals in medicine taking. A working party report. London: Royal Pharmaceutical Society of Great Britain and Merck Sharp and Dohme; 1997

Runciman, W. (1966) *Relative Deprivation and Social Justice: Attitudes to Social Inequality*. London: Routledge.

Russell, B. (1950) *An Inquiry into Meaning and Truth*. London: George Allen and Unwin; New York: W.W. Norton.

Sallybanks, J. (2001) *Assessing the Police Use of Decoy Vehicles*. Police Research Series Paper 137, London: Home Office.

Sayer, A. (1992) *Method in Social Science: A Realist Approach*. London: Routledge.

Schagrin, M. (1963) 'Resistance to Ohm's Law', *American Journal of Physics*, 31(7): 536–47.

Shedd, J. and Hershey, M. (1913) 'The History of Ohm's Law', *Popular Science*, December pp. 599–614.

Shiner, M., Newburn, T., Young, T. and Groban, S. (2004) *Mentoring Disaffected Young People: An Evaluation of 'Mentoring Plus'*. York: Joseph Rowntree Foundation.

Skrabanek, P. and McCormick, J. (1998) *Follies and fallacies in medicine* (3rd edn), Bellingham Tarragon Press.

Smith, M., Clarke, R. and Pease, K. (2002) 'Anticipatory benefits in crime prevention', *Crime Prevention Studies Annual Review*, 13: 71–88.

Smithson, M. (1989) *Ignorance and Uncertainty*. New York: Springer-Verlag.

Snelling, I. (2003) 'Do star ratings really reflect hospital performance?', *Journal of Health Organization and Management*, 17(3): 210–23.

Sridharan, S., Platt, S., Hume, M. and Nakaima, A. (forthcoming) *Taking Complexity Seriously*.

Stewart, M. (1995) 'Effective physician–patient communication and health outcomes: A review', *Canadian Medical Association Journal*, 152(9): 1423–1433.

Strupp, H. (1986) 'The nonspecific hypothesis of therapeutic effectiveness: A current assessment', *American Journal of Orthopsychiatry*, 56(4): 515–20.

Tallman, K. and Bohart, A. (1999) 'The client as a common factor: Clients as self-healers', in M. Hubble, B. Duncan, and S. Miller (eds), *The Heart and Soul of Change: What Happens in Therapy*. Washington DC: American Psychological Association. pp. 91–131.

Taylor, D., MacBean, C., Das, A. and Rosli, R. (2007) 'Handheld mobile telephone use among Melbourne drivers', *Medical Journal of Australia*, 187, 432–434.

Thaler, R. and Sunstein, C. (2008) *Nudge: Improving Decisions about Health, Wealth and Happiness*. London: Penguin.

The Royal Society (2005) *Personalised medicines: hopes and realities*. September 2005, London http://royalsociety.org/policy/publications/2005/personalised-medicines/

Thomas, D. (1979) *Naturalism and Social Science: A Post-Empiricist Philosophy of Social Science*. Cambridge: Cambridge University Press.

Thomson, G., Wilson, N., Weerasekera, D. and Edwards, R. (2008) 'Ninety-six percent of New Zealand smokers support smokefree cars containing preschool children', *New Zealand Medical Journal*, 121: 139–140.

Tolson, D. and Schofield, I. (2011) 'Football reminiscence for men with dementia: lessons from a realistic evaluation', *Nursing Inquiry*, 19: 63–70.

Toulmin, S. (1972) *Human Understanding*. Princeton: Princeton University Press.

Trochim, W. (1985) 'Pattern Matching, Validity, and Conceptualization in Program Evaluation', *Evaluation Review*, 9(5): 575–604.

Tsai, A. and Wadden, T. (2005) 'Systematic Review: An Evaluation of Major Commercial Weight Loss Programs in the United States', *Annals of Internal Medicine*, Vol. 142 (4): 56–66.

Turner, K. and Gordon, J. (2004) 'A fresh perspective on a rank issue: pupils' accounts of staff enforcement of smoking restrictions', *Health Education Research*, 19: 148–158.

Umberson, D. and Montez, J. (2010) 'Social Relationships and Health: A Flashpoint for Health Policy', *Journal of Health and Social Behavior*, 51(Special Issue): S54–66.

US Department of Health and Human Services (2006) *The health consequences of involuntary exposure to tobacco smoke: A report of the surgeon general*. Atlanta, GA: US Department of Health and Human Services, Centers for Diseases Control and Prevention, Coordinating Center for Health Promotion, National Center for Chronic Disease Prevention and Health Promotion, Office on Smoking and Health.

US Department of Health and Human Services (2007) *Children and secondhand smoke exposure: Excerpts from the health consequences of involuntary exposure to tobacco smoke*. A report of the surgeon general. Atlanta, GA: US Department of Health and Human Services, Centers for Diseases Control and Prevention,

US Environmental Protection Agency (2010) Coordinating Center for Health Promotion, National Center for Chronic Disease Prevention and Health Promotion, Office on Smoking and Health. 'National ambient air quality standards', Retrieved from http://www.epa.gov/air/criteria.html.

van Dulman, A. and Bensig, J. (2002) 'Health promoting effects of the physician patient encounter', *Psychology, Health & Medicine*, 7(3): 289–300.

Vase, L., Riley, J. and Price, D. (2002) 'A comparison of placebo effects in clinical analgesic trials versus studies of placebo analgesia', *Pain*, 99: 443–52.

Vermeire, E., Hearnshaw, H. and Van Royen, P. (2001) 'Patient adherence to treatment: three decades of research', *Journal of Clinical Pharmacy and Therapeutics*, 26: 331–342.

Wagenaar, A. and Webster, D. (1986) 'Preventing injuries to children through compulsory automobile safety seat use', *Pediatrics*, 78: 662–672.

Walker, D. and Myrick, F. (2006) 'Grounded Theory: An Exploration of Process and Procedure', *Qualitative Health Research*, 16(4): 547–559.

Wallace, W. (1971) *The Logic of Science in Sociology*. New York: Aldine.

Walshe, K. (2010) 'Reorganisation of the NHS in England', *British Medical Journal*, 341: c3843.

Wansink, B. and Chandon, P. (2006) 'Can "Low-Fat" nutrition labels lead to obesity?', *Journal of Marketing Research*, 43: 605–617.

Weber, M. (1949) *The Methodology of the Social Sciences* (ed./trans. E. Shils and H. Finch), New York: Free Press.

Weiss, C. (2000) 'Which links in which theories should we evaluate?', in P. Rogers, T. Hacsi, A. Petrosino and T. Huebner (eds) *Program Theory in Evaluation: Challenges and Opportunities* (New Directions for Evaluation no 87) San Francisco: Jossey Bass.

Williams, B. and Hummelbrunner, R. (2010) *Systems Concepts in Action: A Practitioner's Toolkit*. Stanford: Stanford University Press.

Wilson, J. and Kelling, G. (2003) 'Broken Windows: The Police and Neighbourhood Safety', in E. McLaughlin, J. Muncie and G. Hughes (eds), *Criminological Perspectives: Essential Readings*. London: SAGE.

Wolfson, M. and Hourogan, M. (1997) 'Unintended consequences and professional ethics: criminalization of alcohol and tobacco use by youths and young adults', *Addiction*, 92, 1159–1164.

Wong, G., Pawson, R. and Owen, L. (2011) 'Policy guidance on threats to legislative interventions in public health: a realist synthesis', *BMC Public Health*, 11: 222.

World Health Organization (2005) Seventh Futures Forum on Unpopular Decisions in Public Health. Copenhagen: WHO Europe.

Zaza, S., Sleet, D., Thompson, R., Sosin, D. and Bolen, J. (2001) 'Reviews of evidence regarding interventions to increase use of child safety seats', *American Journal of Preventive Medicine*, 21(4) 31–47.

Index

Tables and Figures are indicated by page numbers in bold.